The Ward Sister's Survival Guide

The Professional Developments Series

These five books provide you with a wealth of insight into all aspects of nursing practice. The series is essential reading for qualified, practising nurses who need to keep up with new developments, evaluate their clinical practice and develop and extend their clinical management and teaching skills. Up-to-date, and appropriately illustrated, The Professional Developments Series brings together the work of well over a hundred nurses.

Other titles in The Professional Developments Series:

The Staff Nurse's Survival Guide
Relevant to nurses working in all healthcare settings, this brings together chapters on a wide range of clinical and non-clinical issues in patient care, and includes a practical section on looking after *yourself*, too.

Effective Communication
Good communication is an essential aspect of nursing in every healthcare setting, and this title in the series covers a wide range of topics, including counselling, confidentiality, group and team work, compliance and communicating with children.

Patient Education Plus
This book will help you to develop your teaching role with patients and clients, and covers a wide range of clinical topics. Each chapter includes a clearly written and illustrated handout which can be freely photocopied or adapted for use with your clients.

Practice Check!
How well do you communicate with colleagues and patients? How do you respond when difficult situations arise? You can explore your responses to all these – and more – by using this book. Each Practice Check presents brief descriptions of situations which may arise in practice, together with open-ended questions and discussion to enable you to explore the problems and establish your own solutions.

These books are available from the publishers:

Austen Cornish Publishers Limited
Austen Cornish House
Walham Grove
London SW6 1QW
Tel: 01-381 6301

Ask to be included on their mailing list!

The Ward Sister's Survival Guide

A collection of articles first
published in The Professional Nurse
and here revised and updated

Austen Cornish Publishers Limited
London
1990

The Ward Sister's Survival Guide
First published in 1990 by

Austen Cornish Publishers Limited
Austen Cornish House
Walham Grove
London SW6 1QW

© Austen Cornish Publishers Limited

ISBN 1 870065 12 3

Printed and bound in Great Britain by
Richard Clay Limited, Bungay, Suffolk.

Contents

Introduction

'Management' has become a popular word in nursing within the last five years. Nurses have always had a management role, of course, but nowadays the positive benefits of effective management are widely recognised and the development of management skills is actively encouraged – and even sometimes resourced – by employers of health professionals.

The role of the ward sister or charge nurse encompasses a wide range of different management responsibilities, as well as requiring clinical expertise and judgement and many practical and interpersonal skills. These Superwomen and Supermen are often appointed to their posts in charge of a ward (or community team) without any formal management training and often with little support in developing all the skills they immediately need. Newly-appointed ward sisters and charge nurses will have at least begun to develop these skills as staff nurses, and most will have 'acted up' and taken charge of the ward in the absence of the ward managers. But most will feel that there's still a lot to learn.

This book will provide ward sisters and charge nurses with a resource for their professional development. The main focus of the book is on the skills required for **effective management**, including teamwork, interpersonal skills, quality assurance, legal and ethical issues, recruiting and managing staff and product appraisal. Also included are sections on **planning your own professional development**, **managing stress**, on **primary nursing**, **research awareness** and on **managing aggression**. Almost all of the 65 chapters were first published as articles in *The Professional Nurse* magazine, and have been revised and updated for this volume. Some are altogether new. I hope that you and your colleagues will find them useful in your own practice and professional development.

Elizabeth M Horne
Editorial Director, The Professional Nurse
London, November 1989

Your Professional Role

1

Taking charge: a newly appointed ward sister

Elizabeth S. Wright, SRN, DipN, CHSM
Ward Sister, The Middlesex Hospital, London

My experience as a new ward sister is probably typical. I had to learn from my mistakes, with little support or guidance from senior staff, except when I sought it myself. My appointment was fortuitous in that I had the opportunity to "act up" as a ward sister for 15 months, while still in senior staff nurse uniform. This undoubtedly enabled me to learn assertiveness and the ward manager's role quickly, without the sophistication or enforcement of a sister's uniform, and although my abilities were taxed to the limit at the time, the experience proved to have been rewarding when I eventually took up the post of ward sister.

Priorities within ward management

The elements of the ward sister's role may be viewed in order of priority, and at the head of the list in every competent sister's mind must be the patients and the delivery of their individualised care. As a clinical nurse, you must have expertise in assessing the various patients' needs within your specialty. Not only is this essential for you to be able to administer the care yourself, but also to supervise and teach others, and to inspire confidence in your patients and staff. Your dedication and positive outlook should generate similar enthusiasm in all those who work with you.

Staff welfare The welfare of the nursing staff is also of importance, including both trained and untrained staff. Their professional needs must be met and include adequate information regarding their patients and the care required, as well as supervised tuition in their work. This in turn enables the manager to assess and praise, or criticise constructively as appropriate, so the staff can progress and evaluate themselves and the development of their skills (Matthews, 1982). Working closely with colleagues and encouraging trained staff to supervise students is also a sure way of monitoring staff morale.

Communication Maintaining effective methods of communication and liaison with *all* members of the multidisciplinary team is vital. A cohesive atmosphere combined with efficient organisation within a ward leads to both patients and staff feeling relaxed. Effective two-way communication with medical staff is of great importance to ensure that both nursing and medical teams are working harmoniously and efficiently for the good of the patient. Other essential ward staff, such as secretaries, ward clerks, domestics and voluntary workers must also be included.

Efficient communication with outlying departments, the community, and the school of nursing is desirable to maintain healthy diplomatic links. This provides opportunities for ward staff to learn further and observe procedures, in for instance X-ray or outpatient departments or theatres.

Teaching Teaching is an aspect of the ward sister's role that is frequently underestimated, by other staff and by the ward sister herself (Marson, 1984). Teaching may take a variety of forms: demonstration, supervision, or formal theoretical ward tuition.

Whichever form the teaching takes, it is best related to the clinical specialty and practice, so that the learners may benefit and retain most of the instruction. The teaching should be given regularly throughout the learner's allocation on the ward, and be aimed at the level of interest best suited to her stage of training; for example a senior student may wish to learn about ward management and methods of teaching, while a junior may require regular supervision in aseptic technique.

The ward sister should make information available to her trained staff team, and give guidance on methods of teaching, so they can help her supervise the students in her charge. Professional updating in clinical aspects of nursing care, techniques, and equipment available should be sought by the ward sister so that she is aware of current policies and research, and she should in turn encourage her trained staff to further their knowledge and attend study days or courses.

Monitoring standards of care and feedback from patients and their relatives, staff, and other departments, enables you to improve the quality of care or oganisation required within the ward setting. I feel we should be approachable and receptive to constructive criticism in order to encourage others to provide such feedback (Ogier, 1984).

Styles of management

The style of management varies between ward sisters depending on their personality, the clinical setting, their methods of organisation, and perhaps the role model from whom they learnt and developed their style of management. The latter can be autocratic, democratic, or laissez-faire (although the last is considered by many not to be an effective style; Matthews, 1982). My surgical ward is run in a democratic manner with definite autocratic leanings in certain decisions or ward policies.

Taking up a new post as a ward sister in an unfamiliar ward with a well established trained staff team may prove unnerving at first. In such a situation it is probably wise to settle into the position, with the ward run as it has been previously, and then with consultation with trained staff, make gradual changes and alterations, and so imprint your own personality and style upon the ward. Advice from colleagues, managers, and perhaps doctors and ward clerks is always valuable and should be sought, but confidential or personal problems within the ward are best kept to yourself.

Personal qualities and skills

The qualities you need to fulfill the role of ward manager certainly include maturity of personality, assertiveness, and ability to accept responsibility. Dedication to the job and a genuine interest in the chosen field of nursing make a tremendous difference to the atmosphere on the ward.

Basic characteristics of loyalty, honesty, approachability, tolerance, and patience are qualities I search for in prospective staff nurses — and hope to find in myself. The ability to accept advice and constructive criticism is a significant asset if you are to improve yourself, but you must also be able to understand the reasons for destructive criticism. A decisive confident air of leadership promotes the image of a figurehead, from whom staff are more likely to seek guidance.

Personnel management This is another aspect of the ward sister's work which you may not have encountered previously. Counselling skills are an area in nursing that are often taught later rather than sooner in the manager's career, missing the time when she would have most benefitted by it. Counselling involves your patients and their relatives, your nurses, and other staff, and may cover both professional and personal difficulties (Allen, 1982).

Confidentiality between staff is essential, and the reassurance that this exists inspires loyalty and support in trained staff and learners.

Professionalism A professional attitude and conduct should also be maintained consistently because in my view this is a standard to be set, although many ward sisters' views differ on this. How can you be taken seriously and offer criticism if you do not set a high standard and are not viewed with respect?

Forethought and initiative Economic use of time and resources are difficult aspects of management to grasp at first. Foresight in nursing care and equipment use, involving the short-term and long-term needs of the ward, only improve with experience. Setting priorities and planning in relation to staff deployment may be another area that requires practice. Learning to manage complaints from both patient and staff in order to defuse angry situations and settle problems involves much diplomacy and often self-restraint. Experience develops a kind of psychic empathy to atmospheres within the ward and between people. An early awareness of problems enables you to deal with such situations before unnecessary ill feeling or a formal complaint occurs.

Aims and expectations

On reflection, the picture I have drawn of a ward sister seems to be one of a superhuman personality with dynamic abilities; of course this is not realistic, but a leader must have aims just beyond her reach in order to set and maintain a standard for her work and that of the nursing staff.

Overall, I feel that the newly appointed ward sister's position is an unenviable one. Certain expectations of her are held by other staff, patients, and relatives, simply because she wears the sister's uniform, regardless of the number of hours of experience. She either learns fast or falls by the wayside, in which case the ward and everyone else are also affected. The majority of newly appointed ward sisters develop their skills and experience with remarkably little support, and although they are expected to give praise to their staff, who takes the trouble to pat them on the back for their achievements?

References

Allen, H.O., (1982) The Ward Sister – Role and Preparation. Bailliere Tindall, London.
Briggs, A., (1972) The Report of the Committee on Nursing. HMSO, London.
Kings Fund Centre, (1982) Ward Sister Preparation – a Contribution to Curriculum Building (project paper). Kings Fund Centre, London.
Marson, S.N., (1984) Developing the 'Teaching' Role of the Ward Sister, *Nurse Education Today*, **4**, 1.
Matthews, A., (1982) In Charge of the Ward. Blackwell Scientific Publications, London.
Ogier, M.E., (1984) Developing leadership, *Nurse Education Today*, **4**, 1.

Bibliography

Bridge, W., and MacLeod Clarke, J., (1981) Editors. Education Care (Series): Communication in nursing care. HM & M Publishers, Aylesbury.
This multiauthor book covers in great depth the communication styles and techniques most effective in specialist areas of nursing.
Evers, H., (1982) Key Issues in Nursing Practice: Ward Management 1. *Nursing Times* (Occasional Paper), **78** ; 6, 20.
This paper argues that ward management must be considered as a key issue in relation to nursing practice.
Farnish, S., (1982) Thrown in at the deep end, *Nursing Times*, **78**, 404.
This article discusses the reactions of sisters and staff nurses to the preparation currently available for ward leadership, and describes a survey being undertaken to determine nurses' views on this.
Pembrey, S., (1980) The Ward Sister; Key to Nursing. Royal College of Nursing, London.
This classic RCN study of the ward sister's role covers 50 ward sisters and their roles in relation to the management of nursing on an individualised patient basis. Various theories on the management role have been tested in this study in relation to four activities in a daily nursing management cycle.
Redfern, S.J., (1981) Hospital Sisters: Their Job Attitudes and Occupational Stability. Royal College of Nursing, London.
This study investigates the attitudes, perceptions, and opinions of the hospital sister and the relationship of these to satisfactoriness and withdrawal from the job.

2
Nursing as a therapy

RICHARD A. McMAHON, RGN, DipN, MA
PhD Student, King's College, University of London

The role of being a nurse may include other aspects than just 'nursing', for example acting as a doctor's assistant, or a bed maker. However, in general it is those actions leading the patient towards recovery of independence or coping with the inability to achieve it that Orem considers to be nursing.

Though difficult to define, therapy could be regarded as the means employed to heal the diseased person. The word 'heal' is meant in the sense of making whole, rather than curing. If a terminally ill patient has been helped to come to terms with his condition so that he makes plans for his family's future, to a certain extent he has been healed. Not all nursing actions or indeed all nurses are therapeutic, but dynamic interventions which lead the patient towards self-care are healing in that decreased dependence on others is an indication of health and 'wholeness'.

Nursing is not simply 'what nurses do', its major concern has been described more precisely as: '. . . The individual's need for self care action and the provision and management of it on a continuous basis in order to sustain life and health, recover from disease or injury, and cope with their effects.' (Orem, 1980).

A new concept

The concept of nursing as a therapy is relatively new. In the past much of the care of the elderly and the mentally infirm has been influenced to a large extent by the nursing rather than medical staff (Bellaby and Oribabor, 1980). However the legacy of the asylums and the work-house have made much of this care of a custodial nature. In contrast much of the nursing activity in the acute areas has been extended to include the therapies and the technical tasks of doctors, leaving the previous nursing practices to the untrained learners and auxiliaries. It could be said that this subservience to and dependence on the medical profession is a result of the historical male dominance over female, and the unique body of scientific knowledge of the medical profession, among other factors. 'If Florence Nightingale had trained her lady pupils on assertiveness rather than obedience, perhaps nurses would be in a different place now.' (Oakley, 1984).

Nurses are at last starting to identify their profession, in which there is a sharp contrast between the extension of the nurse's role into technical, medicine based practice and its expansion into the many aspects of helping patients overcome their self care deficits, and hence the emergence of the nurse as a therapist.

Three areas in which nursing can be considered therapeutic are the nurse-patient relationship, conventional and unconventional nursing interventions and patient teaching. The concept that nursing has a positive outcome for the patient helps to identify its unique contribution to health care, and should become of increasing importance to nurses.

Nurse-patient relationship   The therapeutic effect of the nurse-patient relationship is difficult to demonstrate, as much nursing research shows that many nurses do not communicate effectively with their patients. For example, Macleod Clark (1983) observed that nurses on surgical wards only spent minimal amounts of time communicating with patients, often in a superficial manner and demonstrating few of the recognised interpersonal skills. However, one area of nursing research into the nurse-patient relationship that has become prescriptive is in relation to the information given pre-operatively to patients. Davis (1985) summarises much of the research into the subject, and writes that: 'There would seem, therefore, to be a substantial body of evidence demonstrating that patient outcomes, related to a model of stress reduction involving both physiological and psychological factors, can be significantly influenced by nurses giving pre-operative information.' Clearly the giving of pre-operative information is a therapeutic nursing action.

Whilst further prescriptive research into the nurse-patient relationship is badly needed, it may be suggested that the nurse may act as a therapist by helping the patient to overcome what Orem (1980) calls the 'self-care deficit'. Patients may be taught the series of physical actions that lead to self-care, such as putting on a shirt using one arm, but unless the patient wants responsibility for his or her own care, this may not lead to successful rehabilitation. To achieve this may require the patient to recognise the dissatisfaction caused by the self-care deficit, a preferable situation and the action necessary in order to achieve it. Patients must also face up to what they cannot achieve, and here counselling may be beneficial. Counselling has several aims, one of which is reducing dependence, which is compatible with Orem's ideas on the nature of nursing and should be an aspect of the practising nurse's role as a therapist.

Conventional and unconventional intervention   The idea that conventional nursing interventions may be therapeutic is more easily accepted but if nursing is to be seen as beneficial to the patient, non therapeutic interventions must be identified and described, and effective interventions proved. However such research is pointless unless it is read and acted upon. Myco (1980) examined the reading habits of a group of nurses, and found that most of those involved in nursing practice did not subscribe to a nursing journal, whilst the vast majority of those who did, read the magazines with the least research, namely the *Nursing Times* and *Nursing Mirror*. Having read research, it is not always easy to implement. The findings may be surprising and difficult to believe and it is often difficult to persuade other members of the nursing team to change but with an increasing emphasis on research awareness in basic and post-basic courses, the implementation of proven nursing interventions may also increase.

Nursing and alternative therapies

Unconventional interventions based on 'alternative' therapies may appear at first sight to many nurses to be of little relevance to nursing. However, a common theme to alternative therapies and recent nursing theory, is that of seeing the person not in terms of a diseased system or organ, but as a whole person, within which physical, psychological, environmental and developmental factors are interrelated. For example Orem views 'man' as: '. . . a psychophysiological organism with rational powers. As a biological organism, man exists, and responds both as an organism and as an object, in an environment with physical and biological components. As a rationally functioning being man formulates purposes about and acts upon self, others and environment'. (Caley et al, 1980).

Nurses are becoming increasingly interested in alternative, or 'holist' therapies because they are non-invasive and can be incorporated into traditional nursing care. It may be argued that at a time when nurses are being asked to question their practice, and discard anything based on heresay and whim, it is unreasonable to ask them to perform therapies with little scientific evidence to support them. The response to this lies not only in the common philosophy of holism to nursing and alternative therapies, but also in the fact that research into the benefits of the use of these therapies by nurses, will identify effective practices.

To a certain extent this process has begun in the case of therapeutic touch. Heidt (1981) examined the effect of therapeutic touch on male and female patients in a cardiovascular unit and found that anxiety was significantly reduced in those receiving therapeutic touch when compared with those that received casual or no touch. Another study looked at the effect of therapeutic touch on Danish women in labour, again with favourable results. In this country Ashton (1984) describes the use of therapeutic touch and massage, and comments on the fact that much counselling goes on during the therapy sessions. Nurses are privileged in the way they touch patients, being allowed to dress, undress and touch them in areas normally unacceptable between strangers. It seems appropriate for nurses to build on this privileged position to the benefit of the patient through therapeutic touch. Therapeutic touch has been an integral part of care at the Nursing Development Units in Oxford. It is just one of a range of holistic therapies that may be of value to nurses in their practice. Others include shiatsu and reflexology.

Patient education   This is a combination of the previous aspects of the nurse-patient relationship and nursing interventions. Pembrey (1984) states that: '. . . we can derive professional nursing as a partnership with the individual, with the nurse working primarily as a teacher'.

Nurses must work with patients and their families acting as advisors, rather then someone who, regardless of patients' opinions, tells them what to do and how to do it. But they must be knowledgeable advisors and teachers and must again teach the patient proven techniques. For example, Watson (1984) examined the practice of advising post-operative patients to have saline baths. When questioned, none of the participatory staff knew of any beneficial effect demonstrated for this practice, rather it seemed to have been passed from nurse to nurse, though interestingly, some of the participating staff were doctors. The regaining of the ability to be independent often involves nurses in teaching the patients or their relatives a new way of approaching an everyday activity and allowing patients to find and adapt their own solutions, which is entirely compatible with Orem's concept of patients redressing the balance of their self-care ability against their self-care deficit.

Management implications

The concept of nursing as a therapy has implications for nurse managers. If the nurse-patient relationship is therapeutic, then the profession should be organised in such a way as to promote this, for example by encouraging primary nursing. If nurses are to be accountable they must have access to research to enable them to choose the best course of action for the patient. Nurse educationalists need to adopt curricula which promote the therapeutic aspects of nursing. Clearly nurse-patient communication requires examination, and also the skills for patient teaching.

References

Ashton, J. (1984) In your hands. *Nursing Times,* **80,** 11, 54.
Bellaby, P. and Oribabor, P. (1980) The history of the present contradiction and struggle in nursing. In Davies, C. (Ed) (1980) Rewriting Nursing History. Croom Helm, London.
Caley, J., Dirkson, M., Engalla, M. and Hennrick, M. (1980) The Orem self-care nursing model. In Riehl, J. and Roy, C. (Ed) (1980) Conceptual Models for Nursing Practice. Appleton Century Croft, Connecticut.
Davis, B. (1985) The clinical effect of interpersonal skills: the implementation of pre-operative information giving. In Kagan, C.M. (Ed) (1985) Interpersonal Skills in Nursing. Croom Helm, London.
Heidt, P. (1981) Effect of therapeutic touch on anxiety level of hospitalised patients. *Nursing Research,* **30,** 1, 32-37.
Macleod Clark, J. (1983) Nurse-patient communication- an analysis of conversations from surgical wards. In Wilson Barnett, J. (Ed) (1983) Nursing Research: Ten Studies in Patient Care. John Wiley and Sons, Chichester.
Myco, F. (1980) Nursing research information: are nurse educators and practitioners seeking it out? *Journal of Advanced Nursing,* **5,** 5, 637-646.
Oakley, A. (1984) The importance of being a nurse. *Nursing Times* **80,** 50, 24-27.
Orem, D.E. (1980) Nursing: Concepts of Practice. McGraw Hill Book Co., London.
Pembrey, S. (1984) Nursing care: profession progress. *Journal of Advanced Nursing,* **9,** 9, 539-547.

Watson, M. (1984) Salt in the bath. *Nursing Times* Occasional paper, **80,** 19, 57-59.

Bibliography
Davies, C. (1980) Rewriting Nursing History. Croom Helm, London.
   Interesting insights into the development of nursing.
Fulder, S. (1984) The Handbook of Complementary Medicine. Hodder and Stoughton, Kent.
   Describes the major alternative therapies.
Hunt, J. (1984) Why don't we use these findings? *Nursing Mirror,* **158,** 8, 29.
   Provides interesting suggestions why nurses are not implementing research that has already been done.
Kagan, C.M. (Ed) (1985) Interpersonal Skills in Nursing. Croom Helm, London.
   Looks at a wide range of issues in nurse communication from a research basis.
Wright, S. (1985) New nurses: new boundaries. *Nursing Practice* **1,** 32-39.
   Examines the relationship between nurses and other therapists.

Your Professional
Development

3

Continuing education – whose responsibility?

JANET DUBERLEY, MSc, SRN, RSCN, RCNT, Dip.Adv. Nurs. Stud, RN
Regional Nurse, Education and Practice, South West Thames Regional Health Authority

Opportunities are growing

In recent years, most of the educational opportunities available to qualified staff have been designed to update knowledge of District policies and procedures, to update clinical practice and developments, and to promote teaching and assessing skills. In other words, the training and educational opportunities have been to a large extent determined by the needs of the employer. But there are gradual changes in this pattern. More and more one sees evidence of how the demands of the user — the qualified nurse — can shape the opportunities available.

Take, for example, the increase in part-time degrees in nursing. The growing numbers of nurses studying with the Open University in subjects related to nursing have played an important role in the development of part-time degrees in nursing at other educational institutions. Qualified nurses demonstrated their demand for further knowledge and since the need was identified new opportunities have been created.

Exchanges and visits by nurses to different clinical areas have also generated an awareness of the different types of opportunity available and the understanding of continuing education being more than attendance at courses. So, if there is a greater awareness, whose responsibility is it to provide, fund, or seek these opportunities?

Areas of activity

Such a question demands an analysis of what is happening in professional continuing education today. We can identify three different types of activity which take place on different planes: role preparation; role development; and career development.

If you look at these activities as the planes of a cube (Figure 1), you can identify more clearly the focus of the various continuing education activities. There are three major areas of activity in professional continuing education for nurses:
• Role development
• Role preparation
• Career development

Role development Activities B to C are those intended to help individuals perform aspects of their role more fully or effectively. All individuals grow into roles; the newly appointed staff nurse, ward sister, or any other staff member neither feels nor performs as effectively as an experienced person in the same or similar role. Educational opportunities aimed at promoting such growth are included within this category, for instance short courses in teaching and assessing, the National Boards' Developments in Nursing courses, specific staff development and role-based programmes, and diploma and degree courses.

Role preparation Activities A to B include those opportunities that prepare individuals to fulfil specific roles, for example the National Boards for Nursing, Midwifery, and Health Visiting, post-basic clinical courses or ''in-service'' courses and study days, with the intention of updating and extending knowledge of clinical and administrative practices. These very different activities may be brought together in the category of role preparation because they prepare and enable the individual to perform a role. While the learning achieved may increase and extend the individual's knowledge it does not necessarily develop her within a given role.

Career development The line from A to C is perhaps different in that nursing has not developed a training programme designed specifically to enable individuals to progress along the career ladder. However, each of the examples cited in the other categories may contribute in part to facilitating career development, or may be actively pursued as part of a career progression plan. For example, studying for the Diploma in Nursing provides deeper insights into the role and function of the clinical nurse but the possession of the diploma also provides access to another role preparation course, that is the Certificate in the Education of Adults and career development, and progression as a nurse teacher.

Where does responsibility lie?
An analysis of this nature is helpful when we look at the areas of responsibility for continuing education. In examining the motives and goals of the individual and/or the employer in seeking and providing the educational opportunities, the responsibility of each becomes clearer — but not necessarily well defined.

The Health Authority There are, of course, organisational responsibilities. The Health Authority is required to inform its staff of established and new policies and procedures and to employ staff prepared for their role, that is as described in the *role preparation* plane of the model.
    The Health Authority also requires its staff to be confident, competent, and skilled practitioners and therefore has the responsibility for enabling its staff to develop within roles — the *role development* plane. The Health

Authority, and larger still the Health Service, requires a steady supply of well prepared and able nurses to fulfil roles other than clinical nursing.

The organisational and management changes that have taken place with the introduction of "general management" have indicated the very real need to pay further attention to *career development*, the third plane.

The nurse herself The individual nurse also faces responsibilities in each of the three planes. The professional nurse is responsible for being properly prepared for her role and for being aware of the organisational policies and practices. She is also responsible for developing her knowledge and skills so she can perform at the expected level.

Finally, the professional nurse has the personal responsibility of seeking and enabling her own career development, of setting goals for attainment and ensuring those goals are reached not only within the career development plane but also in the role development plane.

The responsibility for continuing education can therefore be seen to lie not with any one organisation or individual but in a partnership.

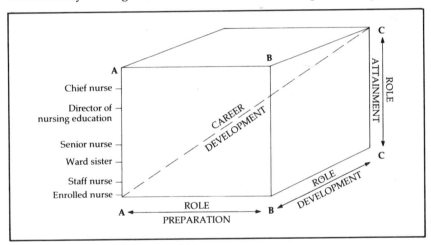

Figure 1. Continuing education activities.

Investigate the options

The opportunities available to qualified nurses are many and varied but are not always known or readily accessible. Finding your way around the maze of opportunities requires guidance. If you are considering further education or a change in career direction, discuss the options with your line manager, colleagues, the senior tutor of post-basic education, the director of nurse education, or the nursing department at a local college.

As mentioned earlier, continuing education is greater than attending courses. Structured visits to other clinical areas, meetings with peers at seminars and conferences, and distance learning programmes may not bear awards or certificates, but because they meet your own specific learning needs they may well be of greater value.

In conclusion, the responsibilities for continuing education lie with both the individual and the organisation; each has the responsibility to seek and to provide. In addition to responsibility being shared, so also are the benefits of continuing education. Therefore, is it not also appropriate that the individual and the employer should to some extent share the funding of the opportunities available?

Bibliography

Davies, C. (1981) Training for Ward Sisters: an Innovative Research and Development Project. *Nurse Education Today* **1,** 2.

DHSS (1982) Professional Development in Clinical Nursing; 1980's Seminar Report, Harrogate. DHSS, London.

Farnish, S., (1982) Thrown in at the Deep Ed. *Nursing Times.* **78; 10,** 404.

Farnish, S., (1985): How are Sisters Prepared? (Occasional Paper). *Nursing Times,* **81; 4,** 47.

Lathlean, J., and Farnish, S., (1984) The Ward Sister Training Project, University of London, Chelsea College; NERU Report Number 3.

Pembrey, S., (1980) The Ward Sister; Key to Nursing. A Study of the Organisation of Individualised Nursing, RCN, London.

Royal College of Nursing (1983) Preparation and Education of Teachers of Nursing: Report of a Working Party. RCN, London.

4
Distance learning for nurses

JACQUELINE M. ISARD, BA, MSc, SRN, SCM, DipN, RNT, MBIM
Nursing and Health Services Adviser, Overseas Development Administration. Lately Senior Lecturer, Distance Learning Centre, Polytechnic of the South Bank

"What do you do?"

"I teach in a unit concerned with distance learning for nurses."

"What's that?"

"Er, distance learning is studying a course at a distance. No. Er, well, you know the Open University . . .?"

"Oh, you broadcast your courses, then?"

"No, no. Not in that sense – our courses are predominantly text based, though we do use audio-tapes and other media . . ."

"Oh, you mean a *correspondence course!*"

In this dialogue the last interpretation of our activities is undoubtedly the least appealing. This is unfair because there have been and are still some excellent courses using this method. Distance learning is, however, more than an old idea dressed up with a new name. The whole technology of education is now much more sophisticated. Educational establishments are more geared to involving students in their own learning, getting them to *use* material while they are learning it. Distance learning, likewise, is no longer a matter of reading a set text (why not read a book?). Nor is it acceptable for students to sit quietly in class while the teacher spills forth pearls of wisdom, a passive member of the teacher-learner partnership. Distance learning challenges the student to be very, very active!

Changing needs and expectations

Rapid changes in society and the profession have given added impetus to this form of education. We are living in a fast-moving, highly technological age where facts learned yesterday are no longer valid. Nursing knowledge, skills, and attitudes have to be in line and in time with these changes. Expectations have also changed. At one time it was not accepted that nurses had lives both at home and at work. The truly devoted nurse was not expected to have family commitments. It is now acknowledged that if a nurse works strange and tiring shifts we cannot reasonably expect her to drag herself to evening classes, especially if she has children and a family that she would like to see from time to time. Distance learning allows her to keep pace with change in her workplace in the warmth of her own home.

Geographical access to courses can be difficult for nurses living and working some way from educational institutions. Many rural districts have nurses scattered in small centres over a large area. It cannot be assumed that staff are going to get to a course of lectures easily. Moreover, their travelling expenses are going to add up!

Some nurses have had unhappy experiences of education and do not relish the intrinsic competition that can take place within a classroom. Distance learning has the advantage of allowing the nurse to take courses at her own pace.

Many authorities are generous in providing fees and study leave. Many are not. In either case, money for continuing education currently derives from the same source as that for direct patient care. Distance learning is no cheaper than conventional courses (in many instances it is more expensive) but the great saving at a time of resource constraint is that clinical areas are not depleted of staff at inconvenient times to attend lectures. Employing authorities, like many industries, may prefer to provide group tutorial support, while the bulk of the studying is done by the student in her own time.

The challenge

In spite of these many advantages, distance learning does not have all the answers. Not all subjects lend themselves to this medium. We use the phrase in our unit to describe this phenomenon as "teaching your student to do brain surgery by post". Principles can be taught and theoretical concepts guided into competent practice, but clinical teaching would need careful planning before being presented in this mode.

Conventionally taught students and their tutors will find this sort of approach quite a challenge to preconceived notions. There is still a lingering feeling that you have to attend lectures in order to learn anything, and distance learning might be perceived as taking control from face-to-face teachers. It would be a pity if such attitudes were widespread, because it is a great opportunity for those in continuing education to do what they are most skilled at — *facilitation*. In such a context the tutor's role would be different, less directive, but skills in leading groups and encouraging students to learn from each other would be essential.

Courses available

The Open University run several courses for health care workers. The best known to nurses is probably P553 "A Systematic Approach to Nursing Care", but others are also available, although less specifically directed at nurses; such as P555 "Mental Handicap: patterns for Living" and most recently, P554 "Child Abuse and Neglect". There is also a course available as part of the undergraduate programme, or as an associate course, called "Health and Disease" (U205).

The Open University has an Open Business School which runs a series of management courses suitable for people working in industry or in the health sector. Many nurses at Sister level and above have completed these short courses which can eventually build up to a Professional Diploma in Management or even to a Master in Business Administration (MBA). The short course "The Effective Manager" has been recognised for exemption from Stage 1 of the Institute of Personnel Management and "Managing People" from Stage 2.

MESOL (Management Education Systems by Open Learning) is an initiative of the National Health Service Training Authority. These courses are being written by the Open University in conjunction with the Institute of Health Service Management. This is an interesting development for nurses and others who wish to extend their education in management but within the health service context.

The Distance Learning Centre at South Bank Polytechnic offers the Diploma in Nursing (shortly to become the Diploma in Professional Studies, a common core with two branches, the Diploma in Nursing and the Advanced Diploma in Midwifery). There are several free-standing courses in the "Managing Care" programme, the overall theme of which is the enhancement of management skills for nursing practice. These include "Improving Teamwork", "Stress in Nursing" and "Teaching Patients and Clients". Modules of the "Research Awareness" course aim to provide a comprehensive guide to understanding the nature of health care research within professional practice.

There is an increasing number of suitable courses becoming available. Not all are written specifically with nurses in mind but this shouldn't detract from their usefulness to the profession. Distance learning is probably the single most revolutionary aspect of continuing education for nurses. It is an opportunity we need to grasp: nursing has great need of it.

Useful addresses

Distance Learning Centre, South Bank Technopark, 90 London Road, London SE1.
    Telephone 01 922 8802.
Associate Study Centre Office, Open University, PO Box 76, Milton Keynes, MK7 6AN.
    Telephone 0908 653449.

5

Can continuing education ease the nursing shortage?

JANET D. DUBERLEY, MSc, SRN, RSCN, RCNT, Dip. Adv. Nurs. Stud. RN
Regional Nurse, Education and Practice, South West Thames Regional Health Authority

Nursing is facing major problems as the shortage of nurses begins to bite, and since there is no single reason for the shortage, there can be no single solution. It seems, however, that continuing professional education (CPE) is currently being used as the panacea to cure all the ills of staff recruitment and retention. I would suggest that at best it could serve as 'First Aid', at worst it could exacerbate the problem unless structural and organisational changes are also made.

What is continuing education?

Generally considered to be a 'good thing' CPE has an aura of common knowledge. However, common knowledge, like common sense, is remarkably uncommon, so I would like to explore the concept of CPE.

Houle (1980) says it relates to a dynamic concept of professionalisation with the ultimate aim "to convey a complex attitude made up of a readiness to use the best ideas and techniques of the moment, but also to expect that they will be modified or replaced. Everyone must expect constant change and with it new goals to be achieved and new understanding and skill to be mastered". This preparation for change is rather nebulous, so what does it mean in real terms? The American Nurses Association (ANA) defines CPE as "learning activities intended to build upon the educational and experimental basis of the professional nurse for the advancement of practice, education, administration, research or theory development to the end of improving the health of the public."

This definition contains a sense of what Houle calls the dynamic concept of professionalisation – the major focus builds on what has gone before to improve the public's health. However, what the learning activities might be is open to interpretation – the definition focuses on the different activities of nursing practice, education, administration and research. There is no mention of the WHAT, or HOW the public's health might be improved. In comparison, the American Medical Association (AMA, 1979) says "continuing medical education is composed of any education and training which serves to maintain, develop or increase the knowledge, interpretive and reasoning proficiencies, appropriate technical skills, professional performance standards or ability for interpersonal relationships that a physician uses to provide the service needed by patients or the public.''

This comprehensive and thought provoking definition does not relate solely to 'keeping up-to-date', nor does it focus on how medicine is practised, but to maintaining, developing and increasing intellectual and cognitive skills as well as psychosocial and psychomotor skills. The definition's goals relate to the ideals of professionalism – the possession of a unique body of knowledge – but also, and especially, to the expert application of that knowledge through the development of the intellectual skills of interpretation and reasoning.

How do employers see CPE?

How do these definitions compare with the way employers might view CPE? The type of CPE supported and promoted by employing organisations give us a clear idea of their perspective. In 1985 Rogers conducted a national review of CPE in nursing, and found a tremendous amount fell primarily into three categories:

In-service training Staff orientation and introduction, dissemination of policy.

Clinical updating Issues and trends in clinical practice and practical skills training.

Post registration clinical role preparation Six to 12 month courses in clinical nursing.

The activities most heavily supported and prevalent in all organisations were in-service training. These were well planned, with records of attendance kept in many cases, especially for those on fire and safety policies. Clinical updating activities were also present in most organisations, but tended to be less well planned and coordinated. Post registration clinical role preparation was provided where appropriate experience was available, but not all experience supported clinical courses.

These findings suggest that employees value the activities they see as contributing to the achievement of their organisational goals – providing a high quality, effective service. To fulfill these goals, staff must be aware of the environment, geography, personnel, operational and safety policies. Surely nurses' clinical knowledge and skills should have at least equal standing?

How do practitioners see CPE?

From the practitioner's point of view, the meaning of CPE may be determined by her or his age, previous experience of preregistration and continuing education and career goals. Cervero (1981) identified four major factors motivating doctors to participate in CPE:

- To maintain and improve professional competence and service to patients.
- To understand oneself as a professional.
- To interact with colleagues.
- To enhance personal and professional position.

The practitioner's view of CPE is different to those of the profession and the employers. It retains the service ideal but focuses more on the individual – CPE has a personal meaning as well as a professional one.

Potential areas of conflict

It is generally believed that responsibility for the continuing high quality of professional practice is equally shared by the profession, the employer and the practitioner, but their priorities may differ. The profession wants to advance its position in service to the public, and the employer wants to provide a high quality and cost-effective service to the public. The practitioner is pulled four ways – serving the public; fulfilling professional ideals; serving the employer, and meeting (or not meeting) personal goals.

This fourth component can cause real conflict. In undertaking CPE and acquiring more knowledge and skills, the practitioner may come to expect more of professional practice and of its financial remuneration. However, while enhancement of the individual's position featured in practitioners' goals, it did not feature in those of the profession or the employer, so the practitioner may not have a forum in which to practise these newly acquired skills or to be recompensed for them.

This conflict, I would suggest, is reflected in current nurse staffing problems. Nurses are expressing frustration, they have a poor self-image, and this contributes to high staff turnover and wastage. Obviously, pay levels and the high cost of living in the south of England have an effect, but I believe that even if the problems over pay were to be rectified tomorrow, the frustration would be evident again in a very short time. Why? Because pay is not the whole problem.

Over the last three years, the nursing shortage has assumed considerable political significance. People are anxious to know why nurses are leaving the profession. Analysis of the 1981 census data in two regional health authorities demonstrates that only 20 per cent of people holding nursing qualifications are currently employed in the profession. This suggests there is not a shortage of nurses, but a shortage of nurses employed in the profession. This in turn suggests there is something about the workplace or practice of nursing that makes people leave.

In 1986, Oxford District Health Authority, concerned about high staff turnover among clinical nurses conducted an extensive study to find the cause of nurses' dissatisfaction. The overwhelming response was that nurses felt unable to provide the care they believed their patients deserved. This was partly due to low staffing levels, but also due to frustration. Having trained in the profession, nurses were increasingly less able to practise nursing – their time was spent doing other things.

Waite (1986) undertook a national survey for the RCN, which came up with similar findings. Nurses who had left the health service or who had seriously considered doing so reported not feeling they were doing a worthwhile job; being unable to use their initiative; poor promotion prospects; not being valued. These sentiments indicate a restricted framework which does not allow nurses to practise nursing. Their expertise is not valued either in monetary terms or in years of professional practice, and they do not have a structure in which they can function as expert practitioners.

When nurses feel frustrated in their profession, they have a number of options. Many simply continue in their frustration – they have a poor image of both themselves and their profession, and take no action 'because it wouldn't make any difference'. Others use their frustration as an impetus for change. These nurses may seek greater challenge by changing jobs within clinical nursing, thus contributing to the high staff turnover in the profession. Others may pursue further education.

Since Rogers' survey of CPE opportunities in 1985, and the recognition of the nursing shortage there has been a great deal of investment in CPE. In some cases it has been used as a carrot to attract and retain nurses, but unfortunately it often only works for the duration of the course. On completion of the course, many nurses either change jobs or leave the profession altogether. I believe this is because employing authorities do not consider how to use the newly acquired skills, which means the nurses remain in their state of frustration and have no alternative but to consider a job change. While by no means all job changes within nursing can be attributed to this, the reality is that with few exceptions, employers have no structure for recognition or acceptance of clinical nurses who pursue education for advanced clinical practice.

Could a structure be created?

In the USA, clinical career structures have developed in a different way than in this country. Using a theoretical model of skill acquisition, Benner (1984) identified distinguishable differences in the competence of nurses with different levels of expertise. This has provided a rationale for the development of a career ladder within clinical nursing. Benner describes five stages of clinical development: novice; advanced beginner; competent; proficient and expert. The latter three are relevant here.

The competent practitioner   This practitioner is typified by the nurse who has been doing the same or a similar job for two or three years. She demonstrates a mastery of and ability to cope with the many contingencies of clinical nursing. Nursing care is conscious, deliberately planned and effective.

The proficient practitioner   This practitioner perceives situations as wholes rather than as aspects of the whole. Previous experience enables the proficient practitioner to recognise when the expected normal picture does not materialise. Decision making is improved because the nurse has a perspective on which of the many aspects are the important ones. Proficient performance is usually found in nurses who have worked in similar clinical settings for three to five years.

The expert practitioner This practitioner has an intuitive grasp of clinical situations. Her enormous background of experience enables her to home in on the accurate region of the problem without time consuming consideration of a wide range of alternative problems and solutions. While the expert practitioner appears not to rely on analytical principles, highly skilled analytical ability is necessary for those situations in which the nurse has no previous experience.

Implications for staff development

In describing levels of clinical expertise, Benner has provided the basis for a clinical career structure based on clinical competence, rather than managerial criteria as we have at present. But such defined career rungs have implications for staff development and continuing education in general. We must re-examine the goals and practice of CPE. It is the possession of cognitive, intellectual and interpretive skills that distinguishes the expert from the competent practitioner. CPE must address how it will facilitate the development of these skills.

However, as stated earlier, education and the acquisition of skills may not assist the retention of qualified nurses. These skills must be valued and recognised by employers. The current review of nursing manpower in terms of demand, supply and skill mix must take on a broader meaning than simply qualified:unqualified ratios. An examination of the level of skill requirements in clinical areas lends itself to the concept of clinical career ladders, to the proper use of scarce nursing resources and to proper levels of remuneration for clinical expertise. Unless this happens, CPE will only serve as First Aid. CPE should support the development of professional practice, but in association with the aims and goals of employing authorities.

References

AMA (1979) Proceedings of the 128th Annual Convention of the Council of Medical Education. July 22–26. Council on Medical Education, Report C.

Benner, R. (1984) From Novice to Expert. Addison Wesley, Mento Park, California.

Cervero, R. (1981) A factor analytical study of physicians' reasons for participating in continuing education. *Medical Education*, **56,** July, 29–34.

Houle, C.O. (1980) Continuing Learning in the Professions. Jossey-Bess, San Francisco.

Oxford District Health Authority (1986) DHA Member Report (Unpublished).

Rogers, J. (1987) Continuing Professional Education for Qualified Nurses. Austen Cornish Publishers and Ashdale Press, London. (Research carried out in 1985.)

Waite, R. and Hutt, R. (1987) Attitudes, Jobs and Mobility of Qualified Nurses. A report for the RCN. Institute of Manpower Studies, Brighton.

Taking Charge of the Ward

6

What is management?

Gillian E. Chapman, SRN, RSCN, BSc, MSc, PhD

Gillian Chapman was Lecturer in Nursing, King's College, University of London when this chapter was written

Every day, clinical practitioners, at staff nurse and sister level, manage. With varying degrees of skill, they manage staff and the use of their time and skills. They control, predict and coordinate a series of complex events in the context of the human dramas of illness, recovery or death. This impressive achievement remains scarcely recognised by their colleagues, who may perceive management as being a restricted set of administrative practices such as writing the off-duty. While mastery of administrative techniques facilitates good management, it is not the essence of management. This chapter discusses the nature of management and those elements of nursing that might be described as managerial. A brief outline of the literature relevant to ward management is followed by a guide to the practical, short-term managerial goals which face the clinical practitioner in charge of a ward during one period of duty. Finally, the long-term managerial goals of the ward sister, and the skills required to sustain them, will be identified.

What is management?

In organisational theory the manager is portrayed as being somewhat like an orchestra conductor – at the centre, controlling parts of the organisation in order to produce a harmonious whole. She is advised to plan, direct, coordinate and control events by exercising leadership and decision-making skills and by using formal administrative techniques of budgeting, record-keeping and so-on. Clinical practitioners observing the sometimes haphazard and confused nature of ward life might be relieved to discover that this view is challenged by some organisational theorists.

Mintzberg (1975), for example, suggests that the orchestra leader view of managers is more folklore than fact. Reviewing research studies in organisational behaviour he notes first, that this view of a manager is not supported by research. In fact, managers work at an unrelenting pace and their tasks are characterised by discontinuity, brevity and variety. Further, managers are action-oriented rather than reflective. The idea that managers have no regular daily duties seems unsupported by the research evidence. Managers not only handle crises, but are regularly involved in negotiations and interactions related to the larger organisation. The idea that managers work with formal communications is also challenged by the evidence which suggests that they prefer verbal exchanges, telephone calls and meetings. The view that management has become a scientific profession backed up by systematic analytical procedures is a powerful one, but neglects the fact that management remains concerned with intuitive judgements about people and situations.

Research studies of ward sisters as managers (Lelean, 1973; Pembrey, 1980; Runciman, 1983) have demonstrated how complex and varied their role is, with discontinuity, fragmentation and brevity characterising their tasks, communications and interactions with others. Indeed, Walton (1984), in a useful text on management techniques contrasts the principles of management described in the literature with the practice of managing in the NHS. He argues that far from rationally planning and coordinating resources and activities of the day, nurses tend to 'get along' with the resources they have; coping and reacting to situations as they arise, rather than anticipating difficulties and planning for them. Despite these reservations, a means is found in hospitals across the country to manage ward and departmental life in a coherent and sustained way.

Managing a ward

Ward management involves the attempt to identify needs and problems, set objectives and plan, implement and evaluate actions. The difference between this and individual patient care is that the whole ward, its environment, equipment and the groups of people within it, is the focus of attention rather than the individual patient.

What are the 'needs and problems' of a ward or unit? Each one will differ, of course, according to the priorities of care and the nursing and medical philosophy. It is vital for each clinical practitioner to make it clear what these might be. For example, nurses on a short-stay, five-day surgical ward might have the overall objective of ensuring safe pre- and postoperative care of patients in the context of a health authority policy or philosophy committed to efficiency and rapid turnover of patients. On the other hand, nurses on a long-term psychiatric ward might stress the development of a secure and consistent relationship with the patient, in order that rehabilitation to the community can be achieved. The important thing is that reasonable and achievable overall nursing objectives are set in keeping with unit philosophy and health authority policy. This is largely a task for the ward sister, together with the nurse manager in liaison with the nursing, medical and administrative teams.

All clinical practitioners in the ward or department should be aware of what these goals are. Once known, the daily organisation of the ward, the priority of problems and the allocation of resources becomes a simpler exercise. For example, the allocation of one nurse to develop a long-term relationship with a patient admitted for day surgery is less important than allocating a skilled nurse to ensure his safe recovery from anaesthetic.

Like the nursing process, the process of management has both short- and long-term goals. For the purposes of this article, a short-term managerial goal will be related to running the ward during one period of duty; long-term goals will be those associated with maintenance of the ward over longer periods of time. Each will be discussed separately.

Managing a shift

What follows is one method of managing a shift while in charge of a ward, based on a judgement of the ward priorities as they relate to the needs of the group of patients under the clinical practitioner's care, and is sequential in nature. In other words, it describes the sequence a nurse in charge of a ward might follow when arriving on duty. Clearly, given the scope of this article, not all the possible problems and actions have been included.

Nurse's prior knowledge Prior knowledge of the type of ward (medical, surgical or psychiatric) together with the number of patients and range of clinical conditions met on the ward will enhance the practitioner's capacity to prepare and think through her management plans. Similarly, knowledge of the ward layout and location of key facilities is essential; for example, clinical rooms, telephones, resuscitation equipment, fire doors and so on. Additionally, when arriving on duty, she should provide herself with an overview of the ward and its work before taking actions or making decisions. The most direct way of doing this is to tour the ward making observations.

Estimate of patient needs/dependency   Direct observation of patients during a brief tour of the ward enhances information on the patient's dependency needs gained from care plans during the handover report. While patient dependency is difficult to measure scientifically, professional judgement about the amount and quality of nursing time required has proved effective (Waite, 1986). Thus, the nurse in charge should assess the number of patients requiring constant nursing, the number requiring frequent nursing (for example, time-consuming treatments or observations) and the number of patients requiring only selective attention. It is important to remember that patients without life-threatening conditions can, at times, require as much attention as those more profoundly ill. For example, a patient requiring dressings for leg ulcers may need more time spent on this procedure than the patient recovering from a myocardial infarction. Once patient needs are known, the next step is to match them with available staff resources.

Establishing staff resources   The nurse in charge next establishes the staff resources available to care for patients. She needs to establish who is on duty, who is off sick, on annual leave, or on a study day, and the skill mix of trained staff to learners, experienced staff to newcomers.

Allocating staff to patients   Using her professional judgement, and based on her estimate of patient dependency, the available staff are allocated to patients, ensuring a balanced caseload for each primary nurse, and matching skills and experience of nurses to patient needs. At this early stage she should inform the nursing administration should she require extra staff.

Inform staff   Clarity of communication about the nurse's delegated duties and responsibilities with respect to the patients she is caring for is essential. The care plan and update received during the report should be enhanced by the nurse in charge checking that the nurse concerned understands and is familiar with the procedures required. Appropriate attachment of learner nurses to trained staff enables trained staff to supervise, monitor and teach learners as required. The fact that less experienced nurses have recourse to senior staff frees the nurse in charge to undertake other managerial duties.

Review organisational components of day   As already noted, once management action has been taken to ensure the continuing care of patients (always the first priority), the nurse in charge is able to review other aspects of the day which require attention. This can take the form of a checklist with which to anticipate problems and delegate tasks. An example of what such a checklist might look like for a general ward is found in Table 1.

Number of empty beds?
Number of admissions: routine or emergency?
Number of transfers: Other wards or hospital? Transport? Time?
Number of discharges:
    Outpatient appointment: Booked?
    Drugs to take home: Ordered?
    District nurse: Arranged? Letter written?
    General practitioner's letter: Written?
    Health education information/advice on recovery: Given?
Number of theatre lists:
    Times?
    Preoperative preparations: Completed? Consent form signed?
    Preoperative medication: Written up? Time?
Drug rounds: Frequency?
Other investigations/treatments: X-rays? Scans?
Special equipment: Needed? Functioning?
Ward round: Nursing recommendations/observations available?
Doctors on call?
Medical teams on take?
Specific tasks: Ordering stores? Meals?
Teaching: Time available?
Liaison with other disciplines: Physio? OT? Dietitian? Ward clerk?
Coffee/lunch/supper breaks: Arranged? Trained staff cover?

Table 1. Organisational checklist.

Decide own priorities/delegate appropriately   Once the clinical practitioner has informed herself of the likely predictable events of the day she can select her own priorities, allocate tasks to herself and delegate others. She is then in the position of being in command of her time and will be better able to respond to unusual or untoward events (like patient complaints, accidents or incidents), or to attend to long-term managerial tasks.

Ending the shift   At the end of each shift information about the ward is collected and communicated to oncoming staff verbally in report and in written form on the patient's care plan. This exchange of information also provides an opportunity to review and evaluate care.

Managing long-term
There are a range of texts available which deal with long-term management issues (Matthews, 1982; Raybould, 1977; Rowden, 1984). It will not be possible to explain these in detail here; however, many of

the topics covered are concerned with techniques and activities aimed at maintaining the ward environment as a place in which patients' conditions improve, and staff and learners achieve job satisfaction (Ogier, 1982). Central to the maintenance of the work environment are the leadership skills of the ward sister. The capacity to motivate and lead a team of nurses depends, in turn, on quite specific managerial skills: first, the capacity to recruit and select staff via the mechanism of effective interviewing; second, the capacity to retain staff both in terms of skills in professional development, appraisal and performance review, and the sensitive planning and allocation of off-duty rotas; third, the demonstration of competence in relation to a range of management techniques, from ward budgeting to quality assurance to research appreciation (Pembrey and Fitzgerald, 1987). Finally, it seems, the perceived integrity and fairness of the manager is of fundamental importance.

References
Lelean, S.R. (1973) Ready for Report Nurse? RCN, London
Matthews, A. (1982) In Charge of the Ward. Blackwell Scientific Publications, Oxford.
Mintzberg, H. (1975) The Manager's Job: Folklore and Fact. Harvard Business Review No. 75409 July/August, 49-62.
Ogier, M.E. (1982) An Ideal Sister? RCN, London
Pembrey, S.E. (1980) The Ward Sister – Key To Nursing. RCN, London.
Pembrey, S. and Fitzgerald, M. (1987) Developing the potential of sisters. *Nursing Times,* 25 March, 27.
Raybould, E. (ed.) (1977) A Guide for Nurse Managers. Blackwell, Oxford.
Rowden, R. (ed.) (1984) Managing Nursing. Ballière Tindall, London.
Runciman, P. (1983) Ward Sister at Work. Churchill Livingstone, Edinburgh.
Waite, R. (1986) Nursing by numbers. *Nursing Times,* 19 February.
Walton, M. (1984) Management and Managing: A dynamic approach. Lippincott Nursing Series, Harper and Row, London.

7

Writing the Off-duty

Brian Gilchrist, MSc, RGN

Lecturer, Department of Nursing Studies, King's College, University of London

Writing the off-duty is, for many people, one of the most frustrating managerial tasks that the sister or charge nurse has to undertake. The need to satisfy simultaneously the needs of the nursing service, the school of nursing, the ward workload and, not least, the individual requests of the ward staff, mean that many hours (often outside work time) are spent every year in juggling these seemingly incompatible demands into a workable rota.

There is no perfect solution to this dilemma, and it is not the author's intention to suggest one. Rather, this paper highlights many of the conflicting factors which must be taken into account, and in doing so will provide the novice with some useful guidelines.

The constraints have been divided into a number of sections, although they are arbitrary and may overlap.

Legal constraints

These are factors which are set down by statute, or by outside bodies over which the manager has no control, but which must be known and understood. They include conditions of employment agreed by the Whitley Council (contained in the Nurses and Midwives Handbook, and updated periodically by 'letters' issued by the DHSS) such as the maximum hours to be worked, the 37½ hour week and any legal requirements such as the need for trained staff to check controlled drugs.

Also included in this category are individual contracts of employment which have been specially negotiated, and which might include agreements about hours or, for example, specific days of the week that the person has been employed to work.

Local constraints

These are factors which have been agreed locally or which form part of managerial rulings that are intended to ensure satisfactory working practices. In some hospitals many of these will be guidelines only, and may be changed with the agreement of the nurse concerned; in others, they may not be altered without the express permission of senior management. The nurse writing the off-duty will need to keep all of the following factors in mind.

Format of the off-duty

Number of consecutive days to be worked Many hospitals now state that no more than a certain number of days in a row can be worked unless there is good reason, such as the request for a certain day off. This, of course, is a maximum and individual wards may decide that within this guideline they wish to nominate some lower number.

Split days off Is this permitted at all? If so, there may be some restriction on how many times a month this can occur.

Weekends There may be an agreement, formal or informal, about the number of weekends off that the staff should receive each month. This might not be the same for all levels of staff, but might apply, for example, only to trained staff, or to the ward sister. In addition, there could be provision for a Friday or a Monday to be routinely added to make a long weekend possible. The situation is further complicated by staff who rotate through night duty, which may affect their allocation of weekends for that particular month.

Night duty Where there is a system of internal rotation the frequency of night duty should be closely monitored to ensure that the planned format is maintained, and that there are the correct number of days off before and after each group of nights allocated.

One further factor that needs to be taken into consideration is the extent to which it is permitted to request holidays during the time of their next night duty, if indeed it is permitted at all.

Daily working hours Set hours may be worked each day, or there may be a facility to vary them so that the ward is covered adequately at certain busy times. If there is an agreement about the number of early and late duties to be worked by each member of staff each week, then these will need to be adhered to once the off-duty is written. It must be remembered that the off-duty does not always start on a Monday.

Days preceding leave days Some hospitals try (and many staff request) to roster an early duty before a day off, and a late one after. The manager needs to decide whether this should be a set policy, or simply a desirable practice.

Pattern rosters In some areas there may already be a 'pattern roster' in use, in which the duties are set down month by month, and the names are simply inserted. Other patterns include a set pattern such as four on, two off, and so on. While such patterns may have some advantages, particularly in terms of predicting days off some time in advance, there does need to be a mechanism which allows staff to change duties, and which allows the manager to alter the pattern if, for example, the lines are not all filled at a particular time.

Holidays There may be set times when certain groups of staff, particularly students, are on holiday. The amount of notice that permanent staff have to give must also be taken into account, as do any limits on the number of staff that can be on holiday at any one time.

Busy days In surgical wards in particular, it is possible to predict the days on which more staff are going to be required to cope with operations, premedications and admission days. In other wards this may be a little more difficult, but factors such as consultants' acute take days can usually be predicted some time in advance.

Acting up On the days when the ward sister 'acts up' for the nursing officer, there would need to be adjustments made to the off-duty to ensure adequate coverage should she be called away from the ward for long periods of time.

Agency nurses Most units now have a policy regarding extra agency nurses to replace shortfalls in established posts, and it may even be possible to write them in to the off-duty without any further approval. However, financial controls generally mean that approval needs to be sought, and if the nursing officer is unable to supply an agency nurse because of either finance or unavailability, then the ward will still need to be safely covered.

Overtime   Is overtime permitted at all? Does it have to be approved in advance?

Local emergency plan   The ward may be part of the local plans for a major emergency, and the staffing levels would need to reflect this.

ENB rulings   National Board inspectors will look very closely at the level of student nurse supervision, and in some cases will even insist on a particular mix of staff grades and qualifications, eg the number of RSCNs covering a paediatric ward.

Night duty   The restrictions which are placed on the number of nights students are permitted to do, or their frequency, may be different from those which apply to trained staff, and ward managers are informed about this by the allocation office.

Examinations   Many students complain that their off-duty affects their performance during examinations. Some schools of nursing will have rulings about the number of days off before exams, or restrictions on night duty, particularly before finals. It is difficult for the person writing the off-duty, however, if the school does not have a mechanism for informing the wards of such dates.

Time in school   There may well be a local ruling about having the weekend (or at least Sunday) off before a week in school, as well as the weekend following a school block. This can create problems if the student then requests a further weekend for a special occasion, thus disadvantaging those students who have not had their 'quota' of off-duty weekends. Other factors which need to be taken into consideration include any rulings about night duty immediately preceeding school, and odd study days that might be scheduled for particular students.

Staff constraints
This is possibly the most difficult area of all, because it is in this area where the greatest potential for conflict lies, and where there is the greatest risk of upsetting staff. It cannot be emphasised enough that many potential problems can be avoided by the simple act of discussing any problems with the nurse concerned *before* the final off-duty is published. A sympathetic, understanding approach will often result in an acceptable solution being reached quickly, with a minimum of upset.

Staff/skill mix
Unfortunately, this is another factor which is often out of the control of the ward manager because of a number of outside influences. The ward establishment is generally reviewed after a close examination of the

workload of a particular ward. In many cases there may be a shortfall simply due to a lack of nurses in post, or because the levels were set at a time when the workload was very different. If this is the situation then the manager would need to make his or her superior aware of the situation, and be prepared to put the case for having the establishment altered.

Such action is clearly demanded by the UKCC Code of Professional Conduct and it may be argued that failure to do so might constitute an "act or ommission . . . detrimental to the safety of patients/clients," although this has yet to be tested. Nevertheless, the responsibility of the ward managers to "act always in such a way as to promote and safeguard the wellbeing and interests of patients/clients" is a strong argument to advance in favour of appropriate staffing levels.

The allocation of learners to the ward is also outside the control of the ward manager, but will clearly have a considerable impact on the construction of the off-duty.

The actual skill mix on a day-to-day basis forms one of the most important factors that needs to be taken into consideration when the off-duty is being written, both in terms of quality and quantity. The mix must include all the necessary expertise, as well as provision for the adequate supervision of junior nursing staff and auxilliary staff.

Another, often controversial, factor that needs to be taken into account at this point is the policy of the hospital with regard to the amount of responsibility that can be expected, or demanded, of the enrolled nurse. Careful attention needs to be paid to the level of knowledge and expertise that is needed to properly manage a ward.

Individual staff

Part-time or fixed duty staff Some members of the ward staff may work only set hours or days of the week. Such people are generally not totally inflexible, and may be prepared to change occasionally where a particular need arises. Such requests should be the exception rather than the rule, however, and need to be approached sensitively. More advantage could be taken of part-time staff, and any move towards flexible hours, crèche facilities and job sharing will add to the potential solutions available for ward staffing.

Personality conflicts Although obviously undesirable, it is sometimes the case that some members of staff are not compatible with each other. Although this should always be the subject of separate management action, part of the solution may be to ensure that contact is kept to a minimum, at least initially; alternatively, the parties may be rostered together at the same time as a senior member of the staff so that the problem can be identified and resolved. Such conflicts can be especially counterproductive on night duty, and should be avoided if possible in that situation.

Staff supervision   Many hospitals now have a staff development programme which may include an element of clinical supervision as part of the requirements of the course. This may mean that the duties of the student and her supervisor may need to be coordinated.

The introduction of various 'mentor' schemes has also increased the pressure to ensure that the student and her mentor are working together for a certain proportion of the time available. It may also be useful for the sister to have worked at least one duty with every student so that when the ward reports are prepared the sister has some knowledge of the student concerned, and is fully responsible for the report, which may be actually written by a staff nurse.

Other situations that need to be taken into account include students who have particular learning needs or those who have been identified as requiring extra supervision and guidance.

In-service education   In addition to the obvious needs of the learners, consideration also needs to be given to the necessity for the trained staff to attend study days, or to have the facility to attend courses for further or higher qualifications. Although such a programme may have been approved by senior management, it may have considerable implications for the off-duty if the leave is needed on a regular basis.

Staff preferences   If a pattern roster is in use, then there will need to be some facility for the staff to change duties.

Where there is no pattern, some sort of request system is generally available. A consistent, written policy is essential for such a system to work properly, and it must take into account such things as who (if anyone) has priority, what length of notice must be given, how many requests are allowed, how much time is given following the publication of a ward change of allocation list, what facilities there are for urgent requests and, most importantly, what the policy of the ward is on changing shifts once the off-duty has been published.

There may have to be variations to cater for particular situations, eg Christmas and New Year, and in these situations the main concern is generally to ensure that everyone is given a reasonable share of both the 'good' and 'bad' duties. Some staff may have a preference for a particular duty for example, to accommodate a regular evening class.

Ensuring cooperation

It can be seen, then, that those writing the off-duty should take into account many different factors, a large number of which are outside their control. Despite this, writing the off-duty is an extremely important part of ward management, and although it does become easier with experience, it still requires the goodwill and cooperation of all staff.

To gain this cooperation, it is perhaps useful to keep a few simple points in mind:

1. Be flexible. The more rigid a structure you attempt to impose, the

more likelihood there is that you will make the whole task more difficult – within the legal constraints, there is considerable scope for variation.

2. Communicate with the staff as much as possible. Many nurses are

	1							2							3							4						
SISTER BROWN	D	D	A	D	/	/	/	A	D	D	/	A	m	m	D	D	A	D	/	/	/	A	D	D	/	A	m	m
SISTER S/N GREEN	/	A	D	A	D	m	m	D	/	A	D	D	/	/	/	A	D	A	D	m	m	D	/	A	D	D	/	/
S/N WHITE	A	D	A	A	D	/	/	/	A	D	A	D	m	m	/	/	N	N	N	N	N	N	N	/	/	/	/	/
S/N BLACK	/	/	N	N	N	N	N	N	N	/	/	/	/	/	/	/	A	D	A	A	m	m	D	/	A	D	D	/
S/N JONES	A	D	D	D	A	m	m	/	/	N	N	N	N	N	N	N	/	/	/	/	/	/	A	D	A	A	m	m
S/N SMITH	D	/	A	D	D	/	/	A	D	A	D	/	/	/	A	D	D	A	A	m	m	/	/	N	N	N	N	N
Student Nurse 1.	/	A	D	A	D	A	D	/	/	A	D	A	D	A	D	/	/	A	A	D	A	M	/	/	N	N	N	N
2.	A	D	/	/	A	D	A	D	A	A	D	/	/	/	/	A	D	A	D	A	D	/	/	A	D	A	D	A
3.	N	N	N	/	/	/	/	/	/	A	D	A	D	A	A	D	/	/	A	D	A	A	D	A	D	/	/	/
4.	M	/	/	N	N	N	N	N	N	N	/	/	/	/	/	/	A	A	D	D	A	D	D	/	/	A	D	A
5.	D	/	/	A	D	A	D	M	/	/	N	N	N	N	N	N	N	/	/	/	/	/	/	A	A	A	D	A	D
6.	/	/	A	D	A	D	A	D	/	/	A	D	A	D	M	/	/	N	N	N	N	N	N	N	/	/	/	/
7.	D	A	A	D	/	/	/	/	A	D	A	D	A	D	/	/	A	D	A	D	A	D	/	/	A	A	D	A
8.	/	A	S/o	M	/	/	A	A	D	S/o	M	/	/	A	A	A	S/o	M	/	/	A	A	D	S/o	M	/	/	A
9.	A	D	S/o	M	/	/	A	A	D	S/o	M	D	/	/	A	D	S/o	M	/	A	D	A	A	S/o	M	/	A	D
10.																												
11.																												
12.																												
13.																												
14.																												

Starts 4/4/88   FOUR WEEK OFF DUTY ROTA

A fixed rota showing staff nurses working one in six and students working one in eight nights.

happy to negotiate around a request if they are reassured that they will be able to have the time off that is crucial, and are often prepared to offer a sensible compromise which will suit all staff and the ward's needs.

3. Remember that nurses are people. Some people do seem to complain more than others, but you cannot expect a nurse to contribute her best to your ward if you roster her six nights leading up to a major exam – what is more likely to happen is that she will take a 'sickness break'.

4. Above all, use your common sense. Would you work the off-duty that you have written? Every line of it? If the answer to either of these questions is 'No' then why should you ask others to?

Many computer programmes are now being developed which can assist the ward manager in this task, and these may be very useful tools. However, the output still needs to be examined closely because, although they may generate an off-duty which is mathematically sound, there may be other, more human, factors to take into consideration.

Finally, it is often a very useful exercise to get other members of the trained staff to take turns at writing the off-duty from time to time. Apart from introducing them to an important managerial skill, another point of view may help to improve the overall standard of the off-duty and it certainly helps acquaint them with the many problems involved.

Writing the off-duty

So how should you proceed? There is no one system that is any better than the rest, but here are some suggested guidelines:

You will need: a sharp pencil; a large eraser; an appropriately ruled sheet of paper; a quiet place where you will not be interrupted; an hour or two; plenty of patience. *In this order:*

1. Write in all the people who have permanent shifts.
2. Write in any other fixed shifts, eg those in school or on holiday.
3. Write in the requests.
4. Add the night duty, and the days off.
5. Now write the off-duty for the trained staff.
6. Add the students last. (This is not because the students are the lowest priority but because trained staff supervision must come first.)
7. Check the numbers for each shift, and adjust according to ward needs.
8. Display the proposed rota for a day or two to allow for a certain amount of negotiation to take place before the final copy is sent to the manager. This will prevent upset and wasted time later on.

There is a certain amount of satisfaction associated with completing a workable roster, but be assured that however good it looks, something or someone is sure to come along and require changes. The only solution in this situation is to keep cool!

Reference
DHSS. The Nursing and Midwifery staff negotiating council conditions of service and rates of pay (The Nurse's and Midwife's Handbook). Standard conditions which are regularly updated.

Bibliography
Matthews, A. (1982) In charge of the ward. Blackwell Scientific Publications London. A useful, practical reference work for all ward managers.
Rowden, R. (1984) Managing Nursing. Ballière Tindall London. Particularly strong on industrial relations aspects of human management.

8

Objectives for care: replacing procedures with guidelines

Gillian Snowley, M.Ed, BSc, RGN, DN,
Deputy Director, Nurse Education, North Lincolnshire School of Nursing

Peter J. Nicklin, M.Ed, RGN, RMN,RNT,
Director of Nurse Education, York Health Authority

Since the inception of the NHS, demands upon the service and its employees have increased. Medical technology, demographic change, consumer expectation and managerial concerns for improved productivity, have all conspired to increase the workload of the caring professions. As these demands have intensified, there has been a tendency to forget the importance of the consumer's identity and personal needs. The nursing profession has recognised and acknowledged this neglect, and attempted to provide a solution by adopting the nursing process as a broad philosophy for the planning and delivery of healthcare.

Definitions of the 'nursing process' vary, but common to all are the assumptions that it is goal-directed, systematic, rational and problem-solving. The registered nurse is accountable for delivery of care, based on an assessment of the individual's needs, and for subsequent measurement of the effectiveness (evaluation) of that care. Implementing the nursing process continues to pose significant problems for the profession. The Nurse Education Research Unit (1986) has provided valuable insights into the difficulties experienced by nurses.

A significant barrier
In 1983, the North Lincolnshire Health Authority acknowledged that the 'nursing procedure manual' was a significant barrier to the successful implementation of the nursing process, as it gave no scope for an individualised and prescriptive approach to care. With its rampant and unbending concentration on task, the perfect completion of which would follow the same format on every occasion, the patient's individual needs seemed insignificant. All patients were expected to respond equally, and all nurses to behave with almost military precision on every occasion, despite any special circumstances which could prevail. The procedure manual restricted professional clinical freedom and became a recipe book for nursing. It also encouraged disregard for the psychosocial aspects of

care delivery.

This was not to say that procedures were inaccurate, or that accuracy in performing procedures was and is unimportant or unnecessary. But they omitted extra dimensions of care which allow total consideration of the patient. The procedure manual tended to dictate specific technical and highly visible nursing actions in a ritualistic manner, with no concern for assessment, planning and evaluation of nursing care. It did not recognise the individual nurse's role in the process of care delivery – except perhaps for the favourite opening instruction: "Tell the patient what you are going to do". Even that became a regulation!

In 1983, North Lincolnshire's chief nursing officer recommended that "guidelines for nursing practice, which reflect acceptable standards of care" be formulated. Membership of the nursing guidelines committee was drawn from all the health units within the district, including the nurse education unit, so all nurses, midwives and health visitors were represented. The authors were members of this group.

Conceptual differences

During the early stages, we experienced some difficulty in grasping the conceptual differences between 'procedure' and 'guideline', and had little idea what the latter would look like. The prospect of reinventing the wheel did not inspire much enthusiasm, so we undertook the obligatory literature search to determine what had been published in this area. There was little or no information from UK sources, but American literature, while describing a guidelines approach, did not seem to offer anything very different, and was not always consistent with Lincolnshire nursing culture. However, we acknowledged that what we were calling 'guidelines' may not have been so defined by the rest of the nursing profession. Informal discussions with colleagues both regionally and nationally did not reveal any formal work of a similar nature, although it may well have existed. Work subsequently published by the Royal Marsden Hospital (Pritchard and Walker, 1984) while sharing some of the characteristics of our guidelines, was not entirely consistent with our philosophy. This meant we could not rely on precedents for guidance, but we were not going to distort someone else's structure to fit our own circumstances. In short, we started from scratch.

Although we did not realise it for some time, we needed to ask the question "what does nursing seek to achieve?" Certainly the procedure manual does not answer this. Once we had recognised the importance of the question, we needed to examine models of nursing to identify the structure of nursing guidelines. We considered Orem's (self-care), Roper et al's (activities of living) and Roy's (adaptation model), but eventually returned to basics – to Virginia Henderson's Basic Principles of Nursing Care (1969), which fulfilled our need for a comprehensive and readily understood model. The committee then began composing guidelines under the headings originally described by Henderson.

To say this was difficult would be an understatement. Our first attempts were either too long, too short, too esoteric, too academic, too trivial, too general or too detailed – and sometimes several of these combined! We had problems with semantics and grammar, and our morale sometimes slumped, but by a process of trial and error, consultation and cooperation, we agreed a style of describing nursing intention which had the potential for improving patient care.

Early guidelines

Our early guidelines were expressed as the aims and objectives of nursing on psychosocial, physiological and educational dimensions. Each had an evaluation component, but their most important feature was that each was generated from available literature and published research, and supported by a bibliography.

By late 1985, the committee had developed and disseminated 17 guidelines to all care points in the district. In addition to Henderson's 14 components of basic nursing care, we acknowledged the need to provide guidance on expressing sexuality; helping patients in pain and the care of the dying and bereaved.

Guidelines were intended to be used by trained nurses who can responsibly and reasonably interpret them with discretion and with the authority which the research base provides. We believed they should encourage thoughtful and individual delivery of care by nurses who are accountable for their own actions. The guidelines were recognised as the basis for teaching nurses in training, and for the use of nursing assistants with trained supervision.

Mixed reception

Not surprisingly, our guidelines had a mixed reception in the clinical areas where they were intended to be used. Their appearance coincided with many other recent changes in the philosophy and implementation of healthcare delivery, both nationally and locally directed. Many nurses regarded them as "just another new idea thrust upon us by nurse managers and nurse educators" – despite the fact that clinical nurses from all specialties were members of the committee, and joint authors of the guidelines. One specific problem was that they were seen as isolated documents, and not as an integral part of a systematic and prescriptive approach to individual care. Suddenly, the procedure manual became a highly valued lifeline, even though in many areas it gathered dust and its whereabouts remained unknown. In considering this dilemma, the committee suggested that guidelines were an important aid to the implementation of the nursing process, and that every opportunity to present them as such be pursued. The Open University's Distance Learning Course P553 – A Systematic Approach to Nursing Care (1984) was widely used within the district, both in the continuing education department and within individual units, where courses were being led by nurse managers. The guidelines were therefore introduced to staff undertaking this course as a tool for goal setting and care planning within whichever nursing model was being used in the clinical area. In fact, they provided suitably phrased goals and objectives which would not disgrace any care plan. Although the committee members recognised a responsibility for ensuring such progress and integration of materials, the real work, on a large scale, was done by clinical nurses themselves, with encouragement and facilitation by management and education.

Despite the suspicion and antagonism with which guidelines were received, enough clinical nurses suggested ways in which they could be improved. Members of the committee were grateful for this information – at least in some areas they had not been ignored. Strong statements of dissatisfaction, accompanied by notes of guidance for change, were far more acceptable than apathy.

Revising the format

Armed with suggestions for a changed format, the committee began the formidable task of revision in 1986. This was almost more difficult than beginning with a blank sheet. The original philosophy remained intact, but presentation of the guidelines now evolved into a staged format of assessment, planning, implementation and evaluation. The original objectives, sometimes the results of agonising search for the right expression, remained; so too did the bibliographies, but each has been updated and refined. The result is Objectives for Care, a source book for all nurses, midwives and health visitors, working in any practice setting. This book is the product of an energetic group who were convinced at the outset of the value of the task which confronted them. Some of us had little idea of its enormity, but the team effort involved was its most encouraging aspect.

The book has now been published and every care point in the district has received a copy to replace the old guidelines folder. No doubt it will attract some criticism, as well as some degree of welcome. We sincerely hope it will not remain out of sight long enough to attract dust!

- *Objectives for Care* is available from Austen Cornish Publishers, Austen Cornish House, Walham Grove, London SW6 1QW. Price £7.50 inc. p+p.

References
NERU (1986) Report of the Nursing Process Working Party. King's College, London.
Pretchard, A.P. and Walker, V.A. (1984) The Royal Marsden Hospital Manual of Clinical Nursing Policies and Procedures. Harper and Row, London.
Henderson, V. (1969) Basic Principles of Nursing Care. ICN, Geneva.
Open University (1984) A Systematic Approach to Nursing Care – An Introduction (P553). OU Press, Milton Keynes.

9

Visiting: should you be more involved?

Judith Ralphs, BSc, RGN
Staff Nurse, St Christopher's Hospice, London

Visitors are a common sight in most wards. Nurses often have mixed feelings about their presence, commonly using an influx of visits as an excuse for a quick cup of tea, while the patients are momentarily distracted from their illnesses and engrossed in family and friends. As nurses, we assume all visits are welcome, but have little informed knowledge of how patients find these times. Yet we have all visited people in hospital and know the atmosphere can be awkward and artificial.

The 'good' visitor	The 'bad' visitor
1. Visits in ones and twos, stays only for half/one hour, generally in the afternoon when patient is up and washed but not yet too tired.	Visits in large groups, stays too long with little regard as to how the patient is feeling.
2. Really wants to come and see the patient.	Makes his visit appear a duty, or spends the time chatting to others, ignoring the patient.
3. Able to sit and relax looking at ease with the patient, feels free to knit or watch TV.	Appears tense, sits on edge of seat, or paces up and down ward looking at watch.
4. Does not pity the patient, but able to laugh and joke, treating the patient as normal.	Dwells on patient's illness, reluctant to be light-hearted, or appears desperately cheerful. – 'You look marvellous', when it is clear the patient is looking pale and ill.
5. Talks about outside matters, family news, gossip. Many patients prefer to talk about anything but their illness – a most unpopular topic.	Reluctant to talk about old times in case of upsetting the patient.
6. Aware of patient's practical needs, ie taking away dirty washing, mouldy fruit.	Patient feels visitor is coming for his own needs, ie 'to have a good moan'.
7. Gives patient choice about next visit. (Half the sample liked planned visits but often were never asked by their visitors.)	Assumes he may come again and that the patient will always be pleased and well enough to see him.

Table 1. What makes a 'good' or 'bad' visitor?

Changing opinions

Opinions about visiting hospital patients have changed over the years. Somerville Hastings believed half an hour a day was enough (1963), the object being to soothe and encourage the patients, not to interest or amuse the visitors (or, it can be supposed, the patient!). Cartwright (1964) found in her study of ward life, that visiting time was enjoyed greatly and broke the monotony and boredom of the hospital routine.

One hospital visiting report, undertaken by the University of Hull in 1966, goes further: "Visiting hours are not merely an interruption of ward routine, they are a means by which a patient is kept in touch with the outside world, which he understands, making it easier to fit in on his return."

Important part of the day

This author's interest has developed through two studies undertaken on patients' views on hospital life. The first study, undertaken, as an undergraduate nurse, investigated ward routine: it was found that visiting hours, along with meal times, were to patients the most important and looked-forward- to part of the day. This finding prompted the author to look at this subject further, as part of an ENB course, 'Care of the Dying'.

A number of patients (18) at St. Christopher's Hospice were asked their views about having visitors. The hospice has open visiting apart from on Monday, which is a rest day; thus there is little external control on visiting.

It was found that most patients appreciated having visitors, but felt there could be improvements. From the results of this study, it was concluded that some people are naturally good at visiting and enjoyed by the patient, whereas others made their visits rather tiresome to all concerned.

Table 1 summarises the information gathered from the two studies, and illustrates aspects of the 'good' and the 'bad' visitors.

Although these studies involve terminally ill patients, the views expressed are valuable to those involved with general patients as the patients in this sample did not class themselves as 'the dying', but wanted to be treated as normal. In any case, most wards have some terminally ill patients.

Keeping in touch

As Gattis (1974) writes:

"Deep subjects are still in the minority, they are still people with a past and a present history, and therefore will want to talk about these things, to keep in touch with the outside world, which is all part of living."

This is all very interesting, but is there a nursing role? This author believes that there is.

Problem	Aim	Action	Evaluation
1. Patient tired by too many visitors	Visitors come in ones and twos for half hour only.	Ask next of kin to arrange with visitors to ring him/her before visiting. If a large group of visitors arrives, ask them to visit two at a time.	Now only two small groups of visitors daily. Able to enjoy these times as not tired out.
2. Visits appear awkward with visitor ill at ease.	Patient and visitor enjoy time together.	Informally ask patient about visiting time; does he think there is a problem? If he does, discuss causes and what would help: nurse joining in. visitor and patient 'do' something together, eg walk in garden. Be friendly to visitor so does not feel a stranger.	How are they now interacting? Body language looks relaxed.

Table 2. Two possible problems that could be added to a care plan.

Grollman (1974) writes:

"Visiting is like a medicine; useful and pleasant at certain times, but can become toxic at higher levels."

Thus nurses can help prevent visiting times – and visitors themselves – from becoming toxic, and make it a pleasant and useful occasion.

Nursing intervention

Perhaps nurses should see it as part of their symptom control.

Four nursing interventions are suggested:

1. Enquire how each patient is finding visiting times – this can be done informally, eg at bath times. Be alert to any hints given, as patients may feel guilty if they have mixed feelings about their visitors. Observe how patient and visitor interact together: do they look relaxed and as if they are enjoying their time together?

2. Assess if there is a problem, eg too many visitors, awkward silences. If a problem is identified, add it to the patient's care plan, along with the aim.

3. Give practical help. Some of the things nurses have done on the author's ward are:

  i. Discuss ideas at report time;
  ii. Have a gentle word with visitors as they enter;
  iii. Place a polite notice at patient's door;
  iv. Join in awkward conversation – lighten the tone if necessary;
  v. Give patients a rest, with periods of time free from visitors. Obviously, all of these things should be done with sensitivity and in consultation with the patient.
4. Evaluate. Informally ask patient how he is now finding visiting times. Observe if visitors have made the desired changes in behaviour.

Table 2 is an example of two possible problems that could be added to a care plan.

Although many visitors are a pleasure, the author believes nurses do have a role to play in their handling. Involvement with managing visiting time will help patients enjoy visitors' time on the ward and to get the most possible out of such important times.

References
Cartwright, A. (1964) Human Relations and Hospital Care. Routledge and Kegan Paul, London.
Gattis, J.W. (1974) in Barton, D. (ed) Death and Dying. Chapter 10. Wavery Press, Baltimore.
Grollman, E.A. (1974) Practical Guide for Living. Beaver Press, Boston.
Somerville Hastings, A. (1962) Visiting in hospital. *British Medical Journal*, No. 5338.
University of Hull (1966) Department of Social Administration. Hospital project visiting report. Unpublished.

10

Triage in accident and emergency

Ann Grose, SRN
Trauma Services Manager, Queen Alexandra Hospital, Portsmouth

The problem that faced our A&E department is not unique. The department is modern, well-equipped and covers a catchment area of 172.29 square miles, within which there is light and heavy industry, a motorway, remote rural areas, a busy rail link with London, the south, the sea and Heathrow Airport.

Over the last 10 years the numbers of attenders, both new and returns, has risen by an average of 1,737.4 per year. In 1985, new patients totalled 59,989, and the returns 8,827.

Nurse staffing levels provide 24-hour cover, including staffing a 10-bedded observation ward. Due to location, the department is subject to large seasonal variations in population; usually, medical cover is increased to take account of this. Early in 1986 it was learned that the department would possibly not get this increase; this posed the problem of how existing staff would cope with ever-increasing patient numbers, resulting in longer waiting times and the frustration and abuse that this could cause.

At various accident and emergency conferences I had heard about triage, a system of sorting patients according to priority, and as a result implemented a system of desk nurse whereby the reception staff had a named nurse to whom they could relate should a problem arise. This, plus the fact that the receptionists were astute, reassured staff that priorities were being dealt with. But would that system help overcome the forthcoming dilemma?

In April 1986, an article appeared in the nursing press (Nursing Times, 1986). I considered how useful it would be if, during busy periods, the triage nurse could see, treat and discharge minor injuries with the patient's permission without referral to a doctor. After discussion with the consultants, who agreed it was a possibility, the next step was to find who was using a triage system, and how it had been set up. Little had been published in Great Britain about the system.

A study carried out in Leicester (Parmer and Hewitt, 1985) gave some clues, as did another from University College Hospital, London (Thayre, 1985). However, most of the reports on triage were American, and not comparable with the situation or resources in this particular A&E

department. Of the numerous papers I read, including that of Blythin (1983), all agreed that the advantages of triage were:
1. Improved standards of care.
2. Reduction of fear and anxiety by improved communication.

Organisation of the trial

Discussions began with consultants and senior nursing staff of the department. In view of the expected medical deficit, it was agreed that a trial on triage would proceed and a senior nurse could see and treat minor conditions. Approval was sought from the health authority to introduce the following:
1. Patients in A&E will be seen in strict order of severity/priority, not time or arrival.
2. Priority will be assessed by a senior nurse, and discussed with a doctor if necessary.
3. No patient will be turned away and refused access to a doctor, but some have to wait a considerable length of time.
4. When the department is very busy, some minor conditions will be seen and treated solely by nurses without automatic reference to a doctor; the full agreement of the patient will be obtained.

Approval by the health authority was given. The department was on its way. Sisters and charge nurses were asked once again if they were committed to the trial; all agreed, with minor reservations, such as:
- Privacy if needed. The triage nurse would use an office next to the reception area.
- Communications for the triage nurse. A telephone from reception would be moved over to the nurse's desk and the intercom (to contact specific areas within the department) placed where it could be used easily by both nurse and receptionist.
- Problems arising with a patient seen, treated and discharged by the triage nurse. Copies of the casualty card for each patient treated would be kept and seen daily by the consultant.

The receptionists were informed of what the nurses were going to do, a short explanation of triage was sent to the local press, and letters were sent to GPs and practice nurses, many of whom took up the invitation to visit the department and discuss triage.

Having alerted colleagues in the community, a great deal of thought went into wording of notices for display around the department. These needed to be brief, and to the point.

Making decisions

Next came the logistics. Where would staff triage the patients? Would they see them before or after the receptionist? Did the triage nurse need telephone and intercom access? Should she use a desk in view of the waiting room, or screen herself off? How would the nurses coming to collect the next patient know the priority of care?

It was decided that the individual would conduct triage in the way that felt most comfortable to him/her. A partitioned office filing box was purchased in which the triage nurse would place casualty cards in priority order. A simple categorisation system was constructed to assess patient priority and enable the trial to be evaluated as follows:

1. Serious injury, chest pain, multiple trauma, collapse.
2. Moderate injury or illness, large limb fracture, epilepsy, overdose, diabetic.
3. Minor injury, sprains, minor small lacerations, minor head injury.
4. Trivial ailments, which could have been treated elsewhere.

Facts and figures   For the trial only, sisters and charge nurses would act as triage nurses, a daily record would be kept from 9am to 9pm of their activities in assessing patients, action taken and advice given.

In the past attendance figures had been kept on colourful graphs, but it was not known exactly what these numbers represented. Staff knew there was a large group of people who should have gone to their GP or health centre or used a plaster or aspirin; and it was thought a fair number of serious injuries or illnesses were also treated. The trial would provide an opportunity to gather facts and figures to assess these theories. Staff were consulted about documentation. They were all aware of the need to complete this, and obviously looked for the least time-consuming format.

Objectives of the trial

1. To assess severity of conditions of patients attending the department, and determine priorities of treatment.
2. To reduce waiting times for patients (other than those arriving by ambulance), particularly the interval between arrival and treatment, and ensure these reflect severity of condition.
3. To direct inappropriate attenders to other sources of advice or treatment, (ie, GP surgeries, health centres).
4. To keep relatives informed about the condition of patients, thus allaying unnecessary anxiety.

A trial ran from 20 July to 30 September 1986. Before this, staff were made familiar with the categories, and what was expected of them. The sisters and charge nurses were asked to complete a questionnaire regarding their role perception. Staff learned that the expected drop in medical staffing would not occur, but it was decided they would still follow the proposal that a nurse may see and treat minor conditions if and when necessary.

Collecting information   From 29 June, for three weeks, information was collected on waiting times by asking both medical and nursing staff to record times of treatment on casualty cards. It was hoped that this information would help when making comparisons before and during triage. It was felt that the public themselves might like to contribute, so a suggestion box was organised in the waiting area.

Triage on trial

The great day dawned. Two of the triage nurses went off sick, and the carefully planned off-duty had to be carefully replanned.

Staff took a while to get used to putting all the times on casualty cards, and were uncertain when there was a category change, eg, a category 1 collapse turns out to be a faint – category 3.

Category 3 was too broad; it needed to be divided, into 3A and 3B. Some reception staff felt threatened by what nursing staff were doing. In the past they have been described as 'gate-keepers', and now that role had been taken from them. Rumour was rife. The sisters and charge nurses had different feelings and approaches to the role of triage nurse. Some found it embarrassing, while others missed the clinical involvement, especially when the ward was busy.

Teething problems   Privacy for the patient talking to the triage nurse left a lot to be desired. Communication with the triage nurse was difficult. From the data collected it appeared that there were fewer seriously ill or injured patients than usual, but that was because documentation stopped at 9 pm, at the end of the triage nurses' shift. It was decided that a true picture could only be gained by categorising patients 24 hours a day. Arrangements were made for data to be summarised every morning. It proved very time-consuming (Monday mornings involved three days' data).

The suggestion box was a surprise. Some of the comments were constructive; all signed correspondence was acknowledged – one young man became a pen pal as he kept replying to our answers. At the end of the triage trial, staff continued to categorise patients for two weeks for a comparison of waiting times. All sisters and charge nurses were again interviewed individually, as were receptionists, on their views of triage. The remaining staff were asked their opinion at a unit meeting.

A worthwhile project

The overall impression of the trial from all staff was that the project was worth doing. Objectives were achieved by assessing priority when the patient arrived in reception and from data collected before the system started. There was a reduction in waiting time for patients in all categories. There were disadvantages, too, which need to be given further consideration. The layout of the department was a problem but could be overcome with small building alterations. Availability of information from other departments practising triage would have been helpful in determining staff training needs, usefulness and type of data collected, the problems experienced and how they were overcome.

Data collected before and during the trial provided evidence on waiting times, categories of patients seen and workload peaks. It really only confirmed what staff already knew. Improved communication between the nurse, patients and relatives resulted in a less hostile waiting room. For triage nurses it had been difficult and, as one sister said: "What box do you tick for gratitude on the face of a patient you spend a long time talking to about their particular problem?"

Hopefully, referrals of inappropriate attenders have helped to educate the public about use of the accident and emergency department.

Outcomes of the trial

Since completion of the trial, the nursing staff and consultants have agreed that the development of triage and the introduction of the nurse practitioner are appropriate ways forward for busy A & E departments such as ours. After joint discussion, a protocol has been drawn up to assist senior nursing staff when practising either role. A bank nurse, recently a sister in the department, has been employed for sixteen hours a week to help practice and establish the triage system, and we were fortunate in having our plans and proposals for a purpose built triage room, accepted and paid for by the hospital League of Friends, this was completed in July 1989 and we have found it to be invaluable. We are currently examining the possibility of improving our facilities for children and we are also considering the use of videos in the waiting area.

We have continued with a suggestion box in the reception area and we respond to all correspondence where there is a name and address. Patients and relatives have commented on the usefulness of the triage nurse, and are much more content when having to wait as they are well informed of the possible length of their stay and the reasons for any delays. When the department is busy, patients are very pleased to be treated by the nurse practitioner; very few refuse the service. In 1986 the total number of attendances in the A & E department totalled 69,430, 70,674 in 1987, and 72,777 in 1988. The upward trend is continuing. We believe that the triage system is contributing to improved effectiveness in the A & E department, even though the demand on our services is increasing.

References:
Blythin, P. (1983) Would youd like to wait over there, please. *Nursing Mirror,* **157,** 23, 36-70.
Shorter Oxford English Dictionary (Vol.II) (1973) page 2358 (and addenda).
Parma, M. and Hewitt, E. (1985) Triage on trial. *Senior Nurse,* **2,** 21-2, 5.
Thayre, K. (1985) Innovations in accident and emergency. *Nursing Mirror Supplement,* **160,** 13, 12-160.
Nursing Times (1986) Accident and emergency uses nurse practitioner. *Nursing Times* (News item), **82,** 14, 60.

11

Managing an operating department

Bernice J. M. West, MA, RGN

Continuing Education Team, Foresterhill College, Aberdeen

Within the theatre suite, a set of powerful constraints combine to make the nurse's role more complex and specialised. The throughput of patients, the technical demands and the risks involved in surgery all make nursing care in operating departments (ODs) especially dynamic and coordinated.

To investigate this highly skilled type of nursing requires inside knowledge and outside objectivity. Several conditions lend themselves to systematic study and enquiry: the routinisation of work, variations in skills required and decision-making concerning patient care.

This chapter summarises and discusses a large-scale research project carried out in 1988. The data-set derives from observation and interviews carried out in 10 theatre suites, including both NHS and private sector hospitals. A report has been completed and circulated to half of the Scottish Health Boards.

The hospitals included in the study varied in size and location. They consisted of three major teaching hospitals, four self-contained provincial hospitals, one large district hospital and two hospitals from the private sector. Together they carry out 69 per cent of all surgery performed in Scotland and cater for 59 per cent of the Scottish population (HMSO, 1983).

The data collected from observations made and staff interviews conducted has been presented and analysed generally (West, 1987). To maintain confidentiality neither specific theatres nor hospitals will be named. The project was primarily concerned with the organisation and planning of care within theatre suites.

Recommendations

For a theatre suite to run smoothly, good organisation is necessary in the OD. Care must be planned in order to integrate a variety of skills, expertise, knowledge and technology in the interest of patients.

Since the recent development of large ODs, senior nursing staff have necessarily assumed more far-reaching responsibilities than the simple supervision of an operating session (Johnston and Hunter, 1984). Issues may arise which test the staffing allocation to the full; for instance, if lists are allowed to run over time on several occasions, staff with other responsibilities will be dissatisfied.

Several organisational goals for staff allocation have been specified in the literature to ensure the smooth running of the department. The theatre timetable should be planned around the commitments of all grades of staff and a sense of responsibility towards the patient, and a team leader should be assigned to each operating session to ensure smooth running of the list (Craig, 1978). Sessions should be organised to avoid peaks and troughs of activity and to allow essential maintenance to be carried out, while time should be set aside to allow team members to discuss any strategies and problems prior to surgery. The patient can then receive a high standard of expertise and care from all staff.

A government document on the building and planning of ODs states that "Concentration of operating facilities gives maximum flexibility and economy in use when programming surgical work; it simplifies supply and disposal arrangements and allows maximum economy in staff, main plant service rooms and running costs of the engineering services. Space economy is achieved by the centralisation of common ancillary accommodation (stores, staff-changing and rest rooms) and provision of recovery space as a single unit close to all theatres" (DHSS, 1970).

The optimum size for good organisation and staff morale has been identified by Philips (1980), who said a complex of no more than eight theatres would satisfy the objectives set out in the government document without causing too many staff-related problems. All of the larger suites in the main teaching hospitals and district hospitals followed strict operating schedules and timetables. The turnover of patients who came through these departments daily meant the staff worked with a high degree of routinisation, and the scope for individual nursing care appeared to be reduced. In some areas staffing levels were not satisfactory, and staff morale at the time of visiting was fairly low.

Established staffing formulae which have been devised with ward-based nursing and nursing workload per patient as their basis are not applicable in the theatre situation (SHHD, 1969; IOR, 1974). In theatre the nursing workload is very high per patient for a short period of time. The peaks and troughs of theatre activity make unusual demands on the staff. Furthermore, the nature of the work varies considerably in one day, unlike the ward situation, where the workload remains fairly constant in terms of type of ward and number of beds.

Recommendations on theatre staffing levels have been set out by the National Association of Theatre Nurses (NATN) (Philips, 1980) who suggest a basic non-medical team of five should be available for each session, the leader of whom must be a qualified nurse. Furthermore, another member should be suitably trained to assist the anaesthetist and care for an unconscious patient. This person can either be an operating department assistant (ODA) or a qualified nurse, but not a member of the ancillary staff (Preston, 1972).

Several sources in the literature have recognised that a high proportion of nursing-time is spent on non-nursing duties (eg Lewin, 1970). Such duties are often domestic or clerical, and not related to nursing, but are essential to the smooth and effective running of an OD (Johnson and Kelly, 1985). This research has suggested that the employment of ancillary staff to ease the nursing workload helps in the efficient running of the department. Specific portering staff ensures the safe and speedy transfer of patients, while a well-trained and highly-motivated domestic team is essential for the smooth running of an OD. A centralised instrument service should be available to help relieve nurses of the task of preparing instruments, and close liaison is necessary with the sterile supply department to ensure nursing time is not wasted chasing up orders. Deliveries of stores and sterile supplies are best planned in advance so that a quantity of large bulky items do not arrive on the busiest day of the week. Nursing assistants or theatre orderlies should be available to deal with the stock when it arrives. Finally, the employment of a secretary or receptionist within the department for clerical and telephone duties relieves the nurse's workload (Johnson and Kelly, 1985).

A new environment
As theatre is a totally new environment and learning situation for student and pupil nurses, there can be little doubt that without associated instruction the theatre experience would be a waste of time (Clarke et al, 1985). A carefully planned teaching programme which implements a clear set of objectives means the learner can obtain a greater understanding of how to provide the physical and psychological care of the surgical patient. As learners are bound by UKCC regulations to obtain theatre experience, it is important that this time is relevant.

This research developed a modular teaching programme suitable for student and pupil nurses in theatre. The modules are designed to introduce the learner to the various nursing roles in the OD and to provide the opportunity for the learner to participate fully as a member of a multidisciplinary team. Each module has been standardised to include aim, method of attainment, content and learning outcomes. The final formulation has been carried out under the auspices of NATN. The resultant document has been produced in collaboration with several nurse educationalist colleagues (Chadwick et al, 1988).

Recent research (Brown and Rowland, 1980) has shown that nurses find work in the anaesthetic room boring and repetitive. To try and overcome the problem of nurse recruitment into the anaesthetic room, Griffiths (1984) suggested a combined in-service teaching programme, suitable for all theatre nurses, which includes work in the anaesthetic and recovery rooms. With this recommendation in mind it is suggested that teaching programmes should be devised for all newly-appointed staff. For qualified nurses and ODAs the report recommends the programme lasts for six months and that specific objectives should be defined for participants to fulfil. The use of structured teaching programmes for all grades of staff can ensure that basic information is relayed to new employees and also that their progress can be monitored.

The full utilisation of teaching programmes requires the cooperation of all experienced staff and the authority of a teaching coordinator. The teaching coordinator should make full use of the resources available from medical or surgical firms, colleges of nursing and the nearest medical school to offer in-service education to experienced theatre staff.

A frightening experience

For most patients, a surgical operation is an important, daunting and frightening experience (Gooch, 1984), and subjective accounts of the care received will dwell a long time in the patient's memory. Frequently the journey from the ward to the operating department is the only part of the theatre experience to be remembered. Research evidence has shown that the most anxious time for surgical patients is being summoned to theatre (English et al, 1983). To alleviate such anxiety, it is important that the patient has been informed of the nature of the journey to theatre and is accompanied by a familiar nurse. (This could be the theatre nurse preferably.) The presence of someone 'on the inside' whom the patient knows is certainly advisable (Thomson-Keith, 1985). Recent studies have suggested the recovery, and/or anaesthetic room nurse is the best person to visit surgical patients (eg, Campbell and Harvey, 1984).

As previously stated, several studies have shown the transmission of relevant information to patients has a beneficial effect on their postoperative recovery (Hayward, 1975; Boore, 1978). Another area of research which warrants attention is the extensive literature dealing with the presence of significant others in ODs – the NATN positively advocate the opportunity for them to accompany patients to the anaesthetic room.

Nursing literature has outlined the benefits of parents accompanying children to the anaesthetic room (eg Glasper, 1988) and some authorities and boards employ a nurse counseller to accompany the parent. Clearly this topic deserves consideration by theatre managers.

Preoperative visits

Further research conducted on the issues of perception and communication has shown that nurses are perceived by other health professionals as the group who give most information to patients (Davis, 1983). However, it is important that the staff involved in this aspect of patient care have been instructed in interviewing and counselling techniques – to convey information competently requires special skills in listening and assessing what the patient says. Ideally, patients should be visited by the nurse who welcomes them into the department and remains with them until anaesthetised. This same nurse should be with them as they recover from the anaesthetic and are returned to the ward.

Apart from establishing an education programme on communication skills for those nurses wishing to participate in preoperative visiting, it is also necessary to organise and establish a good liaison with ward staff. If it is too difficult to visit every patient who comes through a large OD, ward staff should identify those who would benefit most from a theatre nurse visit. This should be included in the nursing assessment of the patient's needs as recorded upon the careplan. To avoid duplication of information and unnecessary accumulation of documentation, the use of one type of recording sheet for care is recommended.

The introduction of theatre careplans or check-lists has focused attention on the recording process but not necessarily on the planning of care. By using one continuous recording sheet for nursing care, the continuity and quality of patient care can be more easily assessed.

In America, elaborate careplans have been designed for each stage of the patient's career through surgery (eg, Thomson-Keith, 1985). However, such careplans are viewed as impractical by British nurses, who often complain of their lack of time for recording care in any detail. Other nurse researchers have focused on those aspects of the nursing process which are most applicable to theatre and so have reduced the concept of nursing care to an administrative check-list for entry into an OD (Shaw, 1983). Clearly some compromise is necessary in the working situation. No easy solution can be offered here; true implementation of the nursing process needs to be carried out alongside an ongoing teaching programme for all staff involved in practice.

Planning patient care

Before deciding on the organisation of a careplan, the theatre nurse should consider the following three areas, and work with her team to develop a conscious awareness of what actually takes place in preparing and caring for a surgical patient (Abdellah et al, 1960). Safety considerations should be observed throughout: when patients are in the department, are on their way to and from the department and especially when they are at the stage of recovery. Methods of planning the patient's safety and avoidance of potential hazards require close consideration.

The continued safeness of the operating room environment for both staff and patients may also be discussed. The safe administration of drugs and anaesthetics along with the precautions taken to avoid iatrogenic injuries to an unconscious patient should be discussed (Gruendeman, 1973).

The principles of asepsis require careful consideration. These involve the environment with all its carriers of contamination including personnel, ventilation systems, scrubbing techniques, preparation of trolleys and disposal of waste. General discussions of both the principles and reasons for each action are necessary.

Finally, the role of the theatre nurse ought to be consciously considered. The interpersonal skills required, along with any psychosocial inhibitions apparent deserve explanation when planning care.

Over the last decade nursing in general claims to be moving away from the practice of carrying out specific tasks on patients, towards an assessment of the patients' needs. A wealth of literature exists on this new ideology of nursing (eg, Abdellah, 1960; Armitage, 1980; Roper et al, 1980), but as yet it is still well ahead of the practice. Nurses have found it difficult to alter their role to become more initiative-taking; Mazza (1981) questions whether the future role of the theatre nurse can be realised. He poses the following question "Will the theatre nurse remain as she is now; assistant to the anaesthetist and surgeon: or will she venture forth as a professional in her own right; or will apathy and disinterest take over and she will disappear from the theatre scene altogether?"

Theatre nurses need to become more involved in consciously planning patient care. Through care planning and preoperative visiting of surgical patients they can expand and develop their unique role.

Nurse manager

The traditional role of the theatre nurse, running an operating session and giving assistance to the anaesthetist and surgeon, is now being questioned. At senior levels of policy making the role of the theatre nurse manager is seen as crucial in developing theatre nursing.

There are common areas where knowledge is now sufficiently clear for new policies to be implemented. These not only cover in-service education and planning of care as indicated here, but also the optimum size of departments, provision for emergency cover, liaison with the private sector and day-care facilities. The scope for future research within ODs is vast. It is to be hoped that other nurse researchers will take up the challenge in the future.

References
Abdellah, F.G. et al (1960) Patient Centred Approaches to Nursing. Macmillan, New York.
Armitage, S. (1980) Non-compliant recipients of health care. *Nursing Times,* **76,** 3,1. (Supplement, 1-3.)
Boore, J.R.P. (1978) A Prescription for Recovery. RCN, London.
Brown, B. and Rowland, S. (1980) The role of the nurse in the anaesthetic room. *NATNEWS* 17, 9.
Campbell, E.M. and Harvey, A. (1984) Continuing individualised care of patients undergoing surgery. Unpublished Report, Western General Hospital, Edinburgh.
Chadwick, D., Heaton, M., Kalideen, D., Kinnear, F. and West, B.J.M. (1988) A meaningful introduction to operating theatres for student nurses. NATN, Harrogate.
Clarke, P.E., Dixon, E., Freeman, D. and Whitaker, M. (1985) Nurse staffing and training in the operating suite. In: Johnston, I.D.A. and Hunter, A.R. The Design and Utilisation of Operating Theatres. Edward Arnold, London.
Craig, B.J. (1978) Team leader concept implemented in the OR. *AORN Journal,* **28,** 4, 1011-16.
Davis, B.D. (1983) Perceptions by nurses, doctors and physiotherapists of pre-operative information giving. University of Edinburgh Nursing Studies Research Unit.
DHSS (1970) Hospital Building Note No. 26. DHSS, London.
English, M. et al (1983) Ordeal. *Nursing,* **13,** 10, 34-43.
Glasper, A. (1988) Parents in the anaesthetic room: a blessing or a curse? *The Professional Nurse,* **3,** 4, 112-15.
Gooch, J. (1984) The Other Side of Surgery. Macmillan Press, New York.

Griffiths, W.)1984) Staffing problems in anaesthetic recovery room nursing. Specialty Supplement, *NATNEWS,* July.

Gruendeman, B.J. et al (1973) The Surgical Patient: behavioural concepts for the operating room nurse. C V Mosby, Saint Louis.

Hayward, J. (1975) Information – a Prescription Against Pain. RCN, London.

HMSO (1983) Scottish Health Statistics. HMSO, London.

IOR (1974) National Nursing Manpower Policies in Scotland. Institute for Operational Research, Tavistock Institute of Human Relations, London.

Johnson, B. and Kelly, L.M. (1985) Theatre control. *NATNEWS,* **22,** 7, 14-15.

Johnston, I.D.A. and Hunter, A.R. (eds) (1985) The Design and Utilisation of Operating Theatres. Edward Arnold, London.

Lewin, W. (Chair) (1970) The organisation and staffing of operating departments. A report of a joint subcommittee of the Standing Medical Advisory Committee and Standing Nursing Advisory Committee. HMSO, London.

Mazza, J. (1981) What changes in operating theatres? *NATNEWS,* **18,** 12, 8-10.

Philips, J. (1980) Big is best? A study into the optimum size of multi-suite operating depts. *NATNEWS,* **17,** 5,7-14.

Preston, B. (1972) A history of the ODA. SODA *News Issue* No 40, 3-5.

Roper, N. Logan, W.W., Tierney, A.J. (1980) The Elements of Nursing. Churchill Livingstone, Edinburgh.

Shaw, H. (1983) What aspects of the nursing process are applicable in theatre nursing and how can they be implemented? *NATNEWS,* **20,** 5, 11-13.

SSHD (1969) Nursing Workload Per Patient as a Basis for Staffing. Scottish Health Service Studies, SHHD, Glasgow.

Thomson, K.E. (1985) Nursing Process – Perioperative role. Introduction Paper presented at World Congress of Theatre Nurses, The Hague.

West, B.J.M. (1978) A comparative study of 10 Scottish theatre suites. Grampian Health Board Scholarship Report.

12

What is resource management?

Shirley Williams, RGN, RHV
Director of Nursing Services (Community) Oxford H.A. Formerly Director of Nursing Services, Radcliffe Infirmary, Oxford

A major complaint voiced by nurses is that they have an ever increasing workload without any commensurate increase in staffing. As a result they are unable to provide what they consider to be an acceptable standard of care. There is considerable evidence to support the claim that workload has risen both in volume and intensity.

- Shorter length of stay has resulted in a rise in the dependency of those patients who are in hospital.
- Quicker throughput may mean the patient due for admission arrives before the patient occupying his or her prospective bed has been discharged. This means the nurses have more patients than beds (and staffing establishments are traditionally set on bed numbers).
- Increasingly sophisticated medical procedures often require added nursing support.

Not surprisingly, the increase in the number of patients treated has resulted in a marked rise in expenditure, particularly in non-staff items such as drugs, X-rays and prosthesis. This has generated considerable alarm in government circles.

Cash limits

In an attempt to control what appeared to be runaway expenditure, 'cash limits' were introduced whereby district health authorities were instructed to ensure they contained their spending within the funds they were allocated. Many health authorities simply passed this directive down the line, and in some cases budget holders found themselves being reprimanded for 'overspending' when they had no idea what money they had been allocated, nor what they were expected to achieve with it.

As a result of cash limits, hospitals found themselves between a pincer movement. On the one hand they were under pressure from the Department to maximise use of their resources, with particular reference to such things as theatre time, while on the other hand they were being reprimanded for expenditure above that which had been allocated by the department, but which had been incurred as a result of the very increase in efficiency which the hospital had been instructed to undertake. The NHS enquiry tried to address this dilemma, and Griffiths said it was necessary for "each unit to develop management budgets which involve clinicians and relate workload and service objectives to financial and manpower allocations".

There was, however, a major obstacle preventing the achievement of Griffiths' aim. The NHS had no idea of the cost of individual components of treatment and care. Previously it had not been deemed necessary to have a pricing policy, since there had been no requirement to 'bill' a patient. However, if Griffiths' ideas were to be realised it would be essential to identify how money was being spent; and work has been going on in this area in a number of pilot sites, on a system of management information known as resource management.

The resource management initiative involves the following:
- Agreeing clear objectives with doctors, nurses and other hospital managers.
- Agreeing with them budgets related to their workload and objectives.
- Giving them greater control over the day-to-day use of resources.
- Providing better information on the actual cost of clinical activity and services used by clinicians and patients.
- Holding budget-holders accountable for their performance.
- Reviewing outcome.

The resource management system will, where these basic principles are applied to a specialty or clinical service, base the information on an individual patient episode, linking the costs to discharge diagnosis, and perhaps ultimately a diagnostic group. Doctors and nurses can then not only understand the potential of their overall budgets to manage their service, but the effects their case-mix has on this.

Thus, with resource management we move from attempting to cope with an unplanned, demand-led workload within a cash limited financial allocation to a position where there is agreement about the amount of work which can be accomplished within available resources. It is imperative that nurses play an assertive proactive role in agreeing workload related budgets, since it is us and only us who can make the necessary statements about what constitutes nursing workload. The way in which we nurses approach this will be determined by our own understanding of the nature of nursing work.

What is nursing?

If we believe nursing consists of the execution of a series of largely predetermined tasks, we are likely to think it appropriate to deploy any nurse to carry out any task in any area. With such a philosophy it is possible to separate the responsibility for the proficient completion of the task from authority over the resources to carry them out. This position is clearly reflected in traditional nurse management arrangements, where ward sisters are held responsible for standards of care on their wards, but have minimal control over the composition of their establishment or deployment of their staff. Their day duty plans can be overridden by the nursing officer or duty nurse who has authority to redeploy their staff; and their responsibility for and authority over night duty is often either tenuous or a subject of outright hostility between themselves and the night sister. In a traditional system the duty nurse, both on day duty and at night, has resources of her own in the shape of a pool or team, which she deploys on a shift by shift basis at her own discretion.

In a task orientated hospital, the approach to resource management would be to devise a system where all tasks were identified and timed and all nursing resources were controlled centrally so that they could be deployed on a shift by shift basis in response to the predicted task-constituted workload and then be 'costed' at patient level. Many hospitals are taking this approach and indeed the production of computerised nurse deployment systems to support them is a new growth industry.

So where should a ward sister start when implementing a resource management system? A report from the Department of Health's Nursing Division (1988) reviewed the issues. It is first helpful to draw up three component functions that could make up a ward based management information system – the functions are:

- workload assessment;
- ward nurse tracking (recording past, present and planned future shift and work patterns of individual staff);
- care planning support.

Workload assessment

Clearly, to decide how many nurses should be on a particular ward at a particular time is not simply a question of measurement – some judgement is also necessary, but existing approaches can vary a great deal in the level of detail they require. Some simply focus on 'nursing tasks', while others go into more detail, classifying patients into dependency groups. Greater complexity and detail does not necessarily bring greater accuracy, however. Schroeder at al (1984), in a trial between two systems found an easy to establish and simple to operate one gave essentially the same results as a more cumbersome task orientated system. They recommended that nurses avoid adopting expensive, detailed task orientated staffing tools, and depend on systems developed in-house by their own nursing staff, which the staff are happy using. This view has also been endorsed by the NHS Management Board (Peach, 1987).

The question of whether the resource management systems should be used to formulate nursing process care plans is a contentious one. It is unlikely that nurses would willingly accept the idea that workload derived task specifications could or should play a role in care planning. Part of the philosophy of individualised care planning is to move away from the mechanical, task-based approach to patient care. It is probably wise, therefore, to keep care planning separate from the resource management system, otherwise the system may end up fulfilling neither of the functions for which it is intended.

Use of computers

Computers can be useful tools in resource management, and their use can have a number of advantages. Information retrieval is quick and easy, and all the information is easily stored without taking up precious space. However, individual ward sisters need to ask whether using a computer will be better for them than a preprinted form to be completed by hand. When nurses are busy and documentation is not seen as a priority, it is just as easy to produce misleading and incomplete computer records as it is hand written ones, so computers should not be seen as a way of imposing a discipline which guards against this. If they are to be used, it should be because the ward sister (and the rest of the staff) feel computerisation will genuinely allow them to operate their resource management system more efficiently and effectively.

Government commitment

The recent White Paper (DoH, 1989) makes it clear the Government is committed to the expansion of the resource management initiative. It is imperative that nurses ensure the opportunities it affords are used for the benefit of patient care, and that the exercise does not merely become a costing mechanism to help the accountants ensure that 'the money follows the patient'.

It is important that hospitals understand the implications of introducing resource management. Merely introducing modern information systems to record clinical and operational activities will achieve nothing except perhaps lots of pretty pie charts. At whatever level a hospital decides it is best to turn its clinical services – involving doctors, nurses and other professionals – it must be based on the principle that the people responsible for care need to be given clear areas of responsibility. This must be supported by an agreed budget which is related to a level and quality of service that can be reasonably be provided within the funds available.

An appropriate management philosophy – and a proper structure within the unit to support it – is an essential prerequisite for the successful introduction of resource management.

References

DoH (1988) The Resource Management Initiative and Ward Nursing Management Information Systems. DoH Nursing Division and Operational Research Services, London.

DoH (1989) Working for Patients. HMSO, London.

Peach, L. (1987) Nurse manpower planning. Letter to regional and district general manager. Ref DA (87) 12.

Schroeder, R.E., Rhodes, A., Shields, R.E. (1984) Nurse activity services: CASH vs GRASP (a determination of nurse staff requirements). *Journal of Nursing Administration*, **21**, 2, 72-77.

Recruiting and Managing Staff

13

Get the best from staff recruitment

Hilary Shenton, SRN, *Managing Director, The Raine Partnership*
Christine Hamm, SRN, *Personnel Consultant, The Raine Partnership*

However attractive the conditions of employment and working environment, and however good the morale, teamwork and opportunities for professional development at your place of work, people will inevitably leave and vacancies will need to be filled. With the current shortage of nurses, employers have to work hard to make their posts attractive. It is also important to make sure appointments are appropriate to the needs of existing staff. This chapter considers the issues arising from staff vacancies and how to fill them most efficiently.

Do you actually have a vacancy?   If someone resigns, it is often the immediate reaction of their colleagues that the post must be refilled. But you do not necessarily have a vacancy when someone leaves: this can be an opportunity to restructure the department so that other staff have increased responsibilities which they are pleased to accept, or the post could be filled by promoting another member of staff, creating a vacancy, or an opportunity for restructuring, elsewhere. It is a good idea to spend at least a couple of days to consider the situation and to look at the needs and skills of others in the department and of the client group. It may be a good opportunity to offer another member of staff training so that they can develop the skills to fulfil the new post in a few months.

Seek out views   The next step is critically important to the success of both the recruitment process and the future employment. The views and needs of *all* relevant colleagues, most importantly those who will be immediately responsible for the newcomer, *must* be sought. Their thoughts on the exact nature of the job, and the ideal skills, personal qualities and level of experience required are essential.

Increasingly, ward sisters and charge nurses are becoming actively involved in the recruitment process for their immediate ward staff. This involvement may make new demands, but will provide the ward managers themselves with the opportunity to build and maintain the team *they* feel is most appropriate for their clients and colleagues.

The staff to be involved in interviewing must also be identified and included in these discussions; there is no point in one group of interviewers shortlisting a candidate who is rejected by someone more senior with different views of the qualities required. Everyone's views must be known before the post is defined and advertised.

Internal or external appointment?

Again, the decision to consider all applicants, including existing staff, or to only look outside *must* be made before the post is advertised – and *everyone* in the relevant departments must be informed. If you decide to use this opportunity to bring in new skills from outside, it is demoralising for existing staff to apply and be rebuffed.

Similarly, if the post is open to internal applicants, they need to know, and should be given a deadline beyond which the post will be advertised externally, unless suitable candidates have applied.

Job descriptions and personnel specifications

Draw up a *brief* description of the job, based on the information and ideas pooled from relevant colleagues (Table 1) and also a list of qualities sought in the 'ideal' candidate (Table 2). These should be circulated to those involved with interviewing; the job description should also be sent to candidates called for interview. The interviewing team should also agree about the parts of both specifications on which they are willing to compromise: the absolutely ideal candidate rarely exists!

Job descriptions should contain:
- Objectives of the job.
- Manager to whom the staff member will report.
- The individual duties of the job (list and detail no more than 12).
- Outline, for each of these duties, where responsibilities begins and ends.

Table 1. The job description.

The ideal candidate:
- Level of experience required.
- Any special experience required.
- Personal qualities needed such as:
    flexibility of attitudes;
    leadership;
    problem-solving ability;
    ability to communicate well.
- Other requirements, such as flexibility to travel.

Table 2. The personnel specification.

Advertising the vacancy

Advertising is not the only way of making a vacancy known, but it is the most effective way of reaching a wide selection of potential candidates.

> **Put the minimum information to attract response:**
> - Job title.
> - A sentence to stimulate interest and make potential candidates want the job.
> - Details of the easiest means of applying.
> - Salary grade.
> - Closing date.

Table 3. The advertisement.

Content Put the minimum amount of information that will attract appropriate candidates to respond (Table 3). It is essential to describe the job clearly but briefly and to highlight particularly attractive opportunities or facilities (such as a professional development course which is available, or well-equipped ward). Include brief details of the *easiest possible* means of applying for the post. This is usually a (correct!) telephone number, and the name of someone friendly and helpful who will be at the extension given (check that they are not on holiday or on a course during the week after the advertisement is placed) and can get an application in the post first class to enquirers the same day.

Design In magazines where there are many advertisements, a large advertisement will attract more attention, and the inclusion of a border or logo may also help to catch the eyes of potential applicants. Advertising is expensive, but so is bridging the gap between staff.

Disruption and increased workload on existing staff should also be considered.

Timing   How urgent is the re-appointment? If the time scale is not at panic proportions, it is probably advisable to avoid advertising just before bank holiday weekend. If another post is coming up you may decide to delay advertising for a week or two so the two can be advertised together in a bigger space. On the other hand, you may feel it would boost the morale of existing staff to advertise early.

Choose the right medium   The only valid measure to assess the effectiveness of magazines or newspapers is the response rate to the advertisements you place. It is also important that the applicants who respond are appropriate for the post, but your wording for the advertisement should ensure this. If you want and need good responses *do not* place your advertisement in a publication where you know you get a very low response rate. You may decide, however, that you want to be seen to be supporting a particular group, and place the advertisement in its journal. Local papers can also be useful.

Handling the applications

If possible, let every applicant know that their application has arrived and is being considered. Inform anyone whose application is obviously inappropriate *straight away,* so that they can get on with more appropriate applications. Once the closing date has passed, let your interviewing team draw up a shortlist for interview. Invite interviewees as early as possible for interview and an informal visit; if candidates have a long distance to travel, these could both be on the same day.

Informal visits   These *must* be informal, and not used as an extra interview. They should give the candidate the opportunity to assess the working environment and the job in a relaxed atmosphere. Their questions should be answered by someone who is enthusiastic about the work; preferably *not* by the person who is leaving.

Interviews   Decide who will be interviewing and how long the interviews will be and inform the candidates of this at the start. The interviewing panel should be kept as small as possible – preferably no more than three people – and interviewers must have the views and requirements and the trust of their relevant colleagues.

It is not easy to assess all the professional skills and personal qualities of a candidate in an interview, but it is possible to get a clear idea of the individual's appropriateness for the job, assessed against the qualities you have identified for the 'ideal' candidate. You need to assess their professional skills and level of motivation, which can be done by asking them to talk about their last (or present) job. Ask what they enjoyed most and least, and what they could handle, given more training. Ask them to identify their training needs, as this will help to build a picture of what they would like most to be doing.

Assessing personal qualities such as leadership and problem-solving ability is difficult, but asking how they have handled problems in previous posts will help. Referees' reports are also important here.

Do not be afraid of 'digging too deep' in an interview: as long as you do not ask unfair personal questions, it is reasonable to find out about the candidate in some depth. After all, it is important for them that they find themselves in the 'right' job, too.

References

At least two references should be sought, one from the current or last employer, and one from a previous employer (or, if newly qualified, from the candidate's school of nursing). An *employer's* reference (even from a non-nursing employer if the candidate was not previously in nursing) is more valuable than that from a colleague (Table 4).

Ask referees for:
- Statement of the candidate's duties.
- Length of employment.
- Sickness and absenteeism record.
- Reliability.
- Ability as a team member.
- Professional conduct.
- Other qualities and skills.

Table 4. The reference.

It is often possible to gain more frank analysis and information and depth from a referee by telephoning them. Most people are now willing to give references in this way; give them the option to think about it and telephone you back. You could ask for a written reference, and then telephone the referee for a more detailed discussion. Always check that the candidate is happy for you to contact their referees before doing so, and work fast.

Offering the job

Once the interviewers have agreed upon the candidate for the post, act fast and offer the post, subject to satisfactory references. This could be done on the same day as the interview, and, if they have already had an informal visit, you should expect an immediate (or reasonably quick) response. Do not wait until the references are in – you may lose the candidate to another employer.

Making the appointment

Once the candidate accepts the job, keep up the momentum and get the starting date agreed, uniform measured and holidays booked. Write immediately to confirm the appointment, terms, conditions and starting date; people are reluctant to hand in their notice until they have the job offer in writing. Also, inform the other applicants as quickly as possible.

It is hoped that if these suggestions for recruitment are followed and some of the ideas for retaining staff, in the article published last month, acted upon, it should be possible to build and maintain reasonable staffing levels – even in the specialties where nurses are few and far between, and in work places located in the heart of cities. Good luck!

14

How to retain nurses

Hilary Shenton, SRN, *Managing Director, The Raine Partnership*

Christine Hamm, SRN, *Personnel Consultant, The Raine Partnership*

Staff recruitment and retention are major responsibilities for any manager, and require skills and organisation which may be new to many nurses. But, with their new responsibilities as ward managers or community care managers, many ward sisters, charge nurses and community nurses are now involved in the appointment of new staff – and with the increasingly important issue of retaining them. This chapter examines some of the issues surrounding staff retention, which will enable you to maintain good staffing levels, despite the increasing shortage of nurses.

Keeping staff

In an environment in which 30,000 nurses a year leave nursing altogether in Britain, and where the number of newcomers to nursing is falling along with the drop in the number of school-leavers, staff retention is a top priority. This is especially true in the particularly difficult specialties such as ITU and surgery, and in the cities. If the work environment is one in which nurses want to stay, obviously the need for recruitment will be minimised. It is also easier to attract staff to a stable working environment than to one in which everyone seems to be leaving.

Continuing education   The provision of appropriate opportunities for continuing education for all staff is vital to enable existing employees to keep abreast of changes and developments, and to feel confident about their present professional role. It is also important to enable individuals to grow and develop their nursing skills, and for those who want to make career progressions to have the support and opportunity to do so. Employers who are seen to be offering appropriate continuing education, or providing the time for nurses to seek it outside, should have no difficulty in attracting staff – and keeping them. However, many employers pay only lip-service to the provision of continuing education, and many do not make the opportunities which *do* exist sufficiently well known to their staff.

The continuing education budget is often the first expenditure to be cut by cost-saving employers, but this is an expensive false economy. The introduction by the UKCC of a mandatory continuing education requirement for all nurses will help to sharpen the focus on this essential requirement for satisfactory employment.

Recognising and developing the skills of individuals All employees, at every level, need to feel that their skills are being recognised and, if possible, used. If they are not, the chances are that the individual will find another job where her skills and potential *are* recognised. Managers can only achieve this by *listening* to their staff and being open and supportive to their needs to develop. Regular appraisal meetings can be the most useful forum for this, but such meetings must be well conducted, and lead to feasible and appropriate action on the manager's part once the need is identified.

Flexible staffing arrangements In an inflexible environment, nurses will leave if their own time availability or home circumstances change in a way that cannot be accommodated by the employer. Often, only small changes may be needed to retain staff – the cost and inconvenience of which will be a lot less than the cost and inconvenience of trying to reappoint. The shortage of nurses is sharpening the focus of employers and employees on the need for more flexibility in patterns of employment. Job-sharing schemes and more creative provision for part-time work are being tried by some employers.

Accommodation and transport These are both big problems for nurses in the cities, particularly in London, where the cost of accommodation is so high. It is not unreasonable for a nurse in his or her late twenties to expect to start buying a flat and to furnish it, but this is almost impossible for most, unless they are willing to share. Travel and rent may cost as much as the outgoings on a mortgage, and many of the London hospitals are certainly losing staff for this reason. Nurses' homes must be of a sufficiently decent standard to be an attractive alternative, and even then may only be seen as a temporary arrangement by staff in their late twenties and beyond.

Some private hospitals are tackling this problem by buying houses some distance away and subsidising both the nurses' rent and travel. Many health authorities do have provision to offer interest-free loans for season tickets, and some have looked at subsidising car purchase. Some health authorities are now making special mortgage schemes available to nurses. But such schemes must be made known to new and prospective staff. The pay review scales dictate the pay and regional weighting allowances which health authorities can offer nurses, but there is still scope for providing the extras – for example, taxis to and from the hospital for those on nights – which may make it possible for nurses to stay.

Security Most hospitals are publicly open places, and the level of petty crime is often a noticeable nuisance to all staff. Much more serious, though, is the apparently increasing risk of physical assault by patients, visitors and hospital intruders. If a hospital, community health centre or practice is based in an area known for such crimes, and if public transport is inefficient and relatively inaccessible, then the problem is compounded, particularly for staff coming off a late shift or going on night duty. A number of measures can be taken to ward off such crimes; several London hospitals have established 'help squads' which are on-call to deal with violent incidents within the hospital. One employer in London (not in health care) has issued all female staff with a loud and high-pitched personal alarm. Employers need to be aware of any such local problems and may need to be inventive with their approaches to the problem; they must be seen to really care about their staff.

Exit interviews

If the environment and conditions of employment reflect the genuine concern and care of an employer for staff, and if there is plenty of opportunity for staff to develop their professional skills and progress their careers, then the problems created by high staff turnover can be minimised. However, it is helpful to have some idea of the overall pattern of reasons staff have for leaving and this can be established by using 'exit interviews'. These must be undertaken by someone other than the individual's immediate manager – personnel staff would be more appropriate – and should briefly establish whether the real reasons for leaving are the same as those already given.

Over a period of months a pattern may emerge suggesting, for example, that a significant proportion of leavers felt that the shift structure was too rigid for their other commitments, or that there was 'no future' for them with their present employer. This is important information which must be acted on to reduce further unnecessary staff losses, and so improve the employer's chance of attracting newcomers.

Including the cost of staff time for interviews, secretarial and administrative time and advertising and possibly recruitment agency fees, it costs about £3,000 to recruit a staff nurse, and £3,500 to £4,500 to recruit a ward sister or charge nurse. These figures will be higher in the specialties where nurses are especially short in numbers. So it is clearly in the interests of a cost-conscious employer to reduce the level of recruitment required to maintain the agreed staffing levels.

15

Job sharing can take the strain out of recruitment

Ann Shuttleworth, BA
Editor, The Professional Nurse

Shortage of labour costs huge sums of money in industry – in health care it costs lives. The projected shortage of nurses is already biting in some specialties and areas, and it is essential for health authorities to retain the staff they have, and attract more recruits – and as the number of 18-year-olds drops, different kinds of recruits. However, unlike industry, they cannot simply pay higher salaries to attract people, so they have to find new ways to persuade people to nurse – ways that compete with the money industry has to offer.

Health authorities have begun to move towards greater flexibility in working hours, to try to attract those people – mainly women – whose other commitments make them unable to undertake full-time work. Part-time work is often characterised by low pay, job insecurity, poor promotion prospects and the lack of fringe benefits. Far more appealing to many is job sharing, an idea which began in the early 1970s as more women decided they wanted families without giving up their careers. They often found the part-time work available was low paid and low skilled, and at a lower level than they had been used to.

A voluntary arrangement

Job sharing is an arrangement whereby two (or more) people voluntarily share one full-time post, sharing salary and benefits between them according to the hours they work. As long as each one works 16 or more hours a week, they are eligible for employment protection. Within this definition, job sharing is completely flexible in how the job is shared, and is at the convenience of the employees and employers concerned. Most people suggest a job share with a partner already in mind, although some have been put in touch with each other after applying for jobs advertised as suitable for a job share. Normal contracts are usually suitable with appropriate ammendments, but sharers may wish to add clauses to cover such eventualities as one wishing to leave.

Advantages

There are many advantages in job sharing, both for employees and employers. The most obvious advantage for the employee is the opportunity to work part-time while retaining the advantages and security of a full-time post. This alone makes job sharing attractive both to nurses wishing to work part-time without moving to a lower grade and those who have taken a career break and want part-time work at the grade they had previously attained.

Job sharing also gives more opportunities for jobs to reflect individuals' interests and skills than part-time work. The increased free time is not only a chance to care for children – it can also be used for the pursuit of research or study interests. In a profession as potentially stressful and demanding as nursing, the opportunity to work in a responsible position only part-time alleviates these problems, while job sharers can offer mutual support and different expertise.

There are also numerous advantages for employers (Buchan, 1987). Trained staff can be retained and are less likely to suffer from job related stress, a major cause of absenteeism. Voluntary job-sharers are also likely to have a high level of commitment since they have shown a positive desire for their job by arranging the job-share, rather than opting for a more easily attained post. They are also likely to be more flexible and able to provide additional cover in peak periods. Working shorter hours, they have often been found to be more productive and able to sustain higher levels of activity.

Disadvantages

While the advantages to both employees and employers make job-sharing attractive, it does have potential disadvantages. Employees' earnings will obviously be limited and promotion prospects may be decreased. A tendency has also been found in job sharers to work more than their half-time, and they may experience some loss of job satisfaction. They will certainly have to ensure their managers do not try to give them too much work and the post is subject to the usual appraisal systems. Sharing the control and responsibilities of the job may cause problems, and must usually be resolved by compromise.

Employers have cited potential disadvantages from their point of view, but in practice these are not always significant (Buchan, 1987). The cost of employing two people – providing uniforms and training, and paying for time spent together in handover is higher, but National Insurance may actually be lower if the post attracts a gross pay of less than £285 a week. The handover time is likely to be minimal, and it has been argued that it leads to increased planning and efficiency.

Job sharers' managers may have to spend more time in supervision and work allocation, although no recorded schemes have reported this as a problem. Staff supervised by the job sharers may find difficulty being accountable to two people, especially if they have different ideas on organisation. Problems may also occur if one sharer wishes to leave.

These disadvantages can be overcome given commitment from those involved, as Judith Lathlean (1987) found in evaluating a job shared ward sister post at the Charing Cross Hospital in London. The sisters found initial resistance from their staff, who knew one of the sisters well and the other not at all. Hackney Job Share, an external organisation, came in to explain to the staff about job sharing and diffuse some of their negative feelings. The first few months involved the sisters in high levels of communication in setting up systems, and they found they had to compromise to reach workable agreements on issues in which they differed. Once systems were operating, the ward settled down and the staff gradually became more supportive and understanding.

While the job share described by Lathlean was not without difficulties, on the whole it was successful and illustrates that job sharing is possible for jobs with managerial responsibilities. Lathlean recommends that health authorities consider job sharers in more posts, and take the initiative in creating opportunities for employees to job share.

New Ways to Work (NWTW) is an organisation committed to advising people on job sharing and other flexible working ideas, such as annual hours and taking career breaks. Started in 1979 as a voluntary organisation, NWTW are now funded by the London Boroughs Grant Scheme to advise both employees and employers. They are currently involved with the Royal Institute of Public Administration in designing a course on job sharing aimed specifically at health authorities.

Health authority interest
They say health authorities are starting to take a little more interest in job sharing, but they are still lagging behind local authorities in actively promoting job sharing schemes. NWTW feel that health authorities are

finding it something of a hurdle to start encouraging job sharers, and most of those employed by health authorities say they have had difficulty in negotiating their posts. There are exceptions, however, including one manager who advertised a post specifically as a job share, and another who has several health visitor job share partnerships.

Obviously, some posts will adapt more easily to a job share than others, and will be more easily broken down. NWTW say, however, that most jobs can be successfully shared, given commitment and flexibility from all concerned. Difficult managerial posts have been shared successfully, allowing people with years of experience to continue to work at the level they are qualified for, rather than leaving employment altogether or working in lower grade jobs. They say it is essential for professional organisations to get involved in encouraging job sharing, as people are most likely to contact them for advice.

Job sharing may not answer all the problems of nurse recruitment, but it could certainly tap an unused and probably frustrated pool of experienced ex-nurses unwilling to return to part-time work at a lower level than they left, and retain many who wish to devote some time to other commitments. If it is to live up to its full potential, health authorities and the nursing unions will have to become more active in publicising the idea and helping potential sharers negotiate their posts.

Useful addresses
New Ways to Work
309 Upper Street
London N1 2TY
Tel: 01-226 4026.

Hackney Job Share Project
380 Old Street
London
Tel: 739 0741.

References
Buchan (1987) A shared future. *Nursing Times*, **83**, 4.
Lathlean, J. (1987) Job sharing a ward sister's post. Riverside Health Authority, London.

16

Part-time staff: a blessing in disguise?

Jean Fisher, SRN, ONC
Sister, St Michael's Hospice, Bartestree, Hereford

As a ward sister with a full-time staff of four, including myself, out of a full complement of 12, to cover the 'day-time' hours from 07.30 to 21.30 hours, all the pleasures and pains of managing part-time staff can certainly be said to be mine. In this particular setting of a small, purpose-built hospice, which is totally charity-run, the stresses and strains – as well as the job satisfaction – encompass both the high and low of nursing morale.

The particular stress encountered here is in coping with pain, and fear, anger and desperation in patients, and also in dealing almost daily with bereaved families. To counteract that the staff has the satisfaction of usually being able to help relieve suffering with good symptom control and that most precious gift – time. More often than not, the nurse may only need an extra five minutes with patients to really make them comfortable or to find out what they are really frightened of.

Those few extra minutes are often just not available to nurses, but to the patient may mean the difference between good nursing and the extra special 'caring' that hospices are all about. All nurses – whether they work in a hospital or hospice – want to give those minutes and they become frustrated when they see less and less time available to spend with patients due to constant pressure and staff shortages. Using part-time staff may provide part of the solution for several problems, including this one.

Increased flexibility

For the employer, one of the greatest advantages of using part-time staff must be increased flexibility. At the hospice all nursing staff (except those employed on the nursing bank) work full shifts in an effort to increase continuity and teamwork. However, there is no doubt that even more flexibility can be obtained (and some considerable financial saving made) by staff working part shifts at peak hours, ie, mornings and 'twilight' shifts. My view is that staff commitment and participation is higher when they are at work for a whole shift and can take part in ward reports, case conferences and decision making.

Almost all continuing education in the form of lectures, video viewing and so on take place in the afternoon during the overlap period. Very few staff off duty at 13.00 hours would be able, or willing, to return at 14.30 hours for a lecture or ward staff meeting. The other important factor in the use of full shift patterns is that staff can be given back 'time owing' during the overlap period. It is known that nurses often work extra time. It is also well known that, more often than not, they do so willingly, to maintain the level of nursing care given to their patients. It is not usually possible for them to be paid for this time. However, this commitment should not be taken for granted – commitment is a two-way process, and therefore 'time off in lieu' should be given at mutual convenience to the unit and the member of staff. The pressure in many areas today usually prevents this, and the extra frustration upon so many others could well become the straw that breaks the camel's back. But 'time off in lieu' might even encourage staff to come in on a day off sometimes for a lecture if that time could be given back during a quiet period.

The other flexibility of part-time staff is that, if necessary, one can *occasionally* ask a part-time nurse to cover an extra part-time shift when unforeseen staffing problems occur. This would obviate the need for agency staff, who are expensive and provide less continuity of care. It is important that staff who are willing to do extra time do not feel that they *have* to do so and that they are not taken advantage of by being asked on a regular basis.

Stress

Stress levels in part-time staff are undeniably lower, which in the hospice situation is vital. The extra time for 'real life' means nurses are more refreshed and have more to offer when they are at work. But what about the effect the number of part-time staff has on the stress levels of their full-time colleagues? In fact, it may *increase* their stress levels a little, in that the onus to provide continuity lies more heavily upon them. However, in many ways this can only be another recommendation for good documentation and the implementation of the nursing process with full-time staff coordinating of nursing teams.

The added stress of working part-time is that it can become more difficult to make useful relationships with patients and their families. However, this may be an advantage if it makes staff less complacent about making contact with patients and relatives. Clinical observations may be much more acute from part-time staff as they have more time away from work and therefore see changes in situations more clearly than staff who are there five days a week.

The small details of the smooth running of the ward are those that break down at times. When the part-time staff nurse hardly ever works the third Tuesday in the month and is therefore not usually required to order stores . . . except when sister is on a day off and the full-time staff nurse is sick . . . then problems can arise. Like most problems there is

usually a solution.

Another advantage for employers in taking on part-time staff is ease of recruitment. Present staff shortages and recruitment problems highlight the outdated historical ideal of nurses being single women, working full-time on a vocational basis, with no life away from work. It is now becoming apparent that few nurses fit into this category today. There are many nurses leaving the profession, or not returning after a break, because of management failure to make it either feasible or acceptable to do so. Hopefully, the increase in crêche facilities, 'back to nursing' courses and the moves towards improved continuing education in nursing, together with flexibility of employer and employee will put this situation to rights. If the idea of job sharing (Cole, 1987) does spread, many high calibre senior nurses may be able to stay in or return to their profession.

Common sense

Most of the staff at St Michael's Hospice are married, and some have children. As their sister, I am always grateful for their common sense approach and skills of empathy as, being younger and single, I still have much to learn in certain situations. If nurses seriously want to take the abnormality and mystique out of ward situations (in hospital, nursing home or wherever the wards may be) they should aim to make them as much like the outside world as possible. This means a good staff mix (single and married as well as more men). The single staff also have their own skills. They may often have new ideas and practices to share, which may be varied as single nurses tend to be less settled. Often, married staff – unless their partners are in the Services – stay in one area for a much longer span of time. Herein lies the answers to a manager's prayer – married staff can provide ongoing continuity and single staff bring new ideas. They can bring the best (or perhaps prevent the worst) from Oxford, East Grinstead or Outer Mongolia!

Skill mix is not just a question of the ratio of trained to untrained staff but also of age group, background and professional expectations. A unit where the turnover of staff is as high as that of the patients is as difficult to manage as one where no one has moved for years. All ward sisters know at some time the frustration of training a bright young staff nurse only to find that once you make progress and she becomes able to be your right hand, the obligatory six months or one year is up and she is off to the next rung of the ladder. We have all done it ourselves and accept its inevitability, but there is no doubt that a nucleus of staff who have been in the team for a while makes for smooth running. The management skills required then are to maintain commitment and prevent staleness and the old adage, 'We always do it this way'. Also, it prevents exclusivity and a clique formation that precludes newcomers from being accepted as part of the team. A clear and agreed ward philosophy should help to prevent these occurring, but the situation needs constant and careful monitoring (Teasdale, 1987; DHSS, 1986; Mallin, 1987; Moores, 1986).

Commitment

Diminished level of commitment among part-time staff is an often quoted problem but is, I suspect, a fallacious one. Certainly among my own staff, the level of caring and commitment is as high in part-time as in full-time staff. The personal areas of responsibility and accountability have never been more clearly stated within the nursing profession and this can only decrease the degree of complacency which exists in some members of various professions. The days of the ward sister 'carrying the can' for every occurrence is being replaced at last. This alone must increase the level of motivation in most trained staff. It may be more difficult for part-time staff, particularly those working on night duty, to participate in continuing education, as often the reason for doing night duty is to dovetail family commitments and work. My own staff seem to have most amenable partners, mothers, neighbours, cousins and aunts who can take care of children for a day to allow them to attend a study day or conference.

Motivation in giving care to an agreed standard is not, or should not be, a problem. Most nurses have high personal standards for bedside care. Why are so many leaving the NHS at the moment? Not because their own standards are inadequate, (or at least only in a very small number of cases) but because they feel they cannot practise at what they consider an acceptable standard. It is the frustration, stress and constant pressure which is driving so many out into the private sector, or abroad, or, most sadly of all, out of nursing altogether. Most nurses want to do their best for patients whether they are on duty for two days a week or five. Certainly the bank staff employed by the hospice, who may come in for a half shift to cover sickness perhaps only once a month, give excellent care to patients and their families (West Dorset H.A., 1987).

I am sure that the level of commitment among staff is high when they are in a position to give good care, as part of a caring team, supported by all tiers of whichever structure they are working within. Staff whose input of care is being respected and appreciated will have higher morale. They will give of their best, perhaps not in every shift – which none of us can – but in a more than acceptable majority.

A valuable part to play

Part-time staff have a valuable part to play in any nursing team. They can provide continuity, stability, maturity and empathy, and enhance the 'normality' of ward environment sought by many team leaders.

The situation in which I work may be said by some to be ideal. It is a small unit, with a small team which works very closely together. It is not attached to a hospital and is not bound by the conservative and short-term views found in some health authorities. The system of part-time staff working full-shift days has been most successful. Working in partnership with patients (Teasdale, 1987) has to begin with partnership with colleagues and managers. Accepting the holistic approach to patient care may well have to begin by accepting a holistic approach to staff needs. Then perhaps better staff will be recruited and retained for longer and they will give better patient care.

References
Cole, A. (1987) Job sharing – partners in time. *Nursing Times*, **83**, 40,
Teasdale, K. (1987) Partnership with patients. *The Professional Nurse*, **2**, 40, 397-9.
DHSS (1986) Mix and match: A review of nursing skill mix. DHSS, London.
Mallin, H. and Wright-Warren, P. (1987) Review mix and match. *Senior Nurse*, **6**, 3,
Moores, B. (1986) Review mix and match document. *Journal of Advanced Nursing*, **12**, 6.
West Dorset H.A. (1987) Standard of Care Quality. West Dorset Health Authority.

17
Appraisal methods: how do you rate yourself?

Elizabeth S. Wright, SRN, Dip N, CHSM
Ward Sister, The Middlesex Hospital, London

Attitudes towards appraisal

A formal system of appraisal is necessary, but which method is most effective? If the whole tactic of appraisal is altered with an aim to improve staff development and career prospects, rather than concentrating solely on criticism of current performance, then the procedure appears much more worthwhile, with long-term planning and objectives designed for the individual's progress, either for her present job or for a different or more senior post.

In the majority of cases within the nursing profession, appraisals are irregular and often serve no constructive purpose for the appraisee. The existence of a staff appraisal interview system compels supervisors to meet with their staff and consult with them on a regular basis, and hence become better informed as to their interests and aspirations (Ansty, 1961). It is insufficient for junior staff nurses to have annual appraisals if they only remain in a junior post for 6 months to a year, and more frequent discussion is necessary to evaluate their progress and needs.

In many professions, including nursing, managers seem reluctant to make any assessment or constructive criticism of their staff. They either avoid doing appraisals or provide ineffective criticisms because they fear to point out weaknesses in performance. This may reflect their inexperience and lack of instruction in methods of appraisal, or possibly their awareness of how difficult it is to make just and accurate assessments, combined with a fear of hostile reactions on confrontation with the appraisee (Fletcher, 1985).

Professional conduct

Being an assessor is a difficult position in which to find yourself, particularly if you work closely with the individual concerned; for instance a sister and a staff nurse working on the same ward. My personal feeling is that one's professional conduct as a senior and therefore a manager, should provide a role model for the staff nurse. The relationship should be friendly and one of approachability and respect, but not familiarity, otherwise the position of assessor loses the credibility necessary for objective criticism to be made. It is to be hoped that the advice will then be received as serious and constructive, and acted upon with intent to improve performance. Managers might find the act of appraisal difficult precisely because they have not maintained a professional relationship with their junior staff.

Current appraisal methods

The most important criterion for a successful method of appraisal is that the manager actually knows the individual concerned, and more importantly her work. Otherwise how can the criticism, good or bad, be justified? How well thought out and personal is the method of appraisal where one person writes a report and another presents it to the individual (commonly a student nurse), often without discussion?

It is preferable that the appraisal is based on first-hand information, but this should include assessment of performance over a substantial period of time, not biased by recent incidents. An overall view of merit is taken into account and should not be marred by personal prejudice.

A common standard by which to assess is difficult to maintain; but in general one should try not to compare to others in a similar post. Assess a person on their own merits in comparison to the standard and experience they should have expected to have attained by that position and after that length of time in the post (Ansty, 1961).

Staff development and career planning

The appraisal may be considered by some managers, and even appraisees, to be an unnecessarily time-consuming process that does not appear to give immediate practical results. An appraisal also involves committing convictions and opinions to paper, which the nurse manager may wish to avoid especially if challenged by the appraisee.

The professional development has long-term implications for clinical practice, but it is not sufficient for the nurse manager to make these assessments and the consequent decisions alone. In order for the most benefit to be gained from the system it is essential that the appraisee is involved in making decisions jointly with the assessor (Pincus, 1982).

I am sure that the fundamental criteria on which to undertake an appraisal, are familiar to all, but they should nevertheless be maintained; such as ensuring a quiet, undisturbed, informal setting, with adequate time set aside. The appraisal needs to be a joint participative exercise between the nurse and her manager in an ambience that is conducive to open discussion, and with strict confidentiality (Stewart, 1978).

The format of the written appraisal form varies greatly between Health Authorities, and the complexity of it depends upon the grade of staff. The actual written evidence of the appraisal is not as important as the two-way discussion. However, it should be completed for reasons of referral and possibly written references at a later date, and as confirmation that the appraisal took place.

Self-appraisal

An increasingly popular and effective method of appraisal that has been implemented recently in Bloomsbury is self-assessment or self-appraisal. Essentially, the appraisee considers their own ability and skills, and fills out their own appraisal form. The principal advantage of this system is that the appraisee has more opportunity than anyone else to note their own performance and understand their own opinions and conscience, related to weaknesses and strengths within that performance. Self-appraisees are also unlikely to become defensive in response to their own critical analysis of their abilities, although this may prove a natural reaction to another person's criticism. Experience shows that appraisees are more willing to act upon weaknesses or problems that they themselves have identified (Fletcher, 1985).

Although the staff nurse fills out her own appraisal form, it is imperative that her manager discusses each description with her, in order to give an outsider's point of view and assist the nurse's insight with guidance on how to make improvements in each area.

Appraisees seem to be modest in their ratings and realistically a manager needs to guide and help develop the appraisee's skills in self-assessment. The manager may assist in improving not only various practical skills, but also the appraisee's insight into areas of professional development. More importantly, the manager can take the opportunity to give the appraisee credit and praise for work and skills completed with thoroughness and initiative.

How do we meet the many needs of newly qualified staff?

A Professional Development Course designed for newly qualified staff nurses being implemented in Bloomsbury, London (one of three pilot schemes in the UK) was evaluated over a 3-year period by a DHSS-funded research team at King's College, University of London. Self-appraisal is incorporated into this course, and is particularly relevant to newly qualified staff who have yet to develop fully the skills of a trained nurse and manager and who require considerable guidance and support in their new role. The project was undertaken in response to the recognised need for nurses' development in both clinical and professional aspects in the newly qualified staff nurse role, as discussed at the national conference on "Professional Developments in Clinical Nursing – The 1980s", which took place in Harrogate in 1981.

It is the belief of those participating in the professional development course that self-appraisal by the course participants is more appropriate than assessment by examination, because the act of self-appraisal and the personal involvement in setting new targets for achievement serves to take the individual further in their personal development.

Emphasis is therefore placed on self-assessment with related discussion. The format used ultimately provides a detailed descriptive profile of the nurses' strengths and weaknesses in relation to the course objectives, and outlines developmental progress by a comparison of pre-course and post-course assessment profiles. The course members' self-assessment is supplemented by their facilitator's and tutors' comments on their progress.

The course has a six-month programme consisting of supervised and supported practice in a designated training area, involving a facilitator for guidance and practical advice (often the ward sister). The course aims to provide the nurses with the necessary background, awareness, and motivation to pursue a continuous programme of personal development, both clinical and professional. It enables them to develop leadership skills, and prepares them to function as responsible members of the profession. The outline of the course comprises two parts: part one consists of practice under supervision, with emphasis on the clinical role of the registered nurse with a problem-solving context; and part two aims at individual development, which incorporates writing skills, teaching methods, research, and career development as well as leadership skills, within a team and as a practising clinician. Other subjects involving some theoretical tuition are models of nursing and legal and ethical aspects of nursing. The final study days of the course include seminar presentations by the participants, based on assignment work done during the course, and a concluding debate on professional issues (Smythe, 1984).

I believe that much of the negative feelings that I have expressed regarding staff appraisal result from the fact that so many managers are not taught proper methods of appraisal, and often carry it out ineffectively. There has to be a better way, and I am sure that self-appraisal incorporated into a professional development scheme is a more positive and effective method of identifying the individuals' needs, and of improving and praising their abilities.

References
Anstey, E., (1971) Staff Reporting and Development. George Allen & Unwin Ltd., London.
Flecher, C., (1985) Means of assessment. *Nursing Times*, **81;** 27,24
Filkins, J., (1985) Going round in circles. *Nursing Times*, **81;** 29,31
Pincus, J., (1982) Staff appraisal and development. *Nursing Mirror*, **155;** 21,47
Smythe, J.E., (1984) Professional development of the newly registered nurse; Guidelines in the Bloomsbury scheme. Unpublished.
Stewart, A.M., (1978) Staff development and performance review. *Nursing Times*, **74;** 16,654.

Bibliography
Dimmock, S., (1985) Starting from scratch. *Nursing Times*, **81;** 30
Jessup, G., and Jessup, H., (1975) Selection and Assessment at Work. Methuen & Co. Ltd., London.
Randell, G., Shaw, R., Packard, P., Slater, J. (1972) Staff Appraisal. Institute of Personnel Management, London.
Raybould, E., (1977) Editor. Guide for Nurse Managers. Blackwell Scientific Publications, London.

Teamwork

18

Teamwork: an equal partnership?

Gill Garrett, BA SRN, RCNT, DN(London), CertEd(FE), RNT, FPCert
Freelance Lecturer, Bristol

From being one of the fundamental tenets in the care of groups such as elderly people and those with mental handicaps, the vital nature of the team approach has become recognised and accepted in all areas of nursing. Many patients have a multiplicity of needs – medical, nursing, therapeutic, social – which no one discipline can hope to meet; only by close collaboration and cooperation can different practitioners bring their skills into concert to attempt to meet them.

Increasingly in recent years, the validity of this contention has been appreciated by both hospital and community workers, and the gospel has been preached. But how effective has the concept been in practice? While no doubt in many parts of the country teams are working efficiently and harmoniously together to the benefit of all concerned, it would seem that in others there are areas of concern which demand urgent consideration and action if the concept is not to prove a meaningless cliché. With this in mind, this chapter considers the prerequisites for effective teamwork, points out a few of the common problems which may arise and offers some suggestions as to how these problems may be ameliorated.

Who makes up the team?
One very basic question to ask before considering the work of the team is who makes up the team? On multiple choice papers, students will indicate the doctor, nurse, therapists, dietitians – all the professional partners in the venture. But integral to every team must be the people most meaningful to the individual patient: her family if she has any, her supportive neighbour, or whoever. If our aim is to rehabilitate the patient or to maintain her at her maximum level of functioning, these are people we neglect at our peril – and much more importantly, at the patient's peril. As professionals we must learn that we do not have a monopoly on care, nor do we have a dominant role in an unequal partnership. The contribution of relatives or friends, as agreeable to the patient, is vital – whether discussing assessments, setting goals or reviewing progress; their non-contribution, if excluded from active participation, may indeed frustrate all professional efforts. Although most of this article

concentrates on those professionals who are conventionally seen as team members (primarily because of the space available), this point cannot be overstressed.

Why are teams necessary?

Perhaps an even more basic question is, why does the team exist? It is easy to lose sight of the fact that its sole *raison d'être* is the patient and her need. An old adage runs, "The patient is the centre of the medical universe around which all our works revolve, towards which all our efforts trend". In economic terms we are quite used to this concept of 'consumer sovereignty', but in our health and social services management at present, all too often our consumer exists more to be 'done to' rather than canvassed for her opinion, offered options and helped to make choices. A thorny question often raised about the multidisciplinary team is, which professional should lead it? An equally important one not so often posed is, who should be the 'director' of team activity? If we recognise the patient as an autonomous, independent person (albeit with varying degrees of support), surely we must have the humility to acknowledge that this directing role falls inevitably to her. For patients with mental or other serious impairment, of course, the question of advocacy then arises – again an issue subject to much current debate.

Having allocated the role of director to the patient, the team leader then becomes the facilitator of action. It has been said that, "Fundamental to the concept of teamwork is . . . division of labour, coordination and task sharing, each member making a different contribution, but (one) of equal value, towards the common goal of patient care" (Ross, 1986). What do these elements demand? To make for efficient division of labour there has to be an accurate assessment of a situation and the input needed to deal with it, a recognition of who is the best person for which part of the job, and the carrying through of the appropriate allocation. Coordination demands the ability to see the overall, the sum of all the individual parts, and to recognise their relative weightings in various circumstances; it needs effective communication skills and the ability to use feedback to take adjustive action as required. Task-sharing demands that team members have an understanding of different roles and their effect upon one another, that they recognise areas of overlap and are prepared to shoulder one another's problems should the need arise. Such demands are not light; they require considerable training and practice to perfect.

Status and power within the team

Consideration of the second part of the Ross quotation brings us to one of the common problems experienced in multidisciplinary teamwork: ". . . of equal value towards the common goal of patient care". Is that how all team members view their own contribution or that of their partners? Status and power imbalances can make for great difficulties in team functioning; tradition accords high status and consequent power to the medical establishment, for example, with much affection but little standing to nurses. But if nurses have been seen as lacking in power and status, even lower on the rungs of the ladder comes the patient; in general, society grants a very low status to ill and disabled people, and institutional care strips all vestiges of power from inhabitants.

For workers who see themselves as being the juniors in teams, the presence and influence of more powerful members may prove intimidating, and consequently they may make only tentative and limited contributions to discussions and meetings. It is important that they realise that, however 'junior', they have a right to contribute, indeed a duty to do so, if they have what has been described as the "authority of relevance" (Webb and Hobdell, 1975) – if they have knowledge relevant to the patient's own feelings of need or wellbeing which must be brought to the team's attention. So often it is those members who spend more time in close proximity to the patient who possess such authority, rather than the senior medical personnel who may visit her only on a weekly basis.

'Follow my leader'   A second problem may arise out of the power and status imbalance, especially when team members have become used to suppressing their views or do not recognise their authority of relevance – regression into the 'follow my leader' phenomenon. There may be the tendency to leave all the thinking to another group member who is perceived as being more prestigious or simply more articulate, often the consultant. His thinking and directions are seen as definitive, with team members abdicating their own professional responsibility to think and speak for themselves and for their patient from their own vantage points. Except in the unlikely event of the team leader being qualified in a multidisciplinary capacity, this obviously acts to the detriment of patient care – we can none of us prescribe or wholly substitute for each other's contributions. A variation on this 'follow my leader' phenomenon is sometimes seen where two leaders emerge from subgroups in a team, each with his or her own following. In addition to the drawbacks already mentioned, the results in situations like this are invariably divisive too.

'Groupthink'   This is the name that has been given to another possible problem in teamwork; it is generally seen in well-established, long-lived teams whose members over time have grown very used to working with each other. Team meetings are always amicable and 'cosy', there is no bickering or dissension and everyone gets on terribly well with everyone else. The group gives the appearance of having its own internal strength, with a marked sense of loyalty and supportiveness. But this denies that disagreement and conflict are facts of life and often signs of constructive enquiry and growth; all too often such teams ". . . become rigid, committed to the status quo . . . less open to input and feedback. Hierarchies become established and bureaucratic qualities emerge which resist questioning and change" (Brill, 1976).

Patient confusion   In case this should all seem a little esoteric, consider for a moment one last very basic possible problem in multidisciplinary teamwork – potential confusion for the patient. Unless each member of the team extends to her the courtesy of an introduction to their personal role, with an explanation of how this fits in with the overall individual plan of care, especially in the acute phase of an illness, the patient (particularly if elderly) may well find so many professionals overwhelming and muddling. If she is to feel in any degree in control of the situation and if any confusion is to be lessened, time must be taken to be sure a personal approach, with all care being presented as part of a concerted whole, and with common goals identified towards which all the team are working.

This last problem, then, is usually amenable to a common courtesy and common sense solution. But what about the others? The problems associated with status and 'follow my leader' have a more deep-seated origin and, although rectifiable in the short term in individual teams, in the longer term they demand a close scrutiny of, and changes in, professional education. 'Groupthink' demands flexibility of individuals and a system which encourages and permits a regular turnover of personnel to maintain healthy group dynamics.

Common core training?

If in effective teams there is no room for professional superiorities or jealousies, what is needed is an open, trusting relationship based on knowledge of, and respect for, one another's professional expertise. But this demands in turn an insight into other trainings and backgrounds to understand one another's terms of reference – the differences in emphasis we have in relation to patient care. While individual effort and inservice training programmes can go some way towards this, the difficulties with late attitudinal change are only too well known. Most of our basic feelings about our own profession and those with which we work are formed during our initial training period. Nursing is currently introducing training programmes based on Project 2000, with a common core foundation programme for all nurse practitioners. Is it not time we were much more adventurous, and explored avenues of common core training for all health professionals? Certain knowledge, skills and attitudes are prerequisites whether we are to be doctors, nurses, therapists or social workers – if we learned them together how much easier it would be to practise them together. The intention of such common training would not be to reduce all teaching to the lowest common denominator, but rather to look at areas of mutual concern, highlighting the unique contribution of each professional, and the bearing this has on the work of the other team members.

Value of difference

Educational change may also help us to recognise the value of 'difference' and the constructive use to which conflict may be put, so that 'groupthink' becomes a less likely problem. Better training in interpersonal skills – including assertiveness – should help the creation of a climate in which there is freedom to differ, to look more dispassionately at dissent, while acknowledging the areas of basic trust and agreement that do exist and can be built upon. The need for turnover in team membership has to be balanced, of course, by the need for reasonable stability over a period of time. Change every five minutes for the sake of it helps no one, but there must be recognition that long-term team stagnation (however well camouflaged) is beneficial neither to the group nor to the professionals within it – and certainly not to the patient and her family.

Realism

This chapter provides only a brief overview of a very important area. Readers' personal experiences may differ considerably from the scenarios which have been outlined. It would seem, however, that most experienced nurses have had the experience of needing to temper idealism in striving for effective teamwork with realism, given the situations in which they work. But recognition of this is in itself a step forward; we must have in mind that "under the aegis of teamwork, strange bedfellows are discovering, in time, that they must *learn* to work together before they *can* work together . . . teamwork is not an easy process to understand or to practise" (Brill, 1976).

References

Brill, N.I. (1976) Teamwork: Working together in the Human Services. Lippincott, New York.

Ross, F.M. (1986) Nursing old people in the community. In: Redfern, S. (ed) Nursing Elderly People. Churchill Livingstone, Edinburgh.

Webb, A.L. and Hobdell, M. (1975) Coordination between health and personal social services: a question of quality. In: Interaction of social welfare and health personnel in the delivery of services: Implications for training. Eurosound Report No. 4, Vienna.

19

Teamwork in psychiatry

Brendan McMahon, BA, SRN, RMN

Clinical Nurse Specialist in Dynamic Psychotherapy, Southern Derbyshire H.A.

Human beings have always needed each other. Medieval societies in Europe were based on the recognition that the peasant, the feudal lord, and the churchman was each necessary to the continued material and spiritual wellbeing of the community, and that the work performed by each was valuable in its own right. As time progressed it became increasingly clear that one individual or family could not hope to acquire all the skills needed to contribute to a civilised life – labour needed to be divided into groups. This process was greatly accelerated by the industrial revolution.

Today, we live in an age of increasing specialisation, and few nurses have the time or skills to mill their own flour or make their own cars! Increasingly, specialisation means that as new skills are acquired, old ones are either abandoned or relinquished to other specialists. We have all lost skills our grandparents took for granted, just as we have learned others which would have amazed them. Something is lost as something is gained, but on the whole, we, as individuals and as society are richer.

Nursing of course, is part of society, and the process of specialisation, of the loss and acquisition of skills, is mirrored within the profession. The increase in knowledge in our time has made, and will increasingly make it impossible for one nurse to acquire the information and skills required to practise generically – we are all specialists now. This presents us with both problems and opportunities. The central difficulty, it seems to me, is how increasingly specialised professions can respond to the need to treat the patient as a whole human being, how we can create effective helping strategies which recognise the patient as a thinking, feeling person who is an integral part of a complex network of relationships and a functioning member of society. I feel our best hope of resolving this dilemma in organisational terms lies in the mutidisciplinary team. This chapter will analyse the strengths and weaknesses of this approach, and reflect on ways to maximise the potential creativity of multidisciplinary working.

Communication and learning

Multidisciplinary team functioning depends on decisions being taken by the team as a whole, not exclusively by one or two powerful members. It requires open communication between all involved professionals, rather than the transmission of information and directives in one direction only.

The team approach requires the capacity to examine relationships between members in an honest, straightforward manner, and necessitates 'role blurring' – the capacity to relinquish rigid conceptions of one's own professional role, and a willingness to learn from others.

A policy or business meeting at which decisions affecting the team are made is a practical necessity and, to function effectively, this meeting must be genuinely democratic, allowing every member, however junior, to contribute to the decision making process. A clinical meeting at which workers are encouraged to share their work with others in a constructive environment is also desirable.

Patients should be allocated to staff on the basis of a careful assessment of the patient's needs, and a well thought out decision about which staff members have the specific skills required to meet those needs most effectively. In a community mental health team, for example, it would be appropriate for a patient with a clearly defined phobia to be referred to a worker with some training in behaviour therapy. However, a team member with no behavioural training might want to work as cotherapist, to acquire the necessary skills to work independently in future, or to prepare for further specialised training: this kind of cross fertilisation is one of the many benefits of multidisciplinary working.

Team meetings should be used to highlight the value of everyone's contribution – although the patient may need the services of different team members at different times, this does not imply that some are more valuable than others. Willingness to learn new skills from others and to pass on our own skills enhances rather than diminishes our professional integrity: it makes us better nurses.

Team members need to spend time getting to know each other if the team is to work effectively. Some teams find a sensitivity group, at which relationships between members can be frankly discussed, to be an effective way of resolving interpersonal problems. A group facilitator from outside the team should be sought if such a group is set up, and it should be made possible for all members to attend. Many teams also find it useful to set aside time occasionally for common group activities, such as policy review or shared learning. All these activities help to promote the team's cohesion and help it move towards a clearer formulation of its aims.

Problems and strategies

Occasionally, one or more workers may be unconvinced about the advantages of multidisciplinary working, or even opposed to it. This can present particular problems if the worker concerned is in a position of authority, such as a consultant. In the last resort, powerful staff members can, of course, prevent a multidisciplinary team from getting off the ground. This reality must be faced, but there are ways of preventing it.

A lengthy process of discussion and planning is necessary before a multidisciplinary approach is initiated, and the views of everyone involved need to be heard. The proposed philosophy needs to be specific, especially insofar as it relates to improved patient care and staff functioning. Much opposition to multidisciplinary working is based on misinformation which can be dispelled. The multidisciplinary approach cannot be imposed, nor can it be carried through by enthusiasm alone. However, managers and consultants are often prepared to tolerate multidisciplinary working if they feel the team knows what it is doing and they are kept informed of what is happening at every stage.

Just as all human groups contain the potential for creativity and cooperation, they also contain the potential for sterility and conflict. This need not be seen in a negative light – without conflict there can be neither learning nor growth for individuals or groups. A potent source of conflict in the team is the wide variety of professional backgrounds that members have, and from which they bring their preconceptions, assumptions and stereotyped attitudes. Traditional rivalries between the different professional groups is another complicating factor. By using team meetings to acquire understanding of how other members work, and encouraging role flexibility within the team, the worst effects of these often unconscious preconceptions can be mitigated. It is even possible for nurses to learn that doctors are capable of sensitivity and humility and for doctors to learn that nurses can take decisions!

Another problem can be posed by the different degrees of autonomy and specialisation to be found within any team. For example, a doctor, psychologist or social worker might be seen as having greater control over the quantity and kind of work she or he does than a community nurse. Although there is a certain amount of truth in this, it need not cause friction or lead nurses to devalue their own skills. All individuals bring something unique to their work, and a primary function of the multidisciplinary team is to assert the value of each individual within it.

Conflict can sometimes arise between the philosophy and practice of the team and the expectations of the professional hierarchies or institutions to which members also owe allegiance. Professional managers can feel threatened by a team over which they may feel they have little control while team members can feel insecure without the support of a professional hierarchy. Our own dependency needs enter into this: although we may not enjoy being told what to do, it is sometimes a comfort not having to think for ourselves. Again this difficulty is often more apparent than real. If regular meetings are held between the team and the relevant professional heads, and between members of particular professional groups within the team and their own managers, fantasies can be dispelled, anxieties reduced, and differences ironed out. Managers can also learn the advantages of allowing their subordinates a degree of autonomy, and team members those of developing their own resources and working more independently. Traditional hierarchical structures provide an element of security, while teamwork requires the ability to tolerate a certain amount of uncertainty – without it, professional and personal creativity becomes impossible.

Honest communication

In my experience, honest communication, whether of a positive or a constructively critical nature, does not occur between nurses as often as it should. Where it does occur, as it should in the multidisciplinary team, it can be unsettling because of its unfamiliarity. Constructive criticism of our work can feel like an attack, and we are often reluctant to engage in it ourselves for fear of upsetting colleagues or causing them to retaliate by criticising us. This attitude is misguided since it denies us the feedback necessary for change to take place – if we are not developing our full potential and are unaware of the fact, we need to hear it from our colleagues. This can happen without too much anxiety being aroused in the team meeting, where everyone is exposed to the same process. The emphasis throughout should be on the positive contribution each member makes, and mutual respect and goodwill are required.

Individuals within a team can sometimes find it difficult to tolerate unfamiliar ways of working in others and, if unchecked this can lead to a tendency towards sterile homogeneity. No two people are alike, and an emphasis on group cohesion at all costs can stifle individual initiative. Teams tend to fall into this trap if they feel exposed to external pressure, and meetings should expose and resolve any conflict. The team must not avoid its problems by imposing uniformity on its members.

Practical benefits

The team approach produces benefits for a very practical nature. Team members have a more accurate perception of their own and each others' skills than workers in hierarchical structures. This makes them less likely to take on work for which they are unfitted, and allows for more effective use of individual and team resources. It is much easier for multidisciplinary teams to arrive at an accurate assessment of patient needs, given tne wide range of experience on which the team can draw, and to ensure a better 'fit' between the specific skills of team members and the specific needs of patients. An overwhelming advantage of this approach is that it resolves the dilemma of how to reconcile increasing specialisation with the need to provide a holistic model of care. Although the difficulties are formidable, its advantages both in terms of the development of team members' professional skills and the improvement in patient care make it well worth the trouble.

20

When disaster strikes: staff support after major incidents

Ian Woodroffe

Hospital Chaplain, Mayday Hospital, Thornton Heath, Surrey

Dealing with a major incident like a fire or a train crash can be an emotional experience for hospital staff. Feelings can range from excitement and interest to concern and grief. Following the Purley train crash, staff support groups were set up at the Mayday Hospital in Thornton Heath, and in giving support, they also gained understanding of staff reaction in this type of situation.

Calm atmosphere

Many staff members commented on how calm they felt while dealing with the initial emergency – some found this amazing among so many terrible injuries and so much suffering. Nursing staff were surprised by the manifestations of shock in many casualties, and felt overwhelmed by how 'good' people were. Despite their injuries, casualties constantly expressed concern for the trouble caused and apologised for being a nuisance. They also became irrationally concerned with detail, apologising for their dirty coat or asking where their other shoe was. Staff found these reactions overwhelming and difficult to understand.

Some staff members who live alone found the crash more difficult to cope with than those who have support at home. They found their journey home stressful, both due to the large scale of suffering they had witnessed and to not wishing to be at home alone. "I had to drive through Purley to get home," said one, "I felt sick when I arrived at an empty house."

Both male and female staff were prone to bursting into tears on the night of the crash, and for three to four days after – particularly on days three and four. Crying was often triggered by trivial incidents unconnected with the crash, and staff found these outbursts embarrassing, particularly in front of colleagues who had not dealt with the initial emergency, as they felt these colleagues would not understand.

Bad dreams

While some staff slept well on the night of the crash due to exhaustion, others could not 'switch off' either that night or the three or four after. Some had vivid and disturbing dreams about what they had seen – many full of anxiety for particular casualties. "I woke up suddenly shaking because I dreamt he had died. Even when I got to work and found he was still alive I had the same dream three days later," said one. On-call managers reported dreaming of a telephone ringing to summon them to another red alert situation.

Emotional reactions also had physical manifestations for some – one woman spoke of "sweating for three days", while others could not eat properly in the week after the crash, or reported starting to shake unexpectedly. These symptoms were discernible from around day three or four after the crash, and continued well into the following week.

Support staff

Reactions from staff not directly involved in caring for crash casualties were interesting. Catering staff felt they had something to offer (which was true), but also felt somewhat detached from the emergency. "We made piles of sandwiches, thinking they would be useful, but not really knowing whether or not they were needed." Chaplaincy volunteers were frustrated at having little to do – they had been sent home because "a lot of people have come in off the street to help, so we don't really need you." The volunteers felt a certain amount of rejection, having been involved with the hospital for years in some cases, yet not being allowed to help in this emergency. Secretarial staff taking calls from anxious relatives found it difficult to deal with them when they got rude and abusive.

The staff taking advantage of the support service after the crash came from many disciplines in the hospital, although no doctors or consultants did so. All reported feeling excited at being involved in a major incident, but also that it was not quite right to be excited about such a tragedy. A week after the crash, feelings were of job satisfaction and 'a job well done'. It seemed important to staff that their managers recognised this, and all said they had been well appreciated.

While there was an outward air of calm in all departments dealing with crash casualties, some people reported feelings of inadequacy, uselessness and helplessness. Others said they felt very alone among all the activity, and it is interesting to note that these people were the ones with managerial responsibility. One thing many staff found hard to accept was the fact that casualties were admitted to hospital with only a number to identify them, although the reasons for this were appreciated.

The following week

In the week after the crash, some staff who had not worked during the initial emergency felt guilty, and were unable to talk about it because of their guilt at 'not having done anything'. Those who had been present, on the other hand were snappy and impatient with colleagues. They felt isolated, a feeling carried over by some to their family and personal relationships, which were also affected by reactions to the crash. Many wanted to talk about their experiences, and felt unable to do so with colleagues who had not been involved or with family and friends.

One thing the crash brought home to staff was how little they often know about patients after they are discharged. They reported feelings of unfinished business, and wanting to know how patients had progressed, or even what their name was, having only known them as a number.

Some staff felt they were expected to return to normal too quickly after the crash. Managers resented being expected to carry out a major organisational change 'imposed from above', only a few days after, and said this was insensitive. It was acknowledged that people need time to adjust to normal working patterns after such a major incident.

Reactions to the media among nurses were strong. While they were aware that casualties had consented to speak to reporters, nurses felt people's privacy was being invaded, and some doubted whether casualties should be asked to speak to the media so soon after an accident.

Dealing with staff reactions

The range of emotions staff can experience in the week or so after dealing with something like the Purley crash mean managers may need to consider giving them time off, or decreasing their workloads for a few days. If this is not possible, managers and colleagues should be aware that these staff may not be able to work to their usual standard for a time. It is also vital to acknowledge and give thanks for everyone's efforts in dealing with major incidents. This should not just include direct care staff – support staff who may not have been directly involved in patient care will also have put in extra effort and have felt some effects of the incident.

Recommendations

- Hospitals need a ready prepared support system for use after a major incident – possibly included in the major incident procedure document.
- Staff support systems should be available for everyday situations.
- Management need to be flexible with staff after a major incident.
- Reactions of staff following a major incident should be recorded, so that enough information can be collated for research into the subject.

The support exercise has shown us that major incidents like the Purley crash have a radical effect on staff involved – whether they are present at the initial emergency or not. While some staff were sceptical about the need for support groups, many needed to share their feelings with others who had been through the same thing. Some even said such support should be available to staff all the time. Hospitals would do well to have a prearranged staff support system set up for use immediately after such an incident – if support is not forthcoming quickly it is not as effective.

21

The Denford meeting – airing staff concerns

Janice Sigsworth, RGN
Formerly Senior Staff Nurse, The Charing Cross Hospital, London, now Ward Sister at University College Hospital, London

There are many factors in health care which can cause stress – the business of caring for ill people in itself can be stressful without the other problems of staffing, pay and communication and 'problem patients' which can crop up. A medical ward in the Charing Cross Hospital, London attempted to alleviate some of the factors causing stress among ward staff by holding a monthly meeting in which problems could be aired and difficulties with patients discussed.

The ward specialises in the care of breathless patients, and is staffed by two job sharing ward sisters, between eight and 12 registered nurses and eight to 12 student nurses. It is run on a primary nursing system, in which registered nurses care for a group of four to seven patients from admission through to discharge, working with other members of the multidisciplinary team.

The Denford meeting

The monthly meeting is known as the Denford meeting, named after Doctor John Denford, by whom it is chaired. Dr Denford is Director of the Cassel Hospital and a psychotherapist in patient community therapy. The meeting is chaired using a method described by Balint (1964). Research seminars had been organised at the Tavistock Clinic to study psychological implications in general medicine.

These seminars attempted to create a free, give and take atmosphere in which everyone could bring up their problems in the hope of gaining insight into them from the experience of others. The material for discussion at the Tavistock clinic was invariably provided by recent experiences with patients. It was essential for the group leader to refrain from making his own comments and criticisms until everyone had had ample time and space to express their thoughts.

As group leader in our meetings, Doctor Denford's role is to make his contributions ones which open up possibilities for the ward staff to discover for themselves some 'right' way of dealing with patient problems, rather than prescribing the right way to them.

The meeting takes place once a month, usually early on a Monday evening, and is held in the ward sitting room, unless patients are watching television, in which case it is held in the sister's office or an empty seminar room. The date of the meeting is publicised several days beforehand. The topic for discussion is decided by the doctors and nurses on the ward and, as suggested by Balint, is based on problems which arise when caring for patients. This is also publicised before the meeting, which usually lasts for an hour, with light refreshments provided by a nominated ward member – not always a nurse!

The meeting opens with brief, informal greetings as described by Balint. There is no reading from prepared reports or manuscripts – group members are asked to report freely on their experiences with the patients. Use of clinical notes is not encouraged but may be used as an aide-memoire. The aim is for group members to include as full an account as possible of their emotional responses to the problem, or even their emotional involvement in the patients' problems.

Such a frank account of the emotional aspects of the nurse/doctor-patient relationship can be obtained only if the atmosphere of the discussion is relaxed enough to enable group members to speak freely. Menzies (1960) states "The core of the anxiety situation for the nurse lies in her relationship with the patient. The closer and more concentrated this relationship the more likely the nurse is to experience the impact of anxiety, therefore the Denford meeting provides an excellent opportunity and environment to discuss and express these feelings." While a solution to the problem is often not found, staff are generally more aware of their own feelings and more clear about the needs of the patient.

Why is the meeting necessary?

As early as 1970 Menzies' attention was repeatedly drawn to the high level of tension and anxiety among nurses. The work situation arouses strong and mixed feelings in the nurse: pity, compassion, love, guilt, hatred and resentment towards the patients who arouse these strong feelings. Menzies examined the techniques employed by the nursing profession to contain and modify anxiety and hypothesised that nurses' struggle against anxiety can lead them to develop socially structured defense mechanisms such as restricted contact with patients through task allocation.

Kelly (1986) concluded in her study that patients who exhibit deviant behaviour are regarded as unpopular, which this supports Stockwell's theory (1984) that when nonconforming behaviour persists, patients come to be regarded as unpopular. Kelly recommended regular ward meetings to discuss difficulties with patients, and the purpose of the Denford meeting is to explore these feelings. Prior to the meetings, the patient who is causing problems has often been formally referred to the psychiatrist because they have been depressed or because members of the nursing or medical staff are concerned about the aspect of their behaviour.

Case study

George, aged 56, had been admitted to the ward six months previously for weight control, and was readmitted for the same reason. Two days following his readmission he suffered a right cerebral vascular accident. Prior to admission George was socially isolated. He had two female friends who appeared very overpowering, and he appeared to dislike them. He presented a number of problems to the nursing staff.

- He was sexually suggestive to the point of rudeness.
- He would not take his medicines when asked.
- He continually demanded food, telling several different nurses at different times that someone had taken his tray before he had finished.
- Initially he was very ill requiring physical nursing care, and was reluctant to become independent when he was over the acute stage.

During the Denford meeting at which George was the subject of discussion, it became obvious that he angered some staff with the disruptions he caused. Some felt sorry for him and wanted to help, but found this difficult because closeness was restricted by his sexual suggestions. Other nurses said he frustrated them or that they gave him one chance to take his medicines or to get out of bed – if he could not be bothered then neither could they and they would just leave him.

It became apparent that George demanded and got extra attention by all this destructive behaviour. For example, when giving George his medications, which would normally take two or three minutes, he would first refuse to take them, then say he would take them, then drop them on the floor which would require readministration and thus the saga continued. Coupled with this mounting anger and frustration, George appeared to give female members of the team more problems. He would have moments in which he would talk about his past life as a seaman and the places he had visited. This made many nurses feel guilty about their difficulties with him, because he showed that he could be a caring, intelligent person. A plan was formulated to overcome the problems George presented.

1. A day plan was drawn up, negiotated with George. This provided a united front so that if George demanded attention at an inappropriate time we could refer to the plan.
2. The problem posed by George's expression of his sexuality would be approached by two methods to meet the needs of the nurses:
   a. to confront him, telling him how difficult it was to be with him because of his comments;
   b. Some nurses felt they could not do this so they said they would ignore him when he made the comments but go to him at other times.

At the end of the meeting everyone felt optimistic about the plans to help staff cope with George and relieved that it was understandable to dislike George. As the reasons for his behaviour had become clear, however, the negative feelings towards him had subsided.

The Denford meetings give both nurses and doctors the chance to appreciate the difficulties and tensions in each other's work. The discussions allow people to share the troubles that difficult patients can cause, and give staff the chance to present a united front once plans are formulated. They are a useful and enjoyable way of reducing stress and, alleviating problems within patients that cause them to behave in a difficult manner.

References
Balint, M. (1964) The Doctor, His Patient and the Illness. Pitman, London.
Kelly, S. (1986) Nurses' perception of the Unpopular Patient. (Unpublished).
Menzies, I.E.P. (1970) Social Systems as a Defence Against Anxiety. Tavistock, London.
Stockwell, F. (1984) The Unpopular Patient. RCN, London.

Effective Communication

22

Respecting clients' dignity

Jo Yeats, RNMH
Staff Nurse, Tatchbury Mount, Calmore, Nr Totton, Hants.

Historically, large institutions were built to provide custodial care for mentally handicapped people which, until recently, was seen as the only possible approach. Individual dignity, self-esteem or independence of the patients were not issues worthy of consideration.

Long, overcrowded dormitories, locked doors, lack of personal privacy and various forms of punishment were regarded as quite normal and segregation of mentally handicapped people from the rest of the community was a matter of course.

These societal beliefs and attitudes led to the denial not only of the services and freedom enjoyed by the rest of the community but to the denial of all basic human rights.

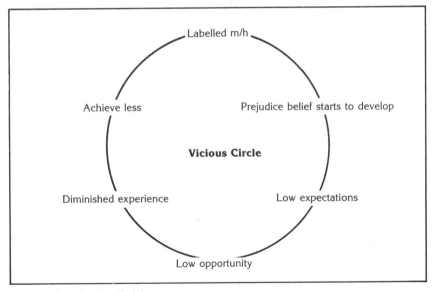

Figure 1. Devaluation Model.

Inherited attitudes

Prejudice still exists against many types of people, not only those with a mental handicap. Labels such as 'punk', or 'the unemployed', lead to whole groups becoming devalued as members of society. Common and often untrue beliefs, founded on fear and ignorance, have been passed down through the generations.

In the past, autocratic decisions were taken about groups of people seen as problems to society, rather than any attempt being made to meet individual need. People with a mental handicap were regarded as unsafe or possessed by the devil, best dealt with in segregation.

Towards the end of the last century, a popular public diversion was to visit the local asylum to view the 'lunatics', where the behaviour of the wretched, untreated inmates confirmed such beliefs.

Such low opinions, which still lurk in many areas of the public consciousness, lead to low expectations of mentally handicapped people. There is therefore little or no opportunity created for them to find a role in society, or for individuals to realise potential ability (Figure 1).

The Jay Report
In 1979, the Jay Committee, chaired by Peggy Jay, put forward proposals to improve the quality of life for those afflicted with a mental handicap and to begin the lengthy process of changing public attitudes. It stated: "Mentally handicapped people have the right to be treated as individuals, to live life to the full and to have access to the same services as 'normal people'."

It went on to say that staff employed should have the "right qualities and attitudes."

These recommendations should be regarded as a blueprint for future planning to promote better living conditions and environments. Some changes have already taken place. Huge institutions are giving way to small family houses and hospital wards are being humanised by allowing the residents to exercise free choice of colours and furnishings. These changes have affected not only the people with a mental handicap but those who care for them, thus preserving the dignity and self-esteem of both groups. The United Nations Declaration of Rights for Disabled Persons (Williams and Shoultz, 1982) states: "Disabled persons have the inherent right to respect for their human dignity." As an employee I believe we must have total respect for the individuals with whom we work to ensure their needs are fully met.

Normalisation
As a philosophy of care, 'normalisation' must come to the fore if carers are to believe and put into practice the principle that people with a mental handicap should have equal opportunity to experience activities enjoyed by their peers. It means improved freedom of choice, and wider participation in many activities with a view to enriching their lifestyle.

Hierarchy of human needs
Each individual must be appreciated as a unique person with a set of

specific needs. In 1970, Maslow (Clarke, 1982) identified the Hierarchy of Human Needs (Figure 2). This demonstrates that everyone has basic physical needs which must be fulfilled before the person can seek to meet the next areas of need in ascending order.

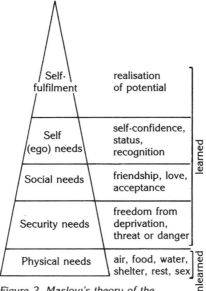

Figure 2. Maslow's theory of the hierarchy of needs.

For each person there are other specific needs and absolute levels of achievement within each layer of this structure. To help a person reach his or her highest possible potential they must be given opportunities to practise until that level of competence is acquired.

For someone with a mental handicap, this could mean gaining complex skills for employment or more basic daily living skills. Respect for a person's beliefs and rights as a human being help to build confidence and generate a high degree of motivation.

Until recently, people with a mental handicap were denied freedom of speech, and therefore self advocacy was impossible. It has been defined as: ''. . . speaking or acting for yourself. It means deciding what is best for you and taking charge of getting it. It means standing up for your rights as a person.'' (Williams and Shoultz, 1982). Skills that need to be taught include knowledge of individual rights, how to value yourself, make decisions and fight for what you believe is right. Many of these skills can be taught — the issues don't have to be large. For example, someone who has lived in a large institution can learn he has the right to a quiet drink at the local pub.

Society's attitudes can only be changed slowly by education. Gradual integration rather than segregation of people with a mental handicap is called for. They must have the same right to education, employment and housing as non-handicapped people enjoy. If society can recognise that they are 'people first', then the concept of integration into the community, respecting the dignity of each individual, would become a reality.

Bibliography

Atkinson, R.L., Atkinson, R.C. and Hilgard, E.R. (1983) Introduction to Psychology. Harcourt Brace, Jovanovich International Edition.

Bogdand, R. and Taylor, S.J. (1982) Inside Out. University of Toronto Press. Clarke, D. (1982) Mentally Handicapped People. Balliere Tindall, London.

Jay, P. et al (1979) Report of the Committee of Enquiry into Mental Handicap Nursing and Care. HMSO, London.

McConkey, R. and McCormack (1983) Breaking Barriers. Souvenir Press (E and A Ltd).

Williams, P. and Shoultz, B. (1982) We can speak for ourselves. Souvenir Press (E and A Ltd).

Williams, P. and Shoultz, B. (1982) Technical Assistance for Self Advocacy Work Book.

23

Encouraging compliance

Ruth E. Smith, BSc, RGN, RMN, DNCert
Support Worker in Rehabilitation, Lothian Regional Council, Department of Social Work.

Jill Birrell, MA(Hons), MSc, AFBPsS, C.Psychol,
Clinical Psychologist, Royal Edinburgh Hospital

'Non-compliance is not restricted to medicine. Not every bit of advice given by solicitors, architects, business consultants and other professionals is followed by those who have sought their services. Clients exercise their judgement, as is their right, when presented with professional advice even though they may not have the experience claimed by their advisers . . . clients' failure to follow advice may have serious consequences, yet these professions tend to see this independence as part of a client's rights and if they study non-compliance at all, do not do so in terms of client deficiency but in terms of necessary improvement in the services they offer.' (Thompson, 1984).

Compliance is generally used to refer to adherence or co-operation — doing as the health professional says concerning health matters. Taking medicine when one is supposed to, going on a prescribed diet or stopping smoking when advised are all examples of compliance. Non-compliance, may cause a breakdown in a treatment programme. It may put an individual at risk of a more serious illness or prolong the current difficulty.

Studies published

An early study by Stockwell (1972) describes the views of nurses in the inpatient setting where patients are described as 'popular' or 'unpopular'. 'Popular' patients are passive in interactions with staff, unquestioning and undemanding. Patients who question their treatment and express views about the nursing care they receive are regarded as 'unpopular'. Perhaps unpopularity and non-compliance have similarities?

Compared with inpatient settings, hospital outpatient clinics and general practice consultations have far greater difficulties regarding compliance — they have a less captive audience. Non-compliance can take many forms, among them failure to turn up for an appointment, failure to file prescriptions, discontinuing medication early, failure to make recommended changes in daily routine and missing follow-up appointments. Studies of a wide variety of illnesses, including coronary heart disease, hypertension, glaucoma and diabetes, have indicated that only 40 to 70 per cent of patients comply fully with physicians' prescriptions and advice. It is also worth noting that problems of non-compliance are often aggravated in elderly people who have no family support to ensure they follow instructions correctly. Macdonald et al (1977) found that twelve weeks after discharge from hospital, half of the elderly people studied were taking less than 50 per cent of their tablets while a further 25 per cent were seriously overdosing themselves. Less than 25 per cent were still taking medicine as prescribed. Clearly consultations often fail to convince patients of the wisdom of the proposed treatment.

Peck (1978) noted that a large number of studies have endeavoured to find an association between compliance and demographic variables such as sex, educational level, age, race, income and religion. If an association is present at all, it is very low. Studies have also been conducted on disease variables and it has been found that the diagnosis, severity of illness, duration of illness, previous hospitalisation and degree of illness or disability also have little or no association with compliance. The only reasonably consistent finding seems to be that psychiatric patients tend to be less compliant than patients with a physical illness.

Most important factors in determining the degree of compliance are more subjective than objective. Patients' satisfaction with contacts with health professionals and beliefs about illness are important. Rosenstock (1966) and Becker (1974) present the Health Belief Model (Table 1).

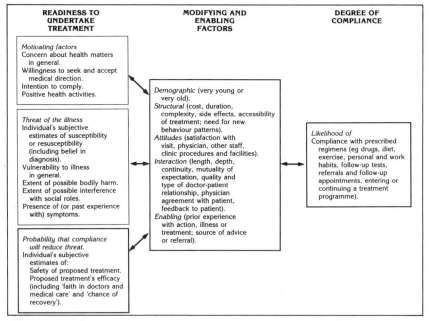

Table 1. Summary of Health Belief Model for predicting and explaining sick role behaviour, adapted from Becker, M.H.: The health belief model and sick-role behaviour reproduced with kind permission of the Society for Public Health Education, Inc.

Clearly patients' readiness to act is paramount. Action comes from their perception of the severity of the disease or possible progression and their perceived susceptibility to illness. If a patient does not believe that an illness is serious or does not believe he or she is likely to become ill, the readiness to act is low, whereas if the patient believes the illness is severe and there is a high chance of him or her contracting it, readiness to act is high. Important too are patients' considerations of the costs and benefits of compliance. They must believe that treatment will be effective.

Increasing compliance

Patients must understand and remember advice if they are to pay attention to it. Compliance is likely to be higher if the doctor or other health professional has a warm and friendly manner, heeds the patient's need for information, talks about non-medical topics and tests out and corrects any misunderstandings the patient may have. Written information seems effective in improving compliance in the short term. Categorisation of material into blocks has also proved useful. For example, saying "I am going to tell you what you must do to help yourself, what treatment you will receive, what tests need to be done" and suchlike, leads to greater recall of information. Also, the more specific the information given, the more compliance will be achieved. Telling a patient to lose half a stone is more effective than simply saying that he or she must lose weight. Supervision by a health worker can effectively increase compliance, as the act of reporting regularly to someone is reinforcing to the patient. When that constant supervision is removed, however, compliance returns to its lower initial rates. Finally, attempts to improve the communication skills of health care workers by further teaching and discussion have also shown promise. Research must continue to look for ways of removing barriers that prevent patients working well with health professionals and as Thompson (1974) states "a fuller understanding of attitude change required if the generally poor record of medical advisers is to be improved".

Bibliography
Fitzpatrick, R. et al. (1984) The Experience of Illness. Tavistock Publications, London and New York.
  The most comprehensive discussion of the literature to date. The book covers most areas of patients' experiences of illness.
Gatchel, R.J. and Baum, A. (1983) An Introduction to Health Psychology. Addison Wesley Publishing Company, London.
  Easier reading than Fitzpatrick et al – covers patients' experiences of illness but with less research data. Chapter seven is a precise summary of the main points.
Rachman, S.J. and Phillips, C. (1978) Psychology and Medicine. Penguin Publications, London.
  Chapter three is a short introductory text.

References
Becker, M.H. (1974) The health belief model and sick role behaviour. *Health Education Mongraph*, **2**, 409-419.

MacDonald, E.T., MacDonald, J.B. and Phoenix, M. (1977) Improving drug compliance after hospital discharge. *British Medical Journal* **2**, 618-621.

Peck, D. (1987) Communication and compliance. *Bulletin of the British Psychological Society,* **32**, 348-352.

Rosenstock. I.M. (1966) Why people use health services. *Millbank Memorial Fund Quarterly,* 94-127.

Stockwell, F. (1972) The unpopular patient. Royal College of Psychiatrists, Series 1, No. 2.

Thompson, J. (1984) Compliance. In Fitzpatrick, R., Hinton, J., Newman, S., Scambler, G. and Thompson, J. (Eds) (1984) The Experience of Illness.Tavistock Publications, London and New York.

The authors are aware that there are no references listed from nursing journals. There appears to be a lack of significant and relevant reports in this area of nursing.

24

What children think about hospitals and illness

Christine Eiser, BSc (Hons), PhD
Research Fellow, Department of Psychology, Washington Singer Laboratories, University of Exeter

Despite the enormous improvements made in caring for sick and hospitalised children since the publication of the Platt report (1959), admission to hospital is still a traumatic event. It is particularly traumatic for young children, who are much less well-informed than adults about ward procedures and treatments. Preschool children in particular may hold quite unpredictable views about what happens in hospitals. Redpath and Rogers (1984) found that some children believed that you went to hospital healthy and became ill while there. This and other research (Eiser and Patterson, 1984) has shown that young children may think that people in hospital always die, or that admission to hospital lasts for years, rather than days or weeks.

Less dramatically, but just as important in terms of how children perceive hospitals, is their confusion about the role of medical staff. In particular, Brewster (1982) showed that young children believed that doctors and nurses deliberately set out to hurt them, and this view was held even more strongly by children with a history of admissions compared with those with only brief experiences.

Punishment

Children differ greatly from adults in their understanding about the cause of illness, its treatment and prevention. There is some evidence that children's thoughts about illness change as they develop. Below seven years of age they may think that illness is a punishment for bad behaviour, or some magical rite.

They commonly think that all illnesses are contagious, and this may lead them to be suspicious of other children in the ward, fearing that they may 'catch' other illnesses (Bibace and Walsh, 1980). They do not understand how treatment can make them better, understandably — why should oral medication or an injection in the arm make a leg feel better?

Explanation of illness to children under seven must also take account of the fact that they have very limited understanding of their bodies (Crider, 1981; Eiser and Patterson, 1983) — they may be aware only that they have a heart, brain, blood and bones inside them. Awareness of their function is also very simple — the heart is for loving and the brain for 'doing sums'.

Misconceptions

Children between seven and 11 years become slightly more sophisticated, though their views are still by no means adult. Illness is caused by contact with 'germs', and there is still the belief that illness is generally spread by contact with others. They do not correctly infer the reasons for treatment. Beuf (1979) found that it was often assumed that a return to a normal diet was a sign of relapse, rather than improvement. By 11 years of age, children know they have a stomach and lungs. The stomach is 'for storing food' and children may not reliably be aware that food is converted to blood and waste. Commonly, they may think they have only one lung, and that they breathe through the mouth.

Increasing sophistication and adult-like concepts emerge from 11 years of age. In particular, children become aware that illness can be aggravated by psychological factors, and that stress or anxiety can influence the course of a disease. They become aware of the connections within the body — that there are digestive, respiratory or circulatory systems for example. Of particular importance, they realise that treatment sometimes makes them feel worse rather than better, and that it may be necessary to endure short-term discomfort in the hope of longer-term cure.

Effect of experience

This approach to understanding how children think about illness should be seen as an approximate guide. Their beliefs are likely to be affected by individual experiences — some children with chronic diseases, for example, can become relatively mature in their understanding, especially of their own disease. Others, particularly young chronically ill patients, may see only that their illness results in parental anxiety. This, and the fact that doctors and parents tend to keep young patients uninformed about their illness to avoid causing them stress, may mean that they remain less sophisticated in their reasoning than healthy children who have little experience of hospitals (Eiser et al, 1984).

In answering paediatric patients' questions, it is important to be aware of the limitations of their knowledge, and that answers may be interpreted very differently from how they were intended. Many medical terms are easily misinterpreted by children, for example, a diagnosis of diabetes may be taken to mean that a child will 'die of betes'; a diagnosis of oedema that 'there is a demon in my belly' (Perrin and Gerrity, 1981). It is also helpful to realise that many young patients believe that all illnesses are contagious, since this is likely to influence their behaviour on the ward.

How else may the stress of hospitalisation be reduced for young children? Undoubtedly it is important that they have some idea as to what to expect on a hospital ward. Generally, attempts to prepare children before admission have been successful in reducing anxiety and/or improving ward behaviour. Many American hospitals provide preparation for children being admitted for routine surgery (Azarnoff and Woody, 1981). The most common methods involve the use of films or videos (Melamed and Seigel, 1975), home visits by nurses (Ferguson, 1979), play therapy (Cassell and Paul, 1967), or pre-admission tours (McGarvey, 1983). Unfortunately, most of this preparation is aimed at the child being admitted for routine surgery and there is little in the way of preparation offered to chronically sick children. It is easy to forget that however minor and routine the procedures may appear to staff, they are potentially very frightening for children. Clearly, it is impossible to provide preparation for children admitted following traumatic injury, so there has been a move to provide children in the general community with information, so that they have some idea about what to expect should they require admission to hospital (McGarvey, 1983). Tours of hospitals appear to be enjoyed by young children, though it is not known if they result in less trauma for those who are later admitted.

Nurses can do a lot to reduce the stress of a child's hospital admission. Play and educational facilities which provide a continuity between home and hospital life are important. In recognising that children have different concerns from adults and by being aware that they are ill-informed about hospital and treatment, the nurse may be better able to answer a child's questions appropriately.

Children are given very little information about their illnesses directly by medical staff (Pantell et al, 1982), and may have to glean knowledge from eavesdropping adult conversation. This inevitably leads to misunderstanding. It is important for all health care professionals to appreciate the trauma hospital admission can cause to children and to ensure that they minimise its effect as much as possible.

References

Azarnoff, P. and Woody, P. (1981) Preparation of children for hospitalisation in acute care hospitals in the United States. *Pediatrics*, **68**, 361-8.

Beuf, A.H. (1979) Biting off the bracelet: a study of children in hospital. University of Pennsylvania Press, Philadelphia.

Bibace, R. and Walsh, M.E. (1980) Development of children's concepts of illness. *Pediatrics*, **66**, 913-17.

Brewster, A.B. (1982) Chronically ill hospitalised cheldren's concepts of their illness. *Pediatrics*, **69**, 355-362.

Cassell, S. and Paul, M. (1967) The role of puppet therapy on the emotional responses of children hospitalised for cardiac catheterisation. *Pediatrics*, **71**, 233-39.

Crider, C. (1981) Children's concepts of the body interior. In R. Bibace and M.E. Walsh (Eds.) Children's conceptions of health, illness and bodily functions. Jossey-Bass, San Francisco.

Eiser, C. and Patterson, D. (1983) "Slugs and snails and puppy-dog tails": children's ideas about the insides of their bodies. *Child: Care, Health and Development*, **9**, 233-40.

Eiser, C. and Patterson, D. (1984) Children's perceptions of hospital: a preliminary study. *International Journal of Nursing Studies*, **21**, 45-50.

Eiser, C., Patterson, D. and Tripp, J.H. (1984) Illness experience and children's conceptualisation of health and illness. *Child: Care, Health and Development*, **10**, 157-62.

Ferguson, B.F. (1979) Preparing young children for hospitalisation: a comparison of two methods. *Pediatrics*, **65**, 656-64.

McGarvey, M.E. (1983) Preschool hospital tours. *Children's Health Care,* **11,** 12-24.

Melamed, B.C. and Siegel, L.J. (1975) Reduction of anxiety in children facing hospitalisation and surgery by use of filmed modelling. *Journal of Consulting and Clinical Psychology,* **43,** 511-21.

Pantell, R.H., Stewart, T.J., Dias, J.K., Wells, P. and Ross, A.W. (1982) Physician communication with children and parents. *Pediatrics,* **70,** 396-402.

Perrin, E.C. and Gerrity, P.S. (1981) There's a demon in your belly. Children's understanding of illness. *Pediatrics,* **67,** 841-49.

Platt Committee, Great Britain (1959) The Welfare of Children in Hospitals. Her Majesty's Stationary Office, London.

Redpath, C. and Rogers, C.S. (1984) Healthy young children's concepts of hospitals, medical personnel, operations and illness. *Journal of Pediatric Psychology,* **9,** 29-40.

25

Counselling: basic principles in nursing

Philip Burnard, MSc, RGN, RMN, DipN, CertEd, RNT
Lecturer in Nursing, Department of Nursing Studies, University of Wales, Cardiff

During the past five years the idea that nurses in all specialties should develop appropriate skills in communicating with and helping their patients has received much attention. Often, however, basic counselling skills are taught without supporting theoretical rationale. This chapter sets out some basic principles based on those found in humanistic psychology theory and in the literature on client-centred therapy, with the aim of offering a 'theoretical scaffolding' on which to build good practice. The principles are presented dogmatically for the sake of clarity but, like all principles, they are open to debate, clarification and development. A further reading list is offered to be used as a guide to tracing the ideas back to source.

The terms 'counsellor' and 'client' are used through the chapter. 'Counsellor' means any grade of nurse acting as counsellor. 'Client' means anyone with whom the nurse is interacting in a counselling capacity. Thus a client may be a patient, a colleague or a friend. Table 1 shows the basic principles of counselling.

1. The client knows best what is best for them.
2. Interpretation by the counsellor is likely to be inaccurate and is best avoided.
3. Advice is rarely helpful.
4. The client occupies a different 'personal world' from that of the counsellor and vice versa.
5. Listening is the basis of the counselling relationship.
6. Counselling 'techniques' should not be overused; however:
7. Counselling can be *learned*.

Table 1. Basic principles in counselling.

The client knows what is best for them   We all perceive the world differently having had different personal histories which colour our views. Throughout our lives we develop a variety of coping strategies and problem solving abilities which we use when beset by personal problems. Central to client-centred counselling is the idea that, given the space and time, we are the best arbiters of what is and is not right for us. We can listen to others, and hear their ideas but in the end we as individuals have to decide upon our own course of action.

Belief in the essential ability of all people to make worthwhile decisions for themselves arises from the philosophical tradition of existentialism. Existentialism argues, among other things, that we are born free and that we 'create' ourselves as we go through life. For the existentialist, nothing is predetermined, there is no blueprint for how any given person's life will turn out. Responsibility and choice lie squarely with the individual.

No one is free in all respects. We are born into a particular society, culture, family and body. On the other hand, our *psychological* make up is much more fluid and arguably not predetermined. We are free to think and feel. One of the *aims* of counselling is to enable the client to realise this freedom to think and feel.

Once a person has to some extent, recognised this freedom, he begins to realise that he can change his life. Again, in humanistic or client-centred counselling, this is a central issue: that people can change. They do not have to be weighed down by their past or by their conditioning (as psychoanalytical and behavioural theory would argue): they are more or less free to choose their own future. And no one can choose that future for them. Hence the overriding principle that the client knows what is best for them.

Interpretation by the counsellor is likely to be inaccurate and is best avoided   To interpret, in this sense, is to offer the client an explanation of his thinking, acting or feeling. Interpretations are useful in that they can help to clarify and offer a theoretical framework on which the client may make future decisions. However, they are best left to the client to make.

As we have seen, we all live in different perceptual worlds. Because of this, another person's interpretation of *my* thinking, acting or feeling will be based on that person's experience — not mine. That interpretation is, therefore, more pertinent to the person offering it than it is to me, coloured as it is bound to be by the perceptions of the other person. Such colouring is usually more of a hinderance to me than a help.

It is tempting for others to lace their interpretations of a person's action with 'oughts' or 'shoulds'. Thus an interpretation can quickly degenerate into moralistic advice which may lead to the client feeling guilty or rejecting the advice because it does not fit into his own belief or value system.

Advice is rarely helpful   Any attempt to help to 'put people's lives right' is fraught with pitfalls. Advice is rarely directly asked for and rarely appropriate. If it is taken, the client tends to assume that 'that's the course of action I would have taken anyway' or, he becomes dependent on the counsellor. The counsellor who offers a lot of advice is asking for the client to become dependent. Eventually, of course, some of the advice turns out to be wrong and the spell is broken: the counsellor is seen to be 'only human' and no longer the necessary life-line perceived by the client in the past. Disenchantment quickly follows and the client/counsellor relationship tends to degenerate rapidly. It is better then, not to become an advice-giver in the first place.

There are exceptions to this principle where advice giving is appropriate; about wound care or medication for example. In the sphere of personal problems, however, advice-giving is rarely appropriate.

Different 'personal worlds' of client and counsellor Because of varied experiences, different physiologies and shifting belief and value systems, we perceive the world through different 'frames of reference'. We act according to our particular belief about how the world is. What happens next, however, is dependent upon how the world *really* is. If there is a considerable gap between our 'personal theory of the world' and 'how the world really is' we may be disappointed or shocked by the outcome of our actions.

It is important that the counsellor realises that her own belief system may not be shared by the client and that her picture of the world is not necessarily more accurate.

A useful starting point is for the counsellor to explore her own belief and value system before she starts. She may be surprised at the contradictions and inconsistencies that abound in that 'personal world'! She is then in a better position to appreciate the difference between her belief system and her client's.

The counsellor's task is to attempt to enter and share the personal world of the client. This is often described as developing empathy or the ability to non-judgementally understand the particular view of the world that a person has at a particular time. That view usually changes as counselling progresses, after which the client may no longer feel the need for the counsellor. When this happens, the counsellor must develop her own strategies for coping with the separation that usually follows.

Counselling is a two-way process. While the client's personal world usually changes, so may the counsellor's. It can, then, be an opportunity for growth for the counsellor as well as the client.

Listening is the basis of the counselling relationship To really listen to another person is the most caring act of all, and takes skill and practice. Often, when we claim to be listening we are busy rehearsing our next verbal response, losing attention and failing to hear the other person. Listening involves giving ourselves up completely to the other person in order to fully understand.

We cannot listen properly if we are constantly judging or categorising what we hear. We must learn to set aside our own beliefs and values and to 'suspend judgement'. It is a process of offering free attention; of accepting, totally, the other person's story, accepting that their version of how the world is may be as valid as our own. Listening can be developed through practice and may be enhanced through meditation. Various experiential exercises have been developed to enable people to learn properly. They need to be used carefully with plenty of time allocated for them.

We need to listen to the metaphors, the descriptions, the value judgements and the words that people use, as they are all indicators of their personal world. Noting facial expressions, body movements, eye contact or lack of it, are all aspects of the listening process.

Many of us have been confronted by the neophyte counsellor whose determined eye-contact and stilted questioning make us feel distinctly uncomfortable! The aim is to gradually incorporate techniques into the personal repertoire. It is important that learner nurses do not adopt, wholesale, a collection of techniques that they have been taught in the school of nursing.

Counselling 'techniques' should not be overused   If we arm ourselves with a whole battery of counselling techniques, perhaps learned through workshops and courses, we are likely to run into problems. The counsellor who uses too many techniques may be perceived by the client as artificial, cold and even uncaring. It is possible to pay so much attention to techniques that they impede listening and communicating.

Some techniques, such as the conscious use of questions, reflections, summary, probing and so forth are very valuable. What one must hope for, is that through practice, such techniques become natural to the counsellor. The process takes considerable time and must be rooted in a conscious effort to appear natural and spontaneous to others.

Counselling can be learned   Counselling is not something that comes naturally to some and not to others. We can all develop listening skills and our ability to communicate clearly with other people, which is the basis of counselling. The skills can only be learned through personal experience and lots of practice, which may be gained in experiential learning workshops for development of counselling skills.

The list of principles outlined here is not claimed to be exhaustive. It attempts to identify *some* of the important principles involved and to explain them. The next stage is to develop counselling theory and skill further through reading and counselling skills courses. The bibliography identifies some sources of further ideas regarding the theory of counselling. These are not the *only* books on counselling but they are up-to-date, readable and currently available in bookshops.

Counselling skills courses are run by a variety of university extra-mural departments; by specialist counselling organisations and, increasingly, as part of the continuing education programmes organised with schools of nursing.

Bibliography
Bond, M. (1986) Stress and Self Awareness: A Guide for Nurses. Heinemann, London.
  A practical book which explores methods of coping with emotions and personal problems.
Burnard, P. (1985) Learning Human Skill: A Guide for Nurses. Heinemann, London.
  An introductory text on self-awareness and experiential learning. Contains a series of exercises on counselling skills training.
Burnard, P.(1989) Counselling Skills for Health Professionals. Chapman and Hall, London.
  A guide to many aspects of counselling theory and skills.
Claxton, G. (1984) Live and Learn: An Introduction to the Psychology of Growth and Change in Everyday Life. Harper and Row, London.
  A stimulating and eclectic approach to the question of how people learn and change. A very readable book.
Nelson-Jones, R. (1981) The Theory and Practice of Counselling Psychology. Holt, Rinehart Winston, London.
  A very comprehensive account of most aspects of counselling.
Rogers, C.R. (1980) A Way of Being. Houghton Mifflin, New York.
  A sensitive book by the late Carl Rogers founder of 'client-centred' counselling, which explores the nature of empathy and the therapeutic relationship.

26

Terminal care: their death in your hands

Suzanne Conboy-Hill, PhD, MPhil, BA, SRN, AFBPsS
Principal Psychologist, Brighton Health Authority

There has recently been a dramatic increase in interest in the care of dying people and research into how this can be given. However, this appears to reflect rather than precede the growth of the hospice movement, and so understanding of the needs of dying people, their families, friends and carers remains scanty in hospitals, despite the fact that increasing numbers of people are being admitted to hospital for terminal care.

Recent improvement in research
This chapter is a short review of psychological and nursing literature in terminal care with some suggested changes nurses might make to ensure the maximum relief of psychological as well as physical pain in dying people.

Much of the research work in terminal care, initiated primarily by such people as Elizabeth Kubler-Ross and Cicely Saunders, has been carried out in America by groups comprising medics, nurses, theologians and psychologists (eg McCusker, 1984; Friel and Tehan, 1980; Davis and Jessen, 1981). While earlier work may be criticised for being largely made up of case histories or anecdotes, the more recent studies have been objective and systematic applications of the scientific method. Nurses in particular have become extremely skilled in this area.

Some interesting findings have been accumulated in these studies, many suggesting that health care personnel are surprisingly ill-prepared to deal with the psychological aspects of dying, so that many terminally ill people get rather a raw deal (Backer et al, 1982).

While most ordinary people would imagine that hospital work must inure its staff to the distress of facing dying people, enabling them to give the best possible care, research shows that both doctors and nurses consistently avoid social contact with terminal patients and that medical students learn early in their careers to become less available to them (eg Doka, 1982; LeShan, 1969; Rabin and Rabin, 1970; Todd and Still, 1984).

It is not clear why this should be, but research has shown that doctors themselves are more, rather than less, afraid of death (Schoenberg and Carr, 1972) and, being in executive control of patient care, frequently deny patients the right to know of their prognosis (Ley, 1977). This puts nurses in the invidious position of knowing the facts but being unable to discuss them with patients or relatives if they are asked.

Effects on nursing care

This may have several effects. Nurses may find ways of talking to dying people without giving any information — perhaps by offering reassurances or platitudes; they may experience conflict which leads to burnout and eventually leave the profession or they may develop patterns of care which avoid social behaviour with dying people. There is evidence for all of these. Nurses describe feelings of helplessness, inadequacy and depression associated with terminal care (Wilson, 1985; Friel and Tehan, 1980; Mandel, 1981). They often use subtle avoidance and conversation-controlling tactics while taking care of the physical needs of dying people (Nicholls, 1984). This poor communication means that people often remain ignorant of the details of their illness while almost everyone else has been given some, if not all, the relevant information.

If research had shown that dying people have no insight into their prognosis and that the distress is clearly confined to health care personnel themselves, then future research should be directed towards enabling staff to 'let sleeping dogs lie' in the most positive way. However, it would seem that patients do have insight into their condition and so are being denied the opportunity to discuss their prognosis and the emotional and practical consequences openly and honestly with those upon whom they would normally rely (Hinton, 1967; Todd and Still, 1984; Antonovsky, 1972).

Closed awareness

The distress associated with this situation, which is known as 'closed awareness', has been observed consistently by those working in the field (eg Hinton, 1967; Cassem and Stewart, 1975; Howells, 1983). Patients themselves have reported relief when open awareness is established (Kubler-Ross, 1969; see also Backer et al, 1982).

This evidence should not be seen as a prescription for routine or ruthless truth telling. Braver (1985) asks, 'Which patient, what truth?', implying a very individual approach is needed, and Hinton (1967) feels that simply telling people is the wrong approach because it suggests that the teller knows everything and the patient nothing. He recommends sensitive interview procedures which allow what Schoenberg and others have called 'graded honesty', and points out how important it is that interviewers be readily available to listen, so that they are always in touch with the patient's current needs.

Should nurses take control?

Nurses are clearly best placed for this role and Benoliel (1972) has gone as far as suggesting that nurses rather than doctors take executive control of care when it becomes predominantly comfort oriented rather than curative. Of course, with current emphasis on an inter-disciplinary team approach to care, it could be argued that no-one should take complete control. However, it is clear that this ideal has a long way to go and nurses may have to exert their authority in some particular way before gaining acceptance as true equals in a team containing medical practitioners.

To do this, nurses will need to:

• confront doctors about their joint role in information exchange, aiming to gain the right to independent practice in dealing with the day to day psychological needs of patients;

• generate research tied to patients' psychological needs and those of their carers (staff and families);

• develop training methods based on research and continuing through basic and post-basic education;

• develop and evaluate ways of stress management for staff working in terminal care (Mandel, 1981).

An authoritative, informed and assertive nursing staff, abandoning what has been described as the traditional doctor/nurse, male/female role model (Field, 1982), may be essential for the development of good psychosocial care of dying people. Only then can honest relationships develop, allowing patients to place trust and confidence in those to whom they must increasingly surrender control.

References

Antonovsky, A. (1972) The image of four diseases held by the urban Jewish population of Israel. *Journal of Chronic Disease*.

Backer, B. A., Hannon, N. and Russess, N.A. (1982) Death and Dying. Wiley & Son.

Benoliel, J. (1972) Nursing care for the terminal patient; a psychosocial approach. I Schoenberg et al. (Eds) Psychosocial Aspects of Terminal Care, 145.

Braver, P. (1965) Should the patient be told the truth? In Skipper, J. and Leonard, R. (Eds), Social Interaction and Patient Care. Lippincott, Philadelphia.

Cassem, N.H. and Stewart, R.S. (1975) Management and care of the dying patient. *International Journal of Psychiatry in Medicine*, **6**, 1/2, 293.

Davies, G. and Jessen, A. (1981) An experiment in death education in the medical curriculum. *Omega J. Death and Dying*, **11**, 2, 157.

Doka, K. (1982) The social organisation of terminal care in two paediatric hospitals. *Omega J. Death and Dying*, **12**, 2, 129.

Field, D. (1983) Study of nurses engaged in terminal care on an acute medical ward. Paper presented to British Psychological Society Conference, York.

Friel, M. and Tehan, C.B. (1980) Counteracting burnout for the hospice caregiver. *Cancer Nursing*, Aug. 285.

Hinton, J. (1967) Dying. Pelican, London.

Howells, K. (1983) Teaching the medical profession about death and dying. Paper presented to British Psychological Society Conference, York.

Kubler-Ross, E. (1969) On Death and Dying. Macmillan, New York.

LeShan, L. (1969) Psychotherapy and the dying patient. In Pearson, L. (Ed), Death and Dying. The Press of Case Western University, Cleveland.

Ley, P. (1977) Psychological studies of doctor-patient communication. In Rackham, S. (Ed), Contributions to Medical Psychology. Pergamon Press.

McCusker, J. (1984) Development of scales to measure satisfaction and preferences regarding long-term and terminal care. *Medical Care*, **22**, 5, 476.

Mandel, H. (1981). Nurses' feelings about working with the dying. *American Journal of Nursing*, **816**, 1194.

Nicholls, K. (1984) Psychological Care in Physical Illness. Croom Helm.

Rabin, D. and Rabin, L. (1970) In Brim, O. et al (Eds), The Dying Patient. Russell Sage Foundation, New York.

Schoenberg, B. and Carr, A. (1972) Educating the health professional in the psychosocial care of the terminally ill. In Schoenberg, B., et al (Eds), Psychosocial Aspects of Terminal Care. Columbia University Press.

Todd, C.J. and Still, A.W. (1984) Communication between general practitioners and patients dying at home. *Soc.Sci.Med.* **18**, 8, 667.

Wilson, C. (1985) Stress in hospice nursing. *News Letter of the British Psychological Society Division of Clinical Psychology*, No 48, 5.

27

Helping clients to come to terms with loss

Teresa Lombardi, RGN, RSCN, RNT, Cert Ed, Dip Counselling
Senior Nurse Manager, Continuing Education, Worthing District School of Nursing

Working with terminally ill people, although rewarding and challenging, is far from easy, for a variety of reasons. It is impossible to identify a 'right and wrong' way of communicating with them, as each client has individual needs and ways of expressing him or herself. Similarly, each situation is different, and as nurses we bring our own individual attitudes, values, beliefs, experiences and skills into them. We also bring our feelings of anxiety and helplessness and our need to 'make it better' for patients or clients, which it is not always possible to do.

Witnessing strong emotions in others and learning to cope with and accept them may remind us of our own areas of difficulty and losses, whether real or feared. This can make us vulnerable to feelings of anxiety, inadequacy and pain. If we are not sufficiently aware of our own values, beliefs and areas of 'unfinished business', it may affect the way we relate to our clients and hinder the development of the qualities of warmth, acceptance, genuineness, empathy and flexibility that are so essential when working with this client group. Finally difficulties arise because ultimately 'effective helping' requires a degree of self confidence and courage and it is often easier to 'opt out' and avoid the situation. This is a normal coping strategy that we all need to do when we are vulnerable. We must care for ourselves as nurses or we will not be free to effectively care for others.

Tasks of mourning
Although each client and situation is different, there are certain principles that can be followed to make our helping skills more effective. It may be useful to consider these within the framework of the four tasks of mourning (Worden, 1983).

When clients are informed of their situation they often feel a sense of disbelief, that 'it is not really happening'. During this first stage the nurse's prime aim is to help the client become aware and accept that the situation is real, it is happening and is not a figment of the imagination. This is essential, as only when reality is accepted can the client progress and experience the pain of grief, ultimately moving through to resolution. One of the best ways to help clients accept their loss is to encourage them to talk. Many clients mentally relive where they were when they first heard of their diagnosis, what happened and who said what. They may need to talk through this again and again, over weeks or even months. While family and friends may grow tired and even impatient the effective nurse is a patient listener who encourages the clients to talk.

Acknowledging grief

The second task of mourning is to acknowledge and experience the pain of grief. Feelings such as anger, guilt and sadness may not be acceptable to either family or friends or to clients themselves. They may therefore try to suppress or even deny their pain in order to avoid burdening, distressing or embarrassing their loved ones, while other clients may think they are 'going mad'. During this stage clients need to be helped to give themselves 'permission' to be angry or sad, or to cry, and must be given opportunity to talk through their guilt and unburden themselves. A nurse's quiet acceptance and acknowledgement of the pain of grief will facilitate this difficult task, which means that clients are not left to carry the burden of their pain with them into the next stage of their lives.

Adjustment

The third task of mourning is that of adjusting to the loss, real or impending. Essentially the nurse helps clients to identify problems and then to explore alternative ways of dealing with them. For example, this may mean identifying short term goals, of looking at today and next week rather than next month or next year. This is an active stage and may involve adopting and coming to terms with a new role or learning new skills such as coping with a prosthesis.

The final stage of mourning involves withdrawing emotional energy from the loss and reinvesting it in another relationship or diverting it to other channels. At this point the intense pain of grief diminishes and although clients will still experience a sense of sadness they will be able to channel their emotions into living and dealing with their lives today.

Skills for effective helping

Effective helping can be viewed as a problem solving activity. Most nurses use a variety of skills throughout the helping process and although there is no standard classification of such skills, for convenience they can be divided into two main stages.

Stage one — attending Effective helpers are those who can establish a caring, non threatening relationship with their clients. Many nurses begin this relationship with an advantage in that the client's trust is already invested in them because of the nurturing nature of the nursing role. Trust will also develop if the nurse can be open and honest — relationships bound by any degree of mutual pretence will lead to feelings of insecurity and non-acceptance in clients (Glaser and Strauss, 1965), who will then be more likely to withdraw into their lonely worlds.

The first contact between nurse and client is crucial in developing and maintaining a warm trusting relationship. The client will have doubts and fears, and some problems will seem too large, too overwhelming or too unique to share. He may ask himself, "Can I really trust this person?", "Is she really interested in me?" "Does she have the time for me?" Answers to such questions will be provided not merely by words but by other more subtle and powerful means of communication. The physical setting, the way the nurse greets the client and her gestures and tone of voice can all convey sensitivity and consideration.

Observing and reacting

From the first meeting nurse and client will engage in the process of observing and reacting to the other. Success in helping depends upon the client's perception of the nurse's manner and behaviour. He will look for, and must experience, empathy, respect and sensitivity. Being with, attending to and listening are supportive and comforting behaviours which convey respect and concern for the client.

At this stage an opening statement such as, "I wonder what worries you have about your illness?" may provide the necessary invitation for the client to take the lead and talk freely while the nurse 'attends'. This involves 'being with' the client physically and psychologically. Body communication, posture, degree of relaxation and eye contact indicate interest in and attention to the client. Attending behaviour encourages the trust that is so necessary for promoting exploration and will also help the nurse listen more effectively.

Listening is an active, complex process and perhaps the most important of all helping skills. It involves first observing and interpreting the client's non-verbal behaviour and then listening to and interpreting his verbal messages. During the process of listening, the skill of reflection can be used by the nurse to sensitively communicate to the client her understanding of his concerns. It is an empathetic response that involves restating in fresh words the client's core feelings. For example:

Client: "I'm bewildered, there's so much to take in and consider, and so many different doctors each with their own ideas."

Nurse: "It all seems so confusing, even overwhelming and almost out of your control."

Client: "Yes, that's it, it feels like that."

An accurate reflection, while not halting the flow of talk can help clarify and bring less obvious feelings into the client's awareness so that they can be 'owned' and acknowledged. Reflection also increases the degree of trust which will ultimately facilitate further exploration.

Stage two — responding   This stage of helping involves maintaining the good relationship developed in the first stage and taking the process further by helping the client explore, clarify and define his problem or area of concern. Responding skills help the client progress through the stages of mourning, the appropriate and effective ones at this stage are those which enable the client to extend and develop his understanding of himself and his difficulties.

Effective helping will be determined by the nurse's ability to respond accurately to the needs and cues provided by the client. This 'staying with the client' demonstrates empathy and acceptance. To achieve this the nurse needs to avoid directing and leading, eg "I don't think you should be spending so much time talking about your illness."; reassuring, eg "That's a common problem, but you'll be alright."; advising, eg "I wouldn't tell your family about this;" or not accepting the client's feelings and hiding behind the professional facade, eg "Your depression will pass, it's just part of the body's response to your treatment."

Staying with the client may also mean staying silent if he needs time to gather thoughts and feelings together. Although there are many different meanings for a silence, it is often a productive time and it is helpful if the nurse simply waits quietly until the client is ready to go on. This is perhaps a very difficult strategy to adopt as we are used to commenting on, advising or teaching.

Other skills

Other responding skills which will help exploration and clarification are probing, questioning and summarising. Prompts and probes are verbal tactics which help clients talk about themselves and define their problems more concretely. A prompt may be a head nod or a simple "Aha" or "I see" while a probe may take the form of a statement, eg "When you were told you had cancer you said you were both relieved and depressed. I'm wondering how you've been since then."

The careful use of questions can also help focus and clarify. These should be open questions, usually beginning with 'how', 'what' or 'who', which leave the respondent free to answer as he wishes, eg "Can you explain what you mean?", or "What was it about your treatment session today that was so upsetting?". Asking too many questions, however, may make the client feel interrogated, anxious and insecure, which will interfere with the rapport between nurse and client. Questions which begin with 'why', such as, "Why did you feel like that?" are also unhelpful, as they lead the client to search for intellectual explanations to justify his feelings.

Summarising

Summarising is the process of tying together all that has been communicated during part or all of a helping session. It can also be a natural means of finishing the session or beginning a new one. This then paves the way for the client to commit himself to further exploration and to developing awareness. Thus, with continuing emotional support the client, finding and utilising his own inner resources, moves on with hope to another day.

These strategies have been identified to help the nurse care for clients who are experiencing loss, but it should be remembered that the nurse has to deal with her own personal feelings of grief in response to the client's situation. In addition she may be constrained by fears that she will make the situation worse for the client through lack of skill. Only the client can judge what is helpful and is likely to seek a nurse who can support, comfort and care, and is herself — a real person with strengths and weaknesses like anyone else.

Bibliography
Brammer, L. M. (1979) The Helping Relationship Process and Skills. Prentice-Hall, New Jersey.
   Provides more in-depth discussion of the issues raised in this paper.
Egan, G. (1982) The Skilled Helper Model, Skills and Methods for Effective Helping. Brooks Cole Publishing Company, California.
   Describes in detail the skills and methods needed for effective helping.
Munro, E. A., Nanthei, R. J., Small, J.J. (1983) Counselling: A Skills Approach. Methuen, New Zealand.
   A clearly-written text with some very practical exercises and examples of helping skills.
Nelson-Jones, R. (1983) Practical Counselling Skills. Holt, Rinehart and Winston, London.
   Applies the theory of counselling in a very practical way using exercises to aid skill development and case studies as examples.

References
Glaser, B. and Strauss, A. (1965) Awareness of Dying. Aldine, Chicago.
Worden, W.J. (1983) Grief Counselling and Grief Therapy. Tavistock Publications, London.

28

Bereavement: the needs of the patient's family

Jenny Penson, MA, SRN, HVCert, Cert Ed, RNT
Senior Lecturer in Nursing Studies, Dorset Insitute of Higher Education

Through this chapter bereaved people are referred to as "family" or "relatives" for ease of comprehension. Terms such as "key people" or "significant others", while rather unwieldy, may more accurately describe the grieving person who is, for example, a life-long friend.

"Bereavement" means "to be robbed of something valued" – this definition seems particularly helpful as it indicates that this someone or something has been wrongly or forcibly taken from you. A key concept to understanding bereavement is that of loss. As Caplan (1964) and others have suggested, the grief experienced after losing someone close to you may be similar to the emotions felt after other types of loss, life transitions such as redundancy, divorce, failing an important exam or losing a much loved pet. As nurses we become aware of the emotions that patients experience after operations such as mastectomy, amputation of a limb or the loss of body image caused by suffering from a disfiguring disease.

When people are bereaved they suffer not only the loss of a person but also a substantial part of themselves, because everything they have shared with that person cannot be repeated with anyone else. The bereavement experience, therefore, is one of strong, violent and sometimes overwhelming reactions. These feelings actually begin from the moment the relative is told that the patient will not recover, referred to by Lindemann (1944) as "anticipatory grief".

The patient

Kubler Ross (1970), states: "We cannot help the terminally ill patient in a really meaningful way if we do not include his family." She determined that family members undergo stages of adjustment similar to the five phases she described for dying patients – denial, anger, bargaining, depression and acceptance as they come to terms with the reality of terminal illness in the family. She advocates that when there is time to do so, the family should be encouraged to express grief as much as possible prior to the death of a loved one which serves to alleviate, to some extent, the pain that is felt afterwards. If members of a family can share these emotions they will gradually face the reality of the impending separation and come to an acceptance of it together.

Unresolved family stress can significantly affect the outcome of the patient's illness, so the care of the family is part of the total care of the patient. It is also about understanding him as a member of the family group, and being aware that he and his family are not separate entities. Each constantly influences the other, thus affecting the health and happiness of both. It is possible that nursing actions may affect the long-term adjustment of the bereaved relatives after the death of the patient.

Molter (1979) studied family needs as they identified them, and looked at whether these were being met, and if so, by whom. The results showed that relatives could identify their needs during an intensive phase of hospitalisation. Their universal and strongest need was for hope. Nurses can go some way towards meeting this need by helping to set short-term goals for the patient. A weekend at home, a visit from a favourite friend, planning something special to enjoy together all helps to relieve that sense of helplessness which is often felt. They also go some way towards providing good memories to look back on. Reassurance that the patient will not be allowed to suffer pain or great distress, that someone will be with them when they die, and that support is available after the death if they need it, are all significant to those for whom no hope of an ultimate recovery can be given.

Hampe (1975) also found that spouses believed that the nurse's primary responsibility was to the patient and therefore they would be too busy to help relatives. One of the principal needs she identified from her study was for the family to be able to visit the dying patient at any time and for as long as they wished. They also wanted prompt help with the physical care and a demonstration of friendliness and concern in their relationship with the nurse.

My own experience indicates that encouraging involvement of the family in the care of the patient may minimise feelings of guilt during bereavement. There is a sense of not having failed when one was needed and the satisfaction of having done something tangible to give comfort and show love.

Hospital or home care?

This must be borne in mind when discussing the pros and cons of hospital versus home care. Where dying at home is possible because both the patient and their relatives want it, and there are enough resources available when needed, the family are likely to feel a sense of achievement, of not having failed the patient. On the other hand, relatives do derive comfort from the security of constant professional expertise and the knowledge that any emergency will be dealt with by a 24-hour service. However, they still need to feel involved and should be encouraged to give to the patient in any way they can. This might range from helping with nursing care to arranging photos and flowers or bringing in special food or drink that the patient may ask for which the hospital cannot supply.

To tell or not to tell

Whether or not to tell the patient of his diagnosis and prognosis is a dilemma which causes much distress to family, patients and nurses. Sometimes relatives are advised by doctors and/or nurses not to be truthful with the patient and this can create a barrier between them, described by Solzhenitsyn (1971) as "a wall of silence" which separates them.

There is an obvious conflict in many relatives' minds between the idea of the patient's right to autonomy to knowing the truth if he wishes it, and the idea of paternalism, having the right to withhold it on the grounds of protecting the patient and giving him hope. Relatives will often say such things as "it will be too much for him", "he will give up", "I know he won't be able to stand it", "he will be frightened". These sort of statements may well be true but they may also reflect the relatives' own fears.

The cue to how much information is given should lie with the patient and the nurse's role with the relatives is often to explain to and sustain them during that gradual realisation that comes to most patients near the end. This may or may not be expressed and shared. However, when a patient and family can openly discuss their situation together, their relationship can be deepened and this can give great comfort to the bereaved person afterwards. It also creates a basis of honesty and trust which facilitates the relationship between patient, family and carers. Ann Oakley (1985) described when her father, Richard Titmuss, was dying: "You said things you never would have said had you not known you were dying – and that is how I knew you were."

That families fail to share their feelings openly with one another when faced with terminal illness may be due to the defence of denial and also a function of experience. Although we, the health workers, have been enlightened about combating this so-called conspiracy of silence which surrounds the topic of death, it is also possible that some families have been over-exposed to that viewpoint. As Bowen, (1978) points out, in spite of whatever attitudinal change that may have taken place the "basic problem is an emotional one and a change in the rules does not automatically change the emotional reactivity."

Support

So, should staff be so involved as to sit and weep with the relatives? Is this what sharing and support is about? Kubler Ross, (1974), suggests that we ask ourselves whether we would judge someone who cared enough to cry for us. "A display of emotions on the part of the therapist is like drugs, the right amount of medicine at the right time can work wonders. Too much is unhealthy – and too little is tragic."

It has been suggested that nurses are in a prime position to meet the family needs through active listening and supporting. They found that relatives wanted support but they tended to feel they should not burden the "too busy" nurses with their problems. It is important, therefore, that a sense of availability is conveyed to families so that they will not feel guilty when sharing fears and worries with the nurse. Families usually appreciate information and explanation about nursing procedures, tests, treatments, medications. This helps them to feel they are part of the life of the patient and increases feelings of control, which can enable them to cope more realistically and effectively with the immediate future.

Relatives who feel that they have not been "told enough" are suffering from a lack of sustained professional interest. Effective nursing care is *planned* care and relatives can and should be involved in this. Short-term objectives for the patient such as an improved night's sleep, can be explained to relatives and are positive indicators that there are always things which can be done to improve the quality of life for the patient.

There is often an accompanying aspiration or, for many people, a desperate need to find that the experience of grieving does have some meaning. This may lead to a turning or returning towards religion, or other philosophies of living. The nurse can often meet this need with tact and sensitivity by introducing the hospital chaplain or family priest at an appropriate moment. Their availability to families as well as patients gives comfort, and helps them to explore their own beliefs and what they mean.

Physical fitness is related to the ability to cope with stress and measures to maintain health may be more acceptable to the family if they are seen in terms of enabling them to support and be with the dying patient. They also serve to reinforce the message that the grieving relative *is* an important individual whose needs are also the nurse's concern. Simple relaxation techniques to promote sleep and encouragement to eat regularly are all part of this care.

Interpersonal skills

It is important, therefore, for nurses to develop interpersonal skills to enable them to meet the needs of the patient's family. The creation of a trusting relationship, the ability to give information in a clear and sympathetic manner, the ability to listen actively to their concerns and to help them to clarify problems and options all involve skills which can be learned and practised.

As Frederick and Frederick (1986) point out, although there is a great deal of controversy surrounding anticipatory grief, it appears that it may be a way of doing some of the work of mourning before the death occurs. In this way, it may soften the impact of the actual death on the bereaved.

The nurse is in a unique position, being in constant contact with the family. Her attention to their needs may have long-term beneficial effects on their adjustment to bereavement and is likely to enhance the quality of their remaining time with the dying patient.

References

Bowen, M. (1978) Family reactions to death. In: Family Therapy and Clinical Practice. Aronson, New York.

Caplan, G. (1964) Principles of Preventive Psychiatry. Basic Books, New York.

Frederick, J.F. and Frederick, N.J. (1985) The hospice experience: possible effects in altering the biochemistry of bereavement. *Hospice Journal*, **1**, 3, 81-89.

Hampe, S. (1975) Needs of the grieving spouse in a hospital setting. *Nursing Research*, **24**, 20.

Kubler-Ross, E. (1970) On Death and Dying. Tavistock, London.

Kubler-Ross, E. (1974) Questions and Answers on Death and Dying. Macmillan, London.

Lindemann, E. (1944) Symptomatology and management of acute grief. *American Journal of Psychiatry*, 101, 141-149.

Molter, N.C. (1979) Needs of critically ill patients: a descriptive study. *Nursing Research*, **8**, 2.

Oakley, A. (1985) Taking it Like a Woman. Penguin, London.

Solzhenitsyn, A. (1971) Cancer Ward. Penguin, London.

Ward, A.W.M. (1976) Mortality of bereavement. *British Medical Journal*, **11**, 700-102.

Quality Assurance

29
Defining Quality Assurance

Lynn M. Dunne, RGN RCNT
Quality Assurance Manager (Acute Services) Queen Mary's Hospital, Roehampton, London

The new Collins Concise English Dictionary (1985) defines as follows:

Quality: a distinguishing characteristic or attribute; the basic character or nature of something; a degree or standard of excellence; having or showing excellence or superiority.

Assurance: a statement or assertion intended to inspire confidence; freedom from doubt; certainly.

Standard: an accepted or approved example of something against which others are judged or measured; a principle of propriety, honesty and integrity; a level of excellence or quality; of recognised authority, competence or excellence.

Monitor: to check (the technical quality of); a person or piece of equipment that warns, checks or keeps a continuous record of something.

Quality of nursing care embodies a certain degree of abstraction. It expresses reality and yet is also synonymous with aspects of desirability. Making the necessary distinction is often difficult especially in relation to individuals, as judgements may be clouded by subjectivity due to individual beliefs, values, expectations and cultural background. To overcome this problem it is suggested that effectiveness of care is measured using specific criteria, statements of performance, behaviour or circumstances (standards), derived from broad goals (values), which represent the views of the department and are acceptable to all concerned. The current wave of interest in nursing quality assurance is almost five years old now. However the idea itself of measuring the quality and effectiveness of nursing care is not at all new. From 1854 to 1870 Florence Nightingale led the impetus for systematic evaluation of both the process of nursing care and its outcome in terms of patient wellbeing. When she and her team of nurses arrived at the Barrack Hospital, Scutari in 1854 the mortality rate was 32 per cent, within six months the mortality rate had fallen to approximately two per cent, arguably the best performance indicator for the effectiveness of her nursing care.

First nursing standards

Florence Nightingale also established what might be described as the first nursing standards in *Notes on Nursing* (Nightingale, 1860), in which she stated that the first rule of the hospital was that it should do the patient no harm. The book went on to describe the importance and benefits of cleanliness and fresh air for patients and underlined the need to prevent overcrowding in hospitals to control infection amongst patients. This point is still relevant today, as many hospitals continue the practice of 'hot-bedding' for daycases. Nightingale also highlighted the importance of nurses being able to observe patients keenly, so that they might detect and report changes in a patient's condition. (Quite apart from the educational ramifications, how often is this point taken into consideration when designing new hospitals?)

Efforts to establish quality assurance programmes began in 1918 in the USA. Rapid growth and development of nursing quality assurance activity took place there throughout the seventies and interest reached Britain towards the end of the decade. This was reflected by the publication of two discussion documents, 'Standards of Nursing Care' (RCN, 1980) and 'Towards Standards' (RCN, 1981), by the Royal College of Nursing.

Characteristics of quality

The two documents attempted to identify the characteristics of high quality nursing care. 'Standards of Nursing Care' (RCN, 1980), addressed the question ''what constitutes good nursing care?'', and the committee agreed that both the process and the outcome of nursing care should be taken into consideration and that by using collective professional judgement it would be possible to determine whether or not good nursing care had taken place. Good nursing care was defined as being planned, systematic and focused on the individual. The nursing process must obviously be used to evaluate the quality of nursing care.

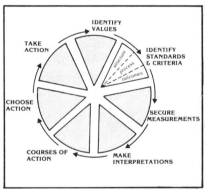

Figure 1. Adapted from the American Nurses' Association model for quality assurance programmes.

There are now numerous tools available to evaluate the quality of nursing care in various clinical settings (future articles will review Monitor, Qualpacs, Rush Medicus Instrument and Nursing Audit). It is still helpful to take one step further back and consider the model or framework from which a quality assurance programme can be developed. Figures 1 and 2 illustrate the models of quality assurance used by the American Nurses'

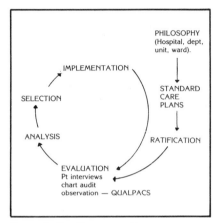

*Figure 2. The Registered Nurses'
Association of British Columbia model for
quality assurance.*

Association and the Registered Nurses' Association of British Columbia, Canada. Both take a similar approach.

The first step in any quality assurance programme is to identify values and a philosophy/ideology for the department and individuals concerned. These will act as the cornerstone for the programme. In America and Canada this means a printed statement (often referred to as a mission statement) that can be found in every nursing office and ward. The mission statement clearly outlines what nursing (in that particular hospital/clinical setting) will and will not do. The next stage is the identification and formulation (writing) of valid, acceptable nursing standards (in Canada these were expressed in standard care plan format as opposed to a list of formal statements which is more popular in the USA). These standards cover such areas as nursing manpower levels, equipment, clinical practice, nurse education (ie ward learning climate) and patient responses to the nursing care delivered.

Evaluate present practice

Having agreed upon their standards the nursing department's next step is to measure present practice against the desired, pre-set standard to determine whether or not the service provided is acceptable or whether some form of remedial action and in-service education needs to be taken. The appropriate course of action is then selected and implemented and the problem/remedial action reassessed to see whether or not the problem has been resolved. Should further action be required, intervention takes place at the appropriate stage of the quality assurance model. Thus the cycle of quality monitoring is continuous, aiming to consistently improve or maintain a high standard of nursing care.

There are three common approaches that can be taken when developing a system to monitor the quality of nursing practice:

Prospective approach   To a certain extent this type of assessment is something of a paradox. You may well be wondering how care can be evaluated before it is given. In reality prospective quality monitoring tends to be the prior identification of types or groups of patients — ie the next 20 patients admitted who are deemed to be at risk from developing pressure sores using the Norton Score (Norton, 1975). Once the patients have been identified evaluation of their care will take place either concurrently or retrospectively.

Concurrent approach   This is an evaluation procedure that takes place while the patient is still in hospital. It tends to focus on the quality of the nursing actions themselves (the process of nursing) and involves direct observation of nurses giving care, questioning patients and chart audit. An obvious benefit to this method is that information can be used to improve a patient's care while he or she is still in hospital should it be found wanting in any respect.

Retrospective approach   A review of care that takes place after a patient has been discharged from hospital. Audits of patient records and charts is the most usual method. Obviously this approach does not have the benefits of concurrent studies (influencing care whilst the patient is still in hospital) but it does allow a comprehensive evaluation of the whole case to take place. Valuable information can be gained about successful nursing care that staff would wish to repeat and likewise unsuccessful nursing intervention that staff should avoid in future.

Whatever method is chosen, the emphasis should be on solving known or suspected problems revealed by the monitoring process which affect patient care or the nursing service detrimentally and cannot be justified.

The quality assurance programme may be designed by an individual or an elected committee but it is important that it is owned and accepted by the staff implementing nursing care to patients. Including some or all of the staff involved in patient care areas (depending on the size of the hospital) in developing the programme would certainly provide a broader perspective and hopefully increase commitment and participation.

Thorough planning

Thorough planning is essential to strengthen and secure the programme and allow participants to be directed and supported.

Many nurses harbour negative feelings towards quality assurance programmes. They are often suspicious of management's motives for such an exercise, fearing cost cutting measures. There is a certain reluctance among the profession to review the care given to patients (as can be seen in its failure to get to grips with evaluation of planned patient care since the adoption of the nursing process by the General Nursing Council in 1977, and personal performance. This is hardly surprising in a system where few hospitals even today practise employee appraisal. It may help to point out to staff that they are already carrying out some quality monitoring activities, nearly all clinical areas have some form of quality control (infection control, review of domestic services), thus proving that quality assurance is not such an alien and theoretical topic.

Figure 3. The relationship (and difference) between the quality monitoring process and quality assurance adapted with kind permission from Lang (1974).

It is important to distinguish between quality assurance and quality monitoring/control (Figure 3). Quality monitoring is a crucial part of any quality assurance programme and is the process whereby current practice is compared with pre-determined standards. It is however not quality assurance (freedom from doubt concerning the degree of excellence). Quality assurance is only present when current nursing practice has been compared with the standard and appropriate action has been taken successfully to remedy the problems identified.

Involving ward staff

Staff frequently need help to realise that unless action is taken on the results of quality control and monitoring, then quality assurance cannot be achieved (Figure 3). Involving ward staff in developing the programme and utilising their experience and skills by asking them to act as assessors/observers is important in overcoming negative feelings and running a meaningful programme. Management must be committed to replacing any staff taken away from clinical areas to participate in the programme, or to pay the necessary overtime.

Quality assurance programmes should only deal with problems that will have a positive effect on patient care or nursing practice when resolved and which can be remedied within existing, available resources (realistic problem solving). Likewise, the prioritising of problems will depend on their effects on patient care and resources. The causes of selected problems must be identified and options outlined for action. Finally the programme must include documentation of problem resolution and indicate to what extent the desired change has been achieved.

The completed quality assurance manual should be available in all nursing departments, with the relevant evaluation reports and action plans. Improvements and problem resolution should be noted and praised and management should be quick to highlight staff who have made particular efforts in this direction. Feedback and knowledge of results regarding a department's quality assessment should be as fast as possible to maintain staff motivation and commitment.

The aim of every nurse and nursing service is surely to provide the highest quality nursing care possible given the presenting situation and resources. It therefore follows that each nursing service must strive to develop a quality assurance programme that accurately measures the level of goal attainment within its clinical areas. To design a successful programme, time must be spent planning well defined goals and objectives, reviewing existing activities that attempt to measure quality and building on them with the cooperation of nursing staff at all levels.

Bibliography
Meisenheimer, C.G. (1985). Quality Assurance: a complete guide to effective programmes. (1st edition). Aspen Systems Corporation, USA.
Bought in USA, may be difficult to obtain in the UK.

References
Lang, N. (1974) A model for quality assurance in nursing. In: A Plan for Implementation of Standards of Nursing Practice. Kansas City Mo: ANA 1975.
Nightingale, F. (1860) Notes on Nursing. Dover Publications Inc., 1969, New York, USA.
Norton, D. (1975) An Investigation of Geriatric Nursing Problems in Hospital. Churchill Livingstone, Edinburgh.
Royal College of Nursing (1980) 'Standards of Nursing Care' – a discussion document. RCN, London.
Royal College of Nursing (1981) 'Towards Standards' – a discussion document. RCN, London.

30

How do we set nursing standards?

Lynn M. Dunne, RGN RCNT

Quality Assurance Manager (Acute Services), Queen Mary's Hospital, Roehampton, London

Nursing standards are valid, acceptable definitions of the quality of nursing care, and cannot be valid unless they contain a means of measuring (criteria) to enable nursing care to be evaluated in terms of effectiveness and quality. When standards are written without criteria (eg 'the patient will not suffer postoperative pain'), the effect is similar to using a ruler without measurements marked on when making a scale drawing. The measurements would have to be guessed, would undoubtedly be wildly inaccurate and they would certainly vary enormously from one individual to another (Mason, 1978).

Implicit in Florence Nightingale's famous statement that the first requirement of a hospital is that it should do the patient no harm (Strauss, 1967) is the idea that nursing care should be of a high standard and through her continued scrutiny of nursing practice she strove to attain this goal. More recently in the UK the Royal College of Nursing, concerned with the promotion of nursing and the ability of its members to provide and maintain an adequate standard of care to their patients, published two authoritative documents on setting, monitoring and evaluating standards of care within the nursing profession (RCN, 1980; RCN, 1981).

What is nursing care?

It is important that before trying to evaluate their individual or collective performances, nurses should have a clear understanding of what 'nursing' and 'nursing care' actually mean. Nursing departments can accept a well known definition of nursing such as 'The unique function of the nurse is to assist the individual, sick or well, in the performance of those activities contributing to health and its recovery (or to a peaceful death), that he would perform unaided if he had the necessary strength, will or knowledge; and to do this in such a way as to help him gain independence as rapidly as possible' (Henderson, 1979). Alternatively they can opt for an in-house definition (mission statement) (Dunne, 1986) that has been ratified by the nursing staff. Which they accept is purely a matter of choice, but it must reflect the values of the nursing service concerned.

The concept of nursing care standards is immediately complicated as the phrase becomes synonymous with both the quality and effectiveness of care. The word 'standards' has both qualitative and quantitative connotations, it may be something that serves as a basis for comparison (a yardstick) or a measure of the level of performance (output) required of an individual. Previous studies of the effectiveness of nursing care have concentrated on the quantitative aspects; however current emphasis is on a more holistic approach, attempting to evaluate the more discrete qualitative issues in nursing care eg interpersonal and communication skills.

'Standards of Nursing Care' (RCN, 1980) suggests that the most suitable method of deciding what constitutes good nursing care is by identifying desired nursing behaviours. Observation of current nursing practice and comparison with predetermined standards would enable nurses to judge whether or not good nursing care had taken place. The report defines desired nursing behaviour as being planned, purposeful, systematic and goal directed, ie the use of the nursing process. 'Towards Standards' (RCN, 1981), in considering how to formulate nursing standards, felt that the writing of checklists, norms and ratios was inappropriate and instead identified eight key factors for professional nursing standards (Table 1).

1.   A philosophy of nursing.
2.   The relevant knowledge and skills.
3.   The nurse's authority to act.
4.   Accountability.
5.   The control of resources.
6.   The organisational structure and management style.
7.   The doctor/nurse relationship.
8.   The management of change.

Table 1. Prerequisites for the professional control of standards of nursing care.

Accountability

Of these eight factors, accountability is the most central to the formation of professional standards. Nurses must also be clear about the extent of their authority, and responsibility and accountability must be matched with the necessary authority to carry out the job effectively. Senior nurses must be prepared to provide the nurse with the tools to do the job — ie manpower, equipment. Devolving accountability to individual nurses may well be the long term answer to improving standards of nursing care but the profession should ask itself if this move is really appropriate now, in a system that still entrusts the majority of its 'basic care' to untrained/unqualified individuals?

Having looked at what nursing standards are and the key areas related to them, how do we set these standards? In his review of the evaluation of the quality of medical care, Avedis Donabedian outlined three approaches (studying the structural variables, studying the process of care and reviewing the outcome of care in patients); these approaches are still widely used by nurses in the field of quality assurance, as most areas of nursing fall into one or more of the three categories (Donabedian, 1966). The three categories when applied to evaluating the quality of nursing care may be defined as follows:

Structure standards These regulate nursing practice and include the organisation of nursing services, recruitment, selection, manpower establishments, provision of necessary equipment, buildings and include all the processes of licensing, eg National Board educational visits to approve facilities for learner/post basic education. They generally tend to indicate minimum expectations or levels of service, eg there will always be at least one RGN on duty on the ward at all times.

Process standards These look specifically at the actions performed by nurses and define the quality of the implementation of nursing care. Nursing departments should develop process standards for all nursing interventions (nursing procedures). Nursing procedures and process standards, although similar, are not the same thing.

Outcome standards The patient's response to planned care, ie the expected change in a patient's condition following nursing intervention, is an outcome standard. Nursing action may result in positive or negative outcomes for a patient (positive outcomes being beneficial and appropriate nursing intervention, and negative outcomes inappropriate nursing care). Outcome standards frequently include some measure of the patient's satisfaction with the care. Many authors define a further category:

Content standards These describe the nature of nursing that is communicated to other groups or disciplines and the basis of nursing decisions, ie information that must be recorded in nursing notes and reported to the multidisciplinary team, communication and teaching of patients and their families or friends (Mason, 1978).

Writing standards
Many standards set for a nursing service will concern clinical work (direct nursing care given to patients), and tend to be written in the form of principles of nursing practice (the foundation of but not quite as detailed as a nursing procedure). The seven steps outlined below can be used when writing any nursing standard (structure, process, outcome or content); here they are illustrated using the example of the process standards set for performing endotracheal suction of a ventilated patient.

1. Select the area of nursing for which the standard is to be written and identify the type (structure, process, outcome, content) eg **process standard:** endotracheal suction of a ventilated patient.

2. Identify the objectives for the standard stating explicitly what you intend to achieve. The objectives may be nurse centred or patient centred:

Nurse-centred objectives
a.   To apply suction to the patient without introducing infection into the respiratory tract.
b.   To prevent trauma to the respiratory tract.
Patient-centred objectives
c.   The patient will not experience hypoxia during the suction procedure, ie PO_2 of no less than 11kPa.
d.   The patient will not experience anxiety or distress during the suction procedure.
3. Specify the nursing action essential to achieve the objectives, eg:
a.   Wash your hands; use sterile equipment and an aseptic technique.
b.   Apply suction only when withdrawing catheter.
c.   Hyperoxygenate patient prior to the procedure (if prescribed) with ventilator or re-breathing bag for one minute prior to suction procedure.
d.   Do not apply suction for more than 15 seconds; suction only until secretions are removed.
4. Where possible specify a time frame for each action, eg apply suction for no more than 15 seconds.
5. Write up the standard in a logical order, eg i. Define subject. ii. Identify objectives. iii. List standards.
6. Review the work done to eliminate ambiguous or irrelevant information that cannot be evaluated, eg suggestions for procedure technique.
7. Test the new standard for acceptability and validity.

Who should write the standards?
In order to decide who should write these standards, it is useful to identify the size of the task, the types of standards to be written and the resources available, eg nurse managers, educationalists and clinical specialists, and to use them as effectively as possible. It is essential that the meaning of any nursing standard is shared, accepted and understood by those who have written it and those expected to implement it.

   Examples of nursing standards that should be found currently in any hospital would include a nursing practice and policy manual that is based on current nursing research findings, the use of specific ward learning outcomes for learner nurses in ward areas, the practice of individualised patient care through the use of the nursing process, adherence to National Board training requirements, staff ratios of trained staff: learners and compliance with the UKCC code of professional conduct.

Location of standards
Once written, all nursing standards should be easily accessed and referred to by the nursing staff either before, during or after nursing intervention. Formulating and measuring nursing standards is not akin to setting a closed book exam or an attempt to catch individuals out, so it is only right and proper that staff should know what is expected of them before their

action and its effects on patients are critically evaluated on either a collective or individual basis.

High quality nursing care does not happen by accident, it must be planned for and evaluated against pre-set standards so that nurses can recognise and repeat good nursing care and avoid mistakes in the future (McFarlane, 1979).

Nurses have a responsibility to society, themselves and their colleagues in the health care services to ensure they provide the highest quality care possible in the presenting situation and resources. Nursing standards are the key to any successful quality assurance programme as they define valid, acceptable, measurable levels of performance and outcome against which current nursing practice must and will be judged and evaluated.

References

Donabedian, A. (1966) Evaluating the quality of medical care. *Millbank Memorial Fund Quarterly*, **4,** 166-203.

Dunne, L. (1986) Developing quality assurance. *The Professional Nurse*, **2,** 2, 47-9

Henderson, V. (1979) Basic Principles of Nursing Care. (11th edition). International Council of Nurses. Geneva, Switzerland.

McFarlane, J.K. (1979) Take aim and shoot for goal. *Nusing Mirror.* (supplement). 19.4.79. xx-xxviii.

Mason, E.J. (1978) How to Write Meaningful Nursing Standards. (2nd edition) John Wiley and Sons Inc, USA.

Royal College of Nusing, (1980) 'Standards of Nursing Care' – a discussion document. RCN, London.

Royal College of Nursing, (1981) 'Towards Standards' – a discussion document. RCN, London.

Strauss, M.B. (1967) Familiar Medical Quotations. (1st edition) J.A. Churchill Ltd, London.

31

Quality Assurance: methods of measurement

Lynn M. Dunne, RGN, RCNT

Quality Assurance Manager (Acute Services), Queen Mary's Hospital, Roehampton, London

Attempts to define quality assurance (Dunne, 1986) and how a nursing service might set acceptable standards of nursing care (Dunne, 1987), have already been made. In the next phase a method of measuring current nursing practice against pre-determined standards must be developed. The four methods reviewed here: Qualpacs, Nursing Audit (Phaneuf), the Rush-Medicus System and Monitor, are among several currently available.

Qualpacs

The Quality Patient Care Scale (Qualpacs) was developed by Mabel Wandelt and Joel Ager at the College of Nursing, Wayne State University, Michigan, USA in the early 1970s, a time that saw a rapid increase in knowledge and literature about quality assurance in North America.

It is a tool based on evaluation of the *process* of nursing (ie how nursing care is delivered to patients), by direct observation. The scale itself lists 68 items of nursing care, arranged under six subsections as follows:

Psychosocial: Individual Actions directed towards meeting the psychosocial needs of individual patients.

Psychosocial: Group Actions directed towards meeting the psychosocial needs of patients as members of a group.

Physical: Actions directed towards meeting physical needs.

General: Actions that may be directed toward meeting either psychosocial or physical needs of the patient or both at the same time.

Communication: Communication on behalf of the patient.

Professional implications: Care given to patients reflects initiative and responsibility indicative of professional expectations.

Two or more trained observers evaluate all interaction between nurses and patients in a clinical area for two hours. Any one of the 68 items is scored on a scale of one to five (Table 1).

Wandelt and Ager advocate that Qualpacs observers complete an orientation programme which allows sufficient time for them to become familiar with the background to the Qualpacs; the cue sheets for each section, individual items and spend some time (two days is suggested) discussing what standards are acceptable and becoming familiar with the

```
1 = Poorest care
2 = Between
3 = Average care (that expected of
    a newly qualified RGN)
4 = Between
5 = Best care
```

Table 1. Qualpacs scoring method.

actual use of the rating scale.

The use of Qualpacs evokes a mixed response from nurses. Those who are against it express doubts about the tool as a reliable, objective method, saying it is both subjective (as it is the opinion of the observer as to whether poor, average or best care has taken place and that is highly dependent on previous experience and personal values). The counter argument to this is simple: if you reject Qualpacs on the basis that it is subjective and therefore unreliable it is tantamount to saying you reject the professional judgement of nurses in matters related to nursing practice (for previous experience and personal values are the basis of professional judgement also), which in turn opens Pandora's Box on such issues as the necessity to have a nurse(s) in charge of nursing.

Many groups and individuals (particularly trade unions) fear that as Qualpacs looks at individual nurses and the care they give to patients, the opportunity exists to use the findings in a disciplinary manner if poor or unsafe practice is observed. Certain steps can be taken to overcome these potential problems. First, only nurses with a clinical involvement should order a Qualpacs assessment or act as observers and second, feedback should be direct between the observers and the ward nurses. Management should not have access to a Qualpacs assessment as part of an investigation or disciplinary procedure. This approach has been used successfully at Burford Nursing Development Unit and is now used throughout Oxfordshire Health Authority.

In its favour it must be said that as a direct observation tool, Qualpacs provides an opportunity to improve care and benefit patients while they are still in hospital. Many people involved in quality assurance feel that direct observation of nursing care is the most effective way of evaluating its quality and is critical to the success of any quality assurance programme.

The Phaneuf Nursing Audit

This audit was developed by Maria Phaneuf in the mid 1970s and, as the name suggests, is an audit of nursing care taken from the patients' notes. Phaneuf herself described nursing audit as a process orientated approach to appraise the nursing process as reflected in the patients' records.

The Nursing Audit reviews 50 separate criteria which are grouped under seven headings as follows:
1. The application and execution of the doctor's legal orders.

2. The observation of symptoms and reactions.
3. Supervision of the patient.
4. Supervision of those participating in care (except the doctor).
5. Reporting and recording.
6. Application and execution of nursing procedures and techniques.
7. Promotion of physical and emotional health by direction and teaching.

The first part of the nursing audit consists of a patient details form (similar to many hospital admissions slips) which Phaneuf suggests can be completed by a member of clerical staff, eg ward clerk, as professional nursing knowledge is not required. The second part of the nursing audit is the evaluation of the patients care using his/her inpatient notes. The criteria are evaluated using yes/no/uncertain categories and scored accordingly. To arrive at the final score the total of the individual component scores is multiplied by the value of the 'does not apply' scores. The quality of nursing care is described in Table 2.

Score	Quality of Care
0 — 40 =	Unsafe
41 — 80 =	Poor
81 — 120 =	Incomplete
121 — 160 =	Good
161 — 200 =	Excellent

Table 2. The Phaneuf Nursing Audit Scoring Method.

Nursing Audit has been widely criticised by many nurses who argue that nurses frequently give care that is not documented and conversely often document care that is never given to the patient. I suggest this somewhat cynical view of nursing practice is neither a typical nor fair representation, despite the profession's many faults, and that Nursing Audit has a useful role to play in evaluating quality as it is quick, simple and comprehensive. Familiarisation and training for assessors is easy too. The biggest barrier to using Nursing Audit in the UK is documentation as audit is only feasible in clinical areas using a systematic approach.

Many feel that Nursing Audit can be a useful part of a quality assurance programme. Burford Nursing Development Unit have successfully combined Qualpacs and Nursing Audit in their quality assurance programme (to overcome the criticisms of using each method independently) thus enabling nursing care to be evaluated as it is given to patients and retrospectively via the nursing records.

Rush Medicus System

The Rush-Medicus System was also a product of the early 70s (1972) and was the result of a collaborative project between the Medicus Systems Corporation and Rush Presbyterian St Luke's Medical Centre in Chicago and the Baptist Medical Centre in Birmingham, Alabama.

The conceptual framework chosen for the system was the Nursing Process which had been implemented at Rush Presbyterian St Luke's Medical Centre and the concept of patient needs. The nursing process was defined as the comprehensive set of nursing activities performed in the delivery of a patient's care; assessment of the problems or needs of the patient, planning for care, implementing the plan of care and evaluating/updating the plan of care.

It was hoped to develop a system that would evaluate all these areas. The concept was further enhanced by evaluating whether patient needs were actually being met in accordance with the care plan.

Once the conceptual framework was decided it had to be broken into logical components. Six objectives and 32 sub-objectives were outlined, which the project team believed defined the nursing care process succintly and with a degree of detail not achieved in previous programmes. The next step was to develop criteria that would evaluate each of the sub-objectives. A total of 357 criteria were developed (Master Criteria List).

The Master Criteria List is held on a computer programme which will produce up to 76 different questionnaires that can be used for patients in accident and emergency departments, labour and delivery wards, psychiatry, nursery, recovery and general medicine and surgery, according to their dependency group. In addition there are nine questionnaires which can be used for the parents of babies in the nursery and 18 ward based questionnaires that can be used in all clinical areas.

Ward areas tend to be evaluated three-to-four times per year in hospitals using the Rush-Medicus System in the USA. Quality monitoring takes place over a calendar month during which 10 per cent of the patient throughput is sampled.

Patients forming part of the quality assessment are selected using a random number table and their permission is then obtained verbally before proceeding. Nurse observers tend to be either staff nurses working at ward level who have completed the necessary observer's training course and belong to the hospital nursing quality assurance observers 'bank', or a small permanent team of observers who carry out all the nursing quality monitoring for the whole hospital.

The Rush-Medicus System has the advantage of having been extensively tested during its development (19 hospitals across the USA). It is now widely used by many hundreds of hospitals throughout the USA and Canada which form a users group that feeds in results to provide comparative scores and allows the tool to be updated. The disadvantages of the system are that it is large and time consuming to administer (most hospitals using Rush-Medicus have a full/part time coordinator) and a computer is a prerequisite to run the programme effectively.

Monitor

Of all the quality assurance systems mentioned in this article Monitor is probably the most familiar. It was developed by Goldstone, Ball and

Collier, (1984) as part of the North West Region Staffing Levels Project and is the adaptation for the UK of the Rush-Medicus System.

Monitor consists of four patient questionnaires each related to one of the four patient dependency categories and a general ward based questionnaire. As with the Rush-Medicus System patients are allocated a questionnaire according to their dependency group. The authors recommend that either a random sample of three patients per dependency category are selected or the whole ward be included. Each questionnaire is divided into four sections:

- Assessment of nursing care.
- Meeting the patient's physical needs.
- The patient's non-physical needs are met.
- Evaluation of nursing care objectives.

Sources of information for the question answers include direct patient questioning/observation, patient's records/charts, observation of the clinical environment and questioning of nursing staff.

Answer	
Yes, Yes always, Yes complete	= 1
Yes sometimes, Yes incomplete	= ½
No	= 0

Table 3. Scoring Method For Monitor.

Answers to questions are scored (Table 3) and a final score is obtained by deducting the non-applicable responses and then dividing the total score by the number of applicable questions and expressing this as a percentage. The authors suggest a score of 70 per cent is desirable. It is recommended that Monitor be carried out in wards once a year.

Monitor has been criticised for suggesting a desirable score. Many feel it is better to allow individual ward sisters and nurse managers to decide what is appropriate for their units. For many, a score of less than 100 per cent on knowledge of cardiac arrest procedure or fire drill is unacceptable, while a temporary lapse in other areas, eg evaluating nursing care objectives may be acceptable in a given set of circumstances, such as high vacancy factor/high proportion of new appointees. It has also been criticised for its method of selecting a patient sample, which differs considerably from the Rush-Medicus System of randomly selecting 10 per cent of the patient monthly turnover, irrespective of their dependency groups. Administration is time consuming, particularly in the scoring of the questionnaires, which if done manually can take one person about two working days to complete.

In its favour it must be said that Monitor is a quality monitoring tool developed by a British team who understand the NHS and nursing in the UK and while it is easy to criticise with hindsight, at least North West Region did more than just talk about quality assurance. Monitor has now been adopted by several health authorities in Britain which enjoy a support and update service from Suppliers, Newcastle Polytechnic.

Which programme?

Quality Assurance is here to stay, of that there can be little doubt. Hospitals considering implementing a quality assurance programme have two distinct choices; they can either create their own in-house programme or adopt a programme that is commercially available. There are advantages to both. In-house programmes can produce a high level of commitment, creativity and cohesion; bought-in programmes avoid the exercise of reinventing the wheel and have an easily identified price tag and running costs with no hidden extras. Whatever method is chosen by nursing managements it must accurately reflect and measure the quality of care delivered to the patients within the relevant clinical areas.

Bibliography

Burford Nursing Development Unit. A compendium of articles published in British nursing journals by staff at BNDU (1983-84). (Available on application to BNDU Burford, Oxfordshire).

References

Goldstone, L.A., Ball, J.A., Collier, M.M. (1984). MONITOR – An Index of the Quality of Nursing Care for Acute Medical and Surgical Wards. (2nd Impression). Newcastle Upon Tyne Polytechnic Products UK.

Pearson, A. (1983). The Clinical Nursing Unit. (1st Edition). Heinemann Medical Books Ltd, London.

Phaneuf, M. (1976). The Nursing Audit. Appleton-Century-Crofts. New York. USA.

Wandelt, M., and Ager, J. (1974). Quality Patient Care Scale (QUALPACS). Appleton-Century-Crofts. New York. USA.

32

Quality Assurance: Update

Lynn M. Dunne, RGN, RCNT

Quality Assurance Manager (Acute Services), Queen Mary's Hospital, Roehampton, London

When Elizabeth Horne, the Editorial Director of The Professional Nurse contacted me in August 1989 with a view to reprinting the three articles I had written for the journal in 1986/87 about quality assurance as chapters I was surprised that in reviewing them there were no substantive changes required. Does this mean therefore that there has been no progress in the field of quality assurance in the past three years? I think anyone working in the National Health Service (NHS) particularly over the past year would agree that is far from the truth and that quality assurance is most definitely on the agenda.

The original three articles looked at the beginnings of nursing quality assurance, setting nursing standards and methods of measuring nursing quality and these areas have remained fairly static, where significant development does seem to have taken place is in the nature of quality assurance programmes, how they should be formulated and introduced into the organisation at all levels. Many people remain unaware that the World Health Organisation (WHO) has a published target that all countries will have quality assurance programmes by 1990.

Quality assurance has its origins in industry at the turn of the twentieth century where emphasis was placed on quality control of the kind typified by the inspection of every third widget on the production line for defects. Some years later in the 1920's the approach began to change when management theorists realised the shortcomings of only using quality control techniques. Quality control is separate from normal work activity; it is product-oriented not skill-oriented and it does not tend to include a description of the action necessary to resolve identified problems. Finally, and most importantly, it is a retrospective activity. The process will only detect defects or problems after they have occurred and not during the process; remedial action is therefore more difficult to effect.

Consequently, a new emphasis was placed on quality assurance, namely that of organisation-wide quality assurance where activity focussed on the people and skills within the organisation as well as on widgets! Organisation-wide quality assurance programmes place emphasis on the preventative aspects of quality assurance and encompass the total organisation. Quality assurance activities are seen as part of normal work activity and as a journey not a final destination.

Overall the cost of such a programme should be cheaper than a large quality control programme although initially it will probably require greater investment in staff training and development. It also goes without saying that the return on the investment for this sort of approach to quality assurance should be much higher for organisations that are people-oriented.

Other approaches to achieving quality assurance in an organisation include the concepts of total quality management and, more recently, quality assurance through the successful management of change as described by Tom Peters (Peters, 1988).

Key criteria for the successful development and implementation of quality assurance programmes

South West Thames Regional Health Authority (S.W.T.R.H.A., 1988) identified four key criteria for the successful implementation of district quality assurance programmes in its Regional Quality Assurance Strategy:

1. Leadership In the original articles, approach to quality placed on the importance of a 'bottom up' approach to quality assurance. This still holds good but in addition activity must be led clearly from the top. In order to do this managers must have a clear vision of the purpose of the organisation which includes agreed organisational goals (objectives), values and desired behaviour. This vision would normally take the form of a written statement (usually referred to as a mission statement).

2. Structure Once the organisation is clear about its 'mission' structure and systems need to be put into place to ensure that it is communicated to every employee. Therefore the organisation needs to have well thought out communication and reporting strategies to ensure a good two-directional flow of information, both top down and bottom up. Consideration also needs to be given to what systems might be required to review quality assurance activity. These may include quality assurance steering groups and medical audit committees and where they will fit in to the organisational structure. In North America these committees tend to report directly to the hospital board of governors.

3. Staff support and development In order to make 'the vision' a reality staff will need support from their immediate line managers and training to develop the necessary skills required of them. The managers' communication and reception skills and knowledge about how to formulate standards and measure performance will be essential to achieve this and will require both financial and time investment (5-10 years) in the organisation. Chris Wilson in his book 'Hospital Wide Quality Assurance' (Wilson, 1987) gives some sound, practical advice on how to set up an adult learning programme for quality assurance. Also the importance of individual performance review (IPR) should be recognised in developing staff awareness and skills in quality assurance activity.

4. Development of grassroots quality assurance programmes

Individual units and departments need to develop their own quality assurance programmes to review the performance of their service on a regular basis. This will again include the definition of the unit or department's purpose and values and will go on to define standards from three perspectives: management (the setting of team goals/objectives); professional and technical requirements; achievement of consumer feedback and satisfaction. Finally, units and departments will have to decide upon suitable mechanisms for monitoring performance in relation to agreed standards.

In summary, quality assurance needs to be built into the culture of the organisation at all levels and not merely inspected out periodically. Clear and effective structures must be in place that facilitate communication and reporting up and down the organisation i.e. quality assurance activity must be bottom up but top led. Senior managers must be prepared to invest time and money in staff development and training in order to have any hope of achieving the desired 'quality result'.

Acknowledgements

This chapter draws much of its inspiration from Valerie Kilroy, Regional Nurse for Quality Assurance and Research for South West Thames Regional Health Authority whom I have been fortunate enough to hear speak on the subject of quality assurance several times and who has been a source of continual encouragement and support to those responsible for quality assurance in Richmond, Twickenham and Roehampton Health Authority.

References

Peters, Thomas, J. (1988). Thriving on chaos. Warner Books, London.
S.W.T.R.H.A. (1988). Regional Strategy for Quality Assurance.
Wilson, Christopher, R.M. (1987) Hospital Wide Quality Assurance – Models for implementation and development. W.B. Saunders, Philadelphia.

33

How well do we perform? Parents' perception of paediatric care

Margaret Ball, BN, RGN, *Teaching Assistant, Department of Nursing Studies*

Alan Glasper, BA, RGN, RSCN, ONC, DN, CertEd, RNT
Lecturer in Nursing Studies

Paul Yerrell, BSc, PhD
Visiting Fellow, Department of Nursing Studies, all at the University of Southampton

Towards the end of 1987, staff on the Paediatric Unit at Southampton General Hospital were worried by staff shortages and associated low morale. There were fears that standards of care could be falling, so there developed a keen interest to measure the quality of care on the unit.

Quality is defined by Roberts (1975) as a grade of goodness, ie it is a measurement. Quality assurance is a process of looking at a given situation and appraising it against a measure or a set standard. In the nursing context this enables nurses to promise and maintain a set standard of care. Setting standards is a vital part in this process which the RCN is pursuing with its standards of care project (Kitson, 1988).

Assessing quality of care

One of the most frequently used frameworks for looking at quality of care is that developed by Donabedian (1976). This is based on three distinct, but interrelated factors; structure, process and outcome. Structure looks at the environmental and resource items and their organisation. Process refers to the planning and delivery of the nursing interventions and outcome is concerned with the result of care. Kitson (1988) has devised a model which can be used to look at these three aspects. She describes the process of quality assurance as cyclic, consisting of describing the problem, measuring it and then taking action. Each of these areas can then be broken down into more specific steps (Figure 1). As the process is cyclic it can be entered at any point.

Quality assurance is a subject very much in vogue. Many tools have been developed, such as Monitor, which has been adapted from an American version by Goldstone (1983). Some of these are being used in the clinical setting to evaluate and measure quality of care. In America,

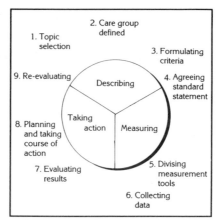

Figure 1. The process of quality assurance.

quality assurance programmes are much more developed than ours, partly because of their private health care system, in which insurance companies demand to know standards of care, but also because of their higher levels of medical litigation. In the UK there has been an increasing recognition of the need for work on quality, which has developed for numerous reasons. Of particular influence has been the implementation of Griffiths style management with its emphasis on cost effectiveness. Also, the public are becoming more medically aware, and their expectations of the health services are increasing.

Quality assurance in paediatrics

Little work has been done on quality assurance in the paediatric field. Some previous work by Maddison (1977) highlighted the importance of seeking the opinion of consumers. Maddison believes parental opinion is most valid in paediatrics in that it reflects that of the child. She further states that she would like to see a grading system for evaluating paediatric wards similar to the stars used to grade hotels. This grade would be strongly influenced by the degree of emotional support offered to children and their parents.

Brykczynska (1987) points out that nurses must work with the child and family, not against them or in spite of them. The child should be viewed as a partner in care, and further work to ascertain children's perceptions of their own care be undertaken.

For the purposes of this pilot study in addressing the staff's worries about care, it was decided to ascertain parental views on the quality of their children's nursing care. This was seen as a way of identifying problems upon which standards of care may be set and further quality work carried out. Although parental opinion is one way of measuring quality of care, it has limitations, because parents' perceptions only relate to perceived quality of care. These do not take into account actual outcome or necessarily reflect the standards of the nursing staff.

The tool chosen to do this was a questionnaire based on some work done at the Hospital for Sick Children in Toronto. It consists of some open-ended questions and some forced choice Likert scale questions in which parents are asked to strongly agree, agree, disagree or strongly disagree to numerous statements (Figure 2). The questionnaire looks at many areas of paediatric nursing care and covers aspects of structure, process and outcome.

A recent article by Ledwith (1988) notes the recent popularity of consumer surveys in the NHS but emphasises that these should look at the quality of information and support, not just overall patient satisfaction. A single criteria to measure quality may be suited to commercial organisations, but is not sufficient in health care. Work on interpersonal communication has shown communication processes and information levels in the health service have a direct effect on consumer satisfaction. The questionnaire was designed to explore these areas.

The effect of staff-client relationships

Barbarin and Chesler (1984) commented that in areas where staff-client relationships are good, quality of care was better than in those where interpersonal relationships were poor. Their study found respect for medical staff strongly related to parents' perceptions of the transmission of information and their evaluation of the staff's technical competence. Francis et al (1969) found mothers were more likely to comply with treatment when staff were understanding, warm and friendly.

Sheridan (1975) has pointed out that children honour those people who tell the truth about procedures, especially where pain is involved. Good communication helps to minimise the disturbance caused by hospital admission. Other work has found parents of hospitalised children to be highly motivated learners (Aufhauser and Lesh, 1973) who then take information to the community where it is most needed.

The questionnaire was administered to the parents of the first 10 children discharged from each of four paediatric wards in the last week of January 1988. Ward clerks were felt to be the best people to administer them, being the most neutral people on the wards with no direct care input. Complete anonymity was guaranteed and the final sample number was 35; five questionnaires were incompletely answered or not returned.

Results of the survey

Overall the results of the questionnaire demonstrated that parents were satisfied with the care they and their children received. Despite the inherent 'halo' effect commonly seen with this type of research, much valuable data was obtained. Only 8.1 per cent described their child's care as fair, while the remaining 91.4 per cent described it as excellent or good (60 per cent excellent; 31.4 per cent good).

Parents particularly liked being able to stay with their children in hospital and 75.9 per cent of the sample were resident during their child's admission. Written comments revealed that parents greatly appreciated the relaxed atmosphere found on the wards, and many were delighted with the play facilities on offer. All respondents felt they could manage their child's care at home following discharge.

The results did highlight some areas of care where parents were not fully satisfied. Several questions were specifically targeted at information-giving, and the results show there is a need for more information to be given to parents; 33.4 per cent indicated that nursing staff did not ask them if they understood what the doctor had told them and a small number said they did not receive adequate information about the ward or about tests and procedures (11.4 per cent). Some parents (8.6 per cent) felt that information given to them was not always consistent and a minority (5.7 per cent) did not feel comfortable asking nurses questions. Several comments in response to the 'open-ended' questions also reflected this need for more information for parents.

The impact of hospitalisation

The impact of hospitalisation on children and families was addressed in several questions. Responses show this is an area where parents are critical: 38.2 per cent felt there was insufficient discussion by nurses on the effect hospitalisation might have on themselves and their families, and a quarter (25.7 per cent) indicated that nurses did not talk to them about what would happen to their children in hospital.

Parents were highly complimentary about their children's nursing care and attitudes among staff. There were some areas, however, where parental expectations were not met: 40 per cent reported that nurses did not involve them in planning care and a similar number reported that nurses never asked them how they would like their child's care to be carried out. The concept of parental involvement in the care of sick children was also highlighted by several comments indicating that parents would like to do more for their children. Two parents specifically reported that the nursing staff did not make them feel comfortable in participating in their child's care while 14.3 per cent believed that some nurses were not familiar with the care their children needed.

A small number of parents reported that nurses did not respond promptly to requests, but believed this was mitigated by the pressure of work. Several commented on the ward environment; some noted that toys and furniture were not very clean. Comments were also received on excessive noise, such as squeaky doors, and such irritations were thought to be controllable. Some parents were concerned about lighting levels. Some said the lights were too bright at night and suggested darker curtains between cubicles, while others felt greater segregation of children into age groups would allow lights to be turned off earlier

For the following statements please check the response which most closely reflects your opinion.	1 Strongly Disagree	2 Disagree	3 Agree	4 Strongly Agree
1. I received consistent information/instructions from each nurse caring for my child during the hospital stay.				
2. I was given adequate information about my child's ward.				
3. I received no information about hospital rules and procedures that might have applied to my family and me.				
4. The nurses always responded to my requests promptly.				
5. The nurses and I discussed how my child's illness or hospitalisation would affect me and my family.				
6. The nurses always asked if I understood what the doctor told me.				
7. I always had trouble getting a nurse when I needed one.				
8. The nurses asked me what I would like to know about my child's illness or hospitalisation.				
9. I feel confident in the nurses caring for my child.				
10. The nurses protected my child's privacy.				
11. I feel confident that I can manage my child's care at home after discharge.				
12. All the nurses caring for my child were familiar with the care he/she needed.				
13. The nurses fully involved me in the planning of my child's nursing care and in the writing of the care plan.				
14. I had to answer a lot of the same questions about my child's needs many times.				
15. If my child was fearful or anxious during any procedures the nurse attempted to reassure, comfort and calm him/her.				
16. I feel the nurses would be willing to stay with my child if he/she was worried or upset about something.				
17. The nurses talked with me and my family about what we could expect to happen during my child's hospitalisation.				
18. I received adequate information about tests and procedures from my child's nurses.				
19. My child received explanation from the nurse that he/she could understand before any procedure was started.				
20. The nurses never asked me how I would prefer my child's care to be carried out.				
21. The nurses helped me feel comfortable in participating in my child's care.				
22. The nurses attended to my child's likes and dislikes as best they could.				
23. The nurses showed genuine interest and concern for my child.				
24. I felt comfortable asking the nurses any questions.				

25. Did you stay with your child during the hospital admission? YES/NO

    If Yes, was it?: a) on the ward
                    b) in a cubicle
                    c) in Victoria House?

26. What in your opinion was most helpful to you during the period of time your child was in hospital? Please comment:

27. What could have made the hospital stay better for you as a parent/guardian? Please comment:

28. How would you rate your child's nursing care on this ward.
    A Excellent   C Fair
    B Good   D Poor

29. Date today ....

Your additional comments would be most welcome. Thank you.

Figure 2. The questionnaire (adapted with kind permission of the Hospital for Sick Children, Toronto).

for younger children.

A few parents wanted to eat with their children and were reluctant to go to the canteen, calling for more eating facilities on the ward. It is interesting that some parents said they wanted tea and coffee facilities when these facilities did exist on all wards.

In conclusion, the majority of parents identified care to be of a good or excellent standard. In respect to information, hospitalisation, parental involvement, and facilities for parents, a minority of parents saw room for improvements. Here we are reminded of Ledwith's reservation that although overall satisfaction is a useful measure, it is not sufficient in the health service.

Addressing parents' concerns

In the interests of the children we care for, we may need to address the concerns highlighted in this work within the financial and manpower constraints imposed upon clinical areas. With regard to information giving, the results encourage nurses to give parents more information both formally and informally. New areas being explored are preadmission programme, a care by parent scheme, ward booklets and discharge information packs. Nurses are also encouraged to examine how to involve parents more fully in their child's care. The advantages of care by parent schemes such as that initiated in Cardiff (Sainsbury et al, 1986) may result in their continued growth and development in the UK.

While responses to the questionnaire indicate areas where nurses could improve care, the task still remains to describe the structure, process and outcome criteria which will allow specific standards to be set, against which a measurement of quality can be made. Restraints of time may well be hindering nurses in this task and perhaps the results of this pilot study will raise awareness and prompt nurses to look at the issues involved.

It will be, of course, for each paediatric unit, as they embark on setting standards in relation to the quality of care, to decide what proportion of time they devote to setting and measuring standards in relation to problems evolving from parents' perceptions. Only when practitioners identify a personal commitment to changing practice and recognise the role parents' views might have in identifying where changes are required, will paediatric units become fully self-evaluating.

References
Aufhauser, T.R. and Lesh, D. (1973) Parents need TLC too. *Hospital*, **47**, 8, 88.
Barbarin, O. and Chesler, M.A. (1984)Relationships with the medical staff and aspects of satisfaction with care expressed by parents of children with cancer. *Journal of Community Health*, 9, 4, 302-13.
Brykczynska, G.M. (1987) Ethical issues in paediatric nursing. *Nursing*, **3**, 2, 862-864.
Donabedian, A. (1976) Measures of quality of care. *American Journal of Nursing*, **76**, 2, 186.
Francis, V. et al (1969) Gaps in doctor – patient communication response to medical advice. *New England Journal of Medicine*, **280**, 535-540.
Goldstone, L.A. et al (1983) Monitor. Newcastle upon Tyne Polytechnic Products Limited.
Kitson, A.L. (1988) Nursing Quality Assurance. Dynamic Standard Setting System. RCN Standards of Care Project, unpublished.
Ledwith, F. (1988) Doing less to achieve more. *Health Service Journal*, 98, 3088.
Maddison, M. (1977) Consumer survey of paediatric wards. *Australian Nurses' Journal*, **6**, 1, 27-28.
Roberts, I. (1975) Discharged from hospital. Royal College of Nursing, London.
Sainsbury, C.P.Q. et al (1986) Care by parents of their children in hospital. *Archives of Disease in Childhood*, **61**, 612-615.
Sheridan, M.S. (1975) Children's feelings about the hospital. *Social Work in Health Care*, **1**, 65-70.

34

Qualpacs – a practical guide

Paul Wainwright, SRN, MSc, DANS, DipN, RNT
Professional Adviser, Welsh National Board for Nursing, Midwifery and Health Visiting, Cardiff

In Chapter 31, Lynn Dunne described several quality monitoring tools available to nurses, including Quality Patient Care Scale, also known as Qualpacs (Wandelt and Ager, 1974). This chapter discusses some of the practical problems involved in putting Qualpacs to work in the ward.

Commitment

The first point to be clear about if you want to measure the quality of care in your area of practice, with Qualpacs or any other tool, is that you and your colleagues really want to do it. To ask nurses to expose their practice to observation and criticism by others is asking a lot, and if there is no commitment to look constructively at the result, the whole exercise will be pointless. The decision to use any quality measuring tool should only be taken after thorough discussion with all the staff involved, including the area manager. An involved and supportive manager is an invaluable ally, who may be able to provide material help with things like photocopying, typing, or extra cover for a meeting of all the ward staff. He or she may offer moral support, share some of the risks and offer a different perspective if things get difficult. The manager may also be able to put you in touch with other helpers, perhaps someone in the school or at district headquarters, who you may not know about. You may even have a standards officer or quality assurance manager to whom you can go for help.

Is Qualpacs the tool for you?

Having thrashed out such questions as: ''do we really want to measure quality and why?'' and: ''what are we going to do with the results of our measurements?'', you can think about which tool to use. Perhaps the most important task at this stage is to decide what quality nursing means to you and your colleagues. Unless you are sure of your values you cannot begin to set standards or measure quality.

If your ward or team has not got a written statement of your nursing philosophy, with some statements about beliefs and values, this is the first step. Measuring quality is a subjective business, involving choices. If no-one agrees beforehand what their preferences are, the result would be like organising a night out at the local Indian restaurant and expecting everyone to enjoy the food, even though nobody else but you likes spices.

Preparing the ground

Assuming you have a philosophy which everyone supports, the next job is to read everything you can find about tools in general. The bibliography at the end of this article will help.

Qualpacs involves watching the care being given, as well as some consideration of charts and records and other aspects of communication. It attaches great importance to individual patient care and involvement and expects the nurse to have good interpersonal skills. If you and your colleagues share these values, Qualpacs may well be the tool for you. However, be wary of measuring only the things you think you are good at. You may get a shock if you find out you are not as good as you thought (which is a good thing to know), but you may also be tempted not to look at things where you know you are weak.

If all the nurse-patient interaction in your area is excellent, but the standard of record keeping is poor or inadequate you might be well advised to use a chart audit of some sort, either instead of, or as well as, Qualpacs.

Validity and reliability

The concepts of validity and reliability are discussed briefly elsewhere in this chapter. You will also find a more detailed discussion in the text of Qualpacs and in Barnett and Wainwright (1987).

Having decided you want to use Qualpacs, the next thing to do is to read the items in the questionnaire and the cues once again. This time you and your colleagues need to ask yourselves: "do we really understand what this item means? How will we recognise this behaviour when we see it, and what represents good and bad performance?" I would advise you not to alter the wording of any of the items in the questionnaire, but you are at liberty to make minor alterations or additions to the cues that go with it. This will enable you to give examples that relate to your area of practice. It will also ensure that everyone in the team has the same understanding of the items.

At this stage, if you have not already done so, you will have to decide who are to be the observers who will carry out the exercise. There is no rule about this, other than that they must be practising nurses who know something about your area of work and, above all, are acceptable to the staff to be monitored. An adverse report is easily rationalised away if it can be suggested that the observers did not know what they were looking at. The observers could be members of staff in the area concerned who will monitor their colleagues at work, from another similar area, from a neighbouring unit, hospital or district, managers, teaching staff, or anybody else who is acceptable, available and willing. Preparing for and carrying out the exercise will require some commitment and time from the observers, so you may need to negotiate with the relevant managers, to create the time by releasing them from duties or providing cover for them.

Training the observers

The observers will then have to be trained to use the tool. This does not take long, perhaps three days in total, but will require some organisation. A friendly tutor or helpful in-service department could be invaluable. Training should include:

- introducing the concept of quality measurement;
- introducing Qualpacs;
- giving everyone time to read through the items and cues;
- discussion of the concepts of validity, reliability and objectivity;
- discussion of the items and cues so that everyone understands and agrees them;
- discussion of the five point, best-nurse-poorest-nurse scale;
- discussion of practical problems — where to sit when observing, how to cope with rapid activities, ensuring privacy and so on;
- practice sessions in clinical areas other than the one to be monitored;
- debriefing sessions to compare scores and establish reliability.

The objective of the practice sessions is that if two or more observers watch the same patients getting the same care without comparing notes at the time, when their scores are checked afterwards they should be very close to each other. The Qualpacs text discusses this and suggests the degree of correlation that should be obtained. If you are not sure about things like correlation coefficients you can probably find a statistician in your district headquarters, or the school of nursing, or at a local college, who will help.

Many modern scientific calculators have a correlation function built in, which makes life simpler. If, having done all this you find your observers produce very different scores, they need to sit down together and go over their notes from the session, comparing their responses to the various situations and finding out where they differed. They should then repeat the exercise and check that their scores are now close enough to be acceptable.

Rating the procedures

The trickiest thing for newcomers to using tools like Qualpacs is the concentration needed to watch a nurse do something, split it up into four or five different components, find those items in the questionnaire, and rate how well they were done. For example, while bathing a patient, a nurse may pay attention to him, treat him in a kind and friendly manner, choose appropriate topics for conversation, utilise the nursing procedure as an opportunity for patient interaction, give the patient information, respond appropriately to him, observe changes in his condition and react accordingly, adapt the procedure to meet his needs, involve him in decision making, record information about him or communicate it to others, as well as maintaining his privacy and dignity and observing acceptable standards of hygiene and cleanliness and making him feel safe!

All of these (and more) are noted separately in Qualpacs, and the same nurse may do them well one minute and poorly the next, with the same patient. She may also chage from patient to patient. However, it is possible to record a surprising amount of detail with great accuracy.

Using the tool

It is essential to plan ahead and make sure everyone involved in the project knows what is happening. You will probably have discussed the project with your manager at intervals, but have a final session to go through all the arrangements. Pick an ordinary day: you are not trying to prove how hard you work or how short staffed you are, so don't choose the morning when there are three lists and two ward rounds all at the same time. Pick the patients to be monitored, randomly if possible, though the final choice will be partly governed by their condition, the layout of the ward, and their willingness to take part. Explain to the patients what is going to happen and ask their permission. Explain what is happening to other staff — domestics, porters and doctors — so that they are not worried by the sight of people with clip-boards busily writing down everything that happens. Don't be afraid to cancel at the last minute if unforseen problems crop up. Introduce the observers to the patients and make sure that everyone knows they are observers, and that they cannot help with care or do anything for patients except in dire emergency.

Subjectivity: If I stand at the end of the bed and look at a patient I may form all sorts of impressions and opinions about him, but these will be subjective judgements based on my experience, knowledge, beliefs and values. Indeed, to say: subjective judgements, is tautology, since judgements are by definition subjective. Much of the work of any profession is based on subjectivity, because no matter how many hard facts you may possess about something, you will always have to exercise judgement when deciding what to do about it. This is not something to be ashamed or frightened of. It is simply a matter of recognising the importance of professional judgement and making sure that it is based on as much good evidence as possible.

Objectivity: The opposite of subjectivity. An accurate thermometer correctly used will give an objective measure of body temperature. No opinion or judgement comes into it.

Validity: To say that a measure is valid is to say that it actually measures what it claims (or is being used) to measure. Thus a clock can give a valid measurement of time and a thermometer can give a valid measurement of temperature.

Reliability: A reliable instrument is one which gives the same result consistently if it is used repeatedly to measure the same thing, by the same or by different people. If a thermometer records a patient's temperature as being sometimes a degree more than it really is, and sometimes a degree less, then it is not reliable. Neither is the clock which sometimes gains and sometimes loses. Of course, some tools may give different results depending who is using them. It is important that all users agree to use the same methods, otherwise the results will be unreliable through no fault of the tool. A tool may be reliable, but not valid, as for example a clock which is always ten minutes fast.

The report
There is no point in spending a lot of time and effort — and therefore money — on an exercise like Qualpacs if you don't intend to use the findings. There must be a commitment from the start to respond constructively to criticism and use the report as the basis for change and improvement. Nevertheless, the staff will have found the experience of being observed quite uncomfortable and will be apprehensive about the outcome. A useful tactic to prepare for the feedback session is to ask the staff to jot down the points they think are going to come out in the report.

Most people have a reasonable degree of insight into their strengths and weaknesses, and will probably err on the critical side if asked to appraise themselves. It should then prove possible to start the feedback with the positive aspects, and you may be able to say of the bad points: "it was better than you expected, though there is room for improvement". People are much more likely to accept that they have faults and to look for remedies if they have identified the faults themselves, and have the opportunity to find their own solutions.

A serious undertaking
Measuring the quality of care in your area is not a task to undertake lightly. This chapter has touched on many of the problems, but has deliberately skimmed the surface in many areas, assuming that you will get hold of Qualpacs and some of the many other articles about it, and read this article in conjunction with them. I do strongly recommend that you seek help from people you trust and spend a lot of time preparing and planning before you do anything. That said, if you wish to recognise your professional responsibility to evaluate the quality of what you do, I wish you well!

Bibliography
Barnett, D. and Wainwright P.J. (1987) Between two tools. *Senior Nurse*, **6**, 4, 40-2.
Barnett, D. and Wainwright P.J. (1987) The reight reflection. *Senior Nurse*, **6**, 5, 33-34.
Burford Nursing Development Unit.(1983-84) A compendium of articles published in British nursing journals by staff at BNDU. Available on application to BNDU, Burford, Oxfordshire.
Burnip, S. and Wainwright, P.J. (1983) Qualpacs at Burford. *Nursing Times*, 36-38.
Dunne, L.M. (1987) How do we set nursing standards? *The Professional Nurse*, **2**, 4, 107-9.
Kemp, N. (1986) What is quality assurance? *The Professional Nurse*, **1**, 5, 124-126.
Kitson, A.L. (1986) Indicators of quality in nursing care: and alternative approach. *Journal of Advanced Nursing*, **11**, 133-144.
Kitson, A.L. and Kendall, H. (1986) Rest assured. *Nursing Times*, 29-31.
Kitson, A.L. (1986) Taking action. *Nursing Times*, 52-54.
Wainwright, P.J. (1987) Peer review: in Pearson, A. (Ed), Nursing Quality Measurement, 15-24. John Wiley and Sons.
Wilson-Barnett, J. (1986) A measure of care. *Nursing Times*, 57-58.

References
Barnett, D., Wainwright, P.J. (1987) A measure of quality. *Senior Nurse*, **6**, 3, 8-9.
Dunne, L.M. (1987) Quality Assurance: methods of measurement. *The Professional Nurse*, **26**, 187-190.
Wandelt, M. and Ager, J. (1974) Quality Patient Care Scale (QUALPACS). Appleton Century Crofts, New York.

35

Self-evaluation can protect your competence

Patrick McEvoy, RMN, SRN, DipN(Lond), RCNT, RNT
Senior Tutor, Department of Post-basic Education, College of Mental Health Nursing, Purdysburn Hospital, Belfast

Who really knows the truth about us but ourselves? Even our professional lives can be a closed book to all but our internal censor. This is why self-evaluation is crucial for professional development. As health professionals nurses, of course, are subjected to formal evaluation at virtually every turn and corner of their careers, which begins during interviews for courses and jobs. It is the primary purpose of examinations and assessments, whether they are formative or summative. Although much stress is placed on the developmental aspect of periodic staff review, appraisal is an all too obvious aspect of the proceedings. Even organisational meetings are sometimes used to evaluate the performance of individuals. Then there are those managers who will remark glibly, 'Call up and see me some time', usually with none of the connotations reminiscent of Mae West. Their covert intention is informal counselling, which can be a polite precurser of a formal warning. Performance indicators and value-for-money scrutinies are recent additions to the arsenal of evaluation which afflicts professionals within the health service.

Measuring quality

Following the Griffiths Report in 1983, an upsurge of interest in the optimal use of limited resources spawned a renewed application of quality assurance methods which had been emanating from the United States since 1980. Techniques such as Qualpacs and Monitor soon became fashionable as measures of quality. These rather obtuse instruments merely measure standards of care within broad parameters. Terms like 'average care', 'above average care', 'best nurse' and 'poorest nurse' do little to inspire the individual practitioner towards excellence in professional practice.

"To use Qualpacs, nurses must clarify their own value systems and identify their own standards," wrote Barnett and Wainwright (1987). This can only be done through enlightened self-evaluation. "Audit/evaluative methods such as Qualpacs measure quality, but these methods alone can only marginally improve quality. There is only one way to substantially improve quality. Every employee in the organisation needs to accept and understand that quality starts and ends with him," said Ryland and

Richards (1987). In other words, only self-evaluation will assure quality of care.

By its very nature, formal evaluation is quantitative rather than qualitative. It is concerned with percentages, grades and measurable results. It produces faithful recording of the nursing process regardless of actual standards of care. It ensures that tutors amass lesson plans, remain in class for the full 60 minutes, and show a presence on the wards without indicating anything of the quality of their teaching. At best, formal evaluation can only enforce minimum standards. It seldom inspires excellence. Regardless of all the interviews, examinations, appraisals and even formal warnings, the real race for excellence is the one you run against yourself.

The reflective practitioner

Self-evaluation is the hallmark of the reflective practitioner. Indeed, it is the hallmark of the mature person in any walk of life. It is a vital ingredient of the hidden curriculum which interlaces every interaction between client and professional. It is all about creating and measuring excellence within professional functions and relationships. Essentially, it involves asking, 'What have I to offer these (patients) (students) (clients) that they are unlikely to get from any other source?' I asked myself this question repeatedly as I penned this article; and my answer has been, ''A series of ideas, beliefs, reflections and bits of humour, hopefully linked together in such a way as to inspire the reader to ask some pertinent questions of himself.'' Perhaps you would like to begin by answering the following questions:

1. I frequently/sometimes/seldom take time out to reflect on my own professional performance.
2. I frequently/sometimes/seldom read stimulating literature which is related to my work.
3. I frequently/sometimes/seldom seek verbal and nonverbal cues from the recipients of my professional endeavours which will assist my efforts at self-evaluation.
4. I frequently/sometimes/seldom feel that I am gaining professional self-confidence as I grow older.
5. I frequently/sometimes/seldom ask myself, ''If I were the purchaser of my own services would I be satisfied with what I am providing?''
6. I frequently/sometimes/seldom feel that I am governed by 'the tyranny of the urgent'.

The last question is the odd one out. While it is desirable that you can answer 'frequently' to the others, it is ideal if you are seldom governed by 'the tyranny of the urgent'. Do you often moan that you have not the time to read professional literature because you are too busy? Is your desk cluttered? Do you always seem to be working under pressure? Worse still, are you a victim of adhocracy or institutional disorganisation? These can blight your professional life. The reflective practitioner will avoid taking on more than he or she can accomplish calmly and effectively. Time, like money, must be budgeted. If nurses were as careful with time as they tend to be with money, their professional effectiveness barometer would take a meteoric rise.

Self-esteem

Self-evaluation is closely related to self-esteem. Self-esteem is the evaluation which an individual makes of his personal worth, competence and significance. Maxwell Maltz (1968) claims that 95 per cent of people feel inferior. He does not say how much of the time or to what degree. Low professional self-esteem may be due to past failures: for example, failure to win a cherished promotion, or a bad experience while teaching in the classroom. Interstaff relationships may also be damaging. There are always those who attempt to boost their own self-esteem at someone else's expense. The astute professional will avoid an inordinate desire to meet other people's expectations. Nor will he feel that he must always be master of his environment. Where people are concerned this is virtually impossible, and will inevitably lead to frustration and feelings of inferiority. This is particularly likely to occur in the clinical setting where staff shortages and expanding needs makes a high degree of control unrealisable.

It may also be perilous to place too much reliance on status symbols to feed one's self-esteem: for example, insistence on the use of titles, letters after one's name, large offices and expensive furnishings. The tutor who insists on being regarded as omnipotent in the classroom has also tied his self-esteem to a status symbol. Such trappings can be superseded through regrading a demand for new qualifications or an emphasis on self-directed learning. Ultimately, retirement will sweep them all away.

Sometimes poor professional self-esteem is a product of the incompetence of others. In a bureaucratic heirarchy people become victims of poor forward planning, lack of communication, unprofessional behaviour, strangulation by red tape and adhocracy. The latter can sometimes be worse than the disease which it attempts to bypass. Reflective self-evaluation can protect a person's self-esteem even within such situations.

Where do we begin with self-evaluation? We must go back over our professional careers and identify those influences that have shaped our present levels of performance. Only when we understand how our present behaviour has developed will we be in a position to evaluate it.

Creating excellence

The reflective professional does not evaluate himself out of mere curiosity, or to compare himself arrogantly with others, or to see how bad he is, but rather to create excellence within himself. For self-evaluation to be effective, we must first develop a concept of the professional we would like to be. This will be personal and subjective; but nonetheless real. Like every other human endeavour, if there is no objective there can be no journey. If we can conceptualise an ideal professional self based upon freely chosen nursing, philosophical, educational and spiritual values, we can continually evaluate ourselves in the light of these. In this way professional self-esteem will be fostered as a personal conviction is developed that the individual is uniquely valuable to the recipients of his or her service, whether patients, clients or students.

Self-evaluation can be a potent source of positive reinforcement. We must try to link self-evaluation with self-reward. What are the rewards and threats which are motivating present behaviour? Self-evaluation linked to self-reward will produce a subtle shift from being externally directed to being internally directed. Individuals who do not learn to reinforce themselves must endlessly seek approval from others. Rewards from others are empty without our own self-regard to back them up.

It is a good idea initially to focus evaluation within our areas of competence. This should result in immediate gratification. As self-esteem is gained, we can move to the less successful aspects of our professional life. For example, we could begin by listing our most satisfying activities, which are most likely to be those that we do well. If self-evaluation shows a consistency in the qualities desired, we can tell ourselves: 'I certainly conducted that meeting smoothly and efficiently'; 'I asserted myself in that situation without damaging anyone's self-esteem'; 'I responded appropriately to that patient who came to me for counselling'.

It is important to be specific in relation to self-reward, and to avoid self-adulation and wishful thinking. The worst of all frauds is to cheat oneself. Share self-evaluation with a trusted colleague, and always remain alert for more objective confirmation of self-judgement. Remember there is often a kernel of truth in all personal criticism, however unfair it may appear at the time.

Journey of self-discovery

Like throwing a pebble into water, the process of self-evaluation continually expands a professional's self-awareness. It is a journey of self-discovery which can make a career more exciting and fruitful. A person evaluating himself can never be completely objective: but then neither will a person appraising another. We all give each other bitter pills to swallow, and we all fall far short of our potential. The success of any method of evaluation must be the extent to which it motivates a person to a more complete development of his talents. Self-evaluation outreaches all other forms of appraisal in that it magnetises a person towards his own centre of excellence.

Bibliography
Bliss, E.C., (1983) Doing it Now. Futura Publications, London.
Hickman, C.R. and Silva, M.A. (1985)Creating Excellence. Allen and Unwin, London.
Kanter, R.M. (1984) The Change Masters. Allen and Unwin, London.
Maltz, M. (1986) Psychocybernetics. Essandes, New York.

Peters, T.J. and Waterman, R.H. (1982) In Search of Excellence. Harper and Row, New York.
Waitley, D. (1984) Seeds of Greatness. Windmill Press, Kingswood, Surrey.
Wayner, M.E. (1975) The Sensation of Being Somebody. Building an adequate self-concept. Zondervan, Grand Rapids.

References
Barnett, D. and Wainwright, P. (1987) Between two tools. *Senior Nurse,* **6,** 4.
Ryland, P. and Richards, F. (1987) Where the buck stops. *Senior Nurse,* **6,** 3.

Primary Nursing

36

What is primary nursing?

Liz Tutton, BSc, SRN
Liz Tutton wrote this chapter whilst she was Nurse Practitioner, Nursing Development Unit, Oxford

The concept of primary nursing emerged from the University of Minnesota hospitals in the late 1960s (Manthey et al, 1970). In her book on primary nursing, Manthey indicates that in her work area there was general dissatisfaction with the existing system of team nursing, where a group of nurses had a generalised responsibility for a group of patients (Manthey, 1980). Nurses felt that care was fragmented, communication channels were extremely complex and no one was totally responsible for patient care. This chapter discusses the Oxford Nursing Development Unit, which was closed on 5th April 1989. It is hoped that this regrettable decision by the Health Authority will not inhibit the continuing development of primary nursing in Oxfordshire and elsewhere.

''Primary nursing is a system for delivering nursing service that consists of four design elements: allocation and acceptance of individual responsibility for decision making to one individual; individual assignment of daily care; direct communication channels; one person responsible for the quality of care administered to patients on a unit 24 hours a day, seven days a week'' (Manthey, 1980). These four elements could be seen as responsibility, patient allocation, communication and care giver as care planner.

Responsibility

The primary nurse takes full responsibility for decision making in patient care, with an 'associate' nurse taking responsibility for carrying out the care planned for the patient when the primary nurse is off duty. An associate nurse is a qualified member of staff who is developing the skills to become a primary nurse. He or she is responsible to the primary nurse, who can be contacted, if necessary, when off duty. In some settings using primary nursing, all nurses act as primary nurses for a small number of patients and also work as associate nurses with other patients for whom another colleague is the primary nurse.

The primary nurse accepts three major responsibilities. She collects all the information, including research findings, needed to care for her patients and makes it available to her colleagues. She also assesses the patient and produces a written plan of action and criterion for evaluation. Finally the primary nurse accepts responsibility for planning and co-ordinating the patient's discharge.

Patient allocation

The patient is allocated to one primary nurse who has a group of associate nurses working for her when she is off duty, and when on duty has the responsibility of administering total care to her patients. An important aim of this is to eliminate the performance of isolated technical tasks which lead to patient centred nursing.

One of the purposes of primary nursing is to simplify the system for communication between all professionals concerned with each patient. The primary nurse communicates directly with everyone involved in her patients' treatment, including the doctor, pharmacist, dietitian, physiotherapist and also patients themselves, and takes responsibility for obtaining and disseminating information to relevant members of the health care team. Communication at hand over periods is simplified by the primary nurse handing over directly to the associate nurse caring for her patients. Continuity of care leads to nurse and patient becoming more knowledgeable about each other, which allows for improved relationships. This gives the nurse more chance of therapeutically using her skills of teaching, guiding and helping and allows the patient to become more actively involved in his or her care and make more informed decisions.

It would seem logical that the care plan would be most useful and practical if the person who formulates it actually gives the care. In this way the patient's real needs are more likely to be stated in it.

Oxford Nursing Development Unit

The Oxford Nursing Development Unit (ONDU) at the Radcliffe Infirmary was closed following a funding decision by Oxfordshire Health Authority in 1989. It was a unique example of primary nursing. The beds were designated as nursing beds rather than as 'medical' beds, so the nurse carried full autonomy and responsibility for patient care.

Based on the principles and philosophies of the Loeb Center in New York, ONDU was a unit run for patients needing intensive nursing care as opposed to 'doctoring'. The concept of nursing as a therapy is relatively new, and the idea that nursing has a positive outcome for patients is of increasing importance to nurses (McMahon, 1986). Patients were admitted to the unit as soon as they are medically stable, and stayed until they were fit for discharge. Priority was given to expansion rather than extension of the nurse's role: building up nurse- patient relationships: using communication and counselling skills, education and teaching to allow patients to make informed choices, and making use of nurses' unique position to give physical care. Patients were involved in planning their own care if they so wish, and make their own decisions about daily activities. There were no routines to be followed, visiting hours were open and family participation encouraged.

Primary Nursing is a system for delivering nursing care (Manthey, 1980) and it provides an ideal environment for the use of the nursing process and nursing conceptual models. ONDU used primary nursing in conjunction with the Roper, Logan and Tierney (1980) model of nursing based on the use of 12 activities of daily living. The unit had four types of staff, in common with other primary nursing centres:

Primary nurse   Primary nurses take a case load of eight patients each, carrying full responsibility and accountability for their care. They assess, plan, implement and evaluate this care, leaving a written plan for associate nurses to implement in their absence. If a change in this plan of care is needed, the nurse practitioner is contacted and will either give a verbal instruction or visit the unit.

Associate nurse   These are trained nurses, often part-time, who carry out the care planned by the primary nurse, under whom they are divided into teams. They have a case load of eight patients.

Ward orderlies or care assistants   Ward orderlies help with domestic or non-nursing tasks so that the nurse can remain at the bedside with the patient. They help with bathing, kitchen work and general domestic duties and are directly accountable to the primary nurse.

Ward coordinators   These are clerical assistants who perform duties such as filing, ordering stores, arranging patient appointments, typing and general telephone duties. 'Walkie-talkies' facilitate quick communication between nurse practitioners and ward coordinator, which again frees the nurse to be with the patients.

ONDU showed that patient centred nursing within the framework of primary nursing improves patient satisfaction, quality of nursing care and leads to shorter stays in hospital for patients. The closure of the unit to 'save money' was a regretable short-term decision.

Bibliography
Bowes Ferres, S. (1975) Loeb Center and its Philosophy of Nursing. *American Journal of Nursing*, **75**, 5.
   Describes the setting up, running and philosophy of the Loeb Center.
Lee, M.E. (1979) Towards better care 'Primary Nursing' *Nursing Times*, Occasional Paper, **75**, 33.
   Lee suggests that the clinical nurse should take responsibility for good quality nursing care. She discusses primary nursing as a means of making this responsibility explicit.
Marram, G.D. et al (1974) Primary nursing: a model for individualised care. Mosby.
   An in-depth study of nursing organisational systems, including some studies on the effects of primary nursing.
Roper, N., Logan W. and Tierney, A. (1986) The elements of Nursing (Second Edition) Churchill Livingstone, Edinburgh.
   A description of the nursing model based on activities of living which can be used as a basis for assessing and planning nursing care.

References
McMahon. R. (1986) Nursing as a Therapy. *The Professional Nurse*, **1**, 10, 270-272.
Manthey, M. (1970) Primary Nursing, *Nursing Forum*, **IX**, 1, 65-83.
Manthey M. (1980) The Practice of Primary Nursing. Blackwell.

37

The role of the associate nurse

Sarah Burns, RGN, SCM, DN(Lond), DNE(Lond)
Lecturer/Practitioner, John Radcliffe Hospital, Oxford

Since primary nursing was implemented at the John Radcliffe Hospital, much attention has been focused on the primary nurse role (Tutton, 1986; MacMahon 1987). Primary nursing is the system whereby all patients and clients are allocated to a primary nurse on entering care. This nurse is then responsible for their nursing round-the-clock as long as it is needed. She is both responsible and accountable for the care she plans and gives. However, the primary nurse can rarely be the sole provider of this care and is therefore assisted by associate nurses. It is important to examine the role of the associate nurse, as without a clear understanding, it may be interpreted as having low status, which we at the John Radcliffe have found not to be true.

Throughout the period of nursing development those nurses who function exclusively as associate nurses have coped extremely well with the perceived threat to their own role, which was caused by uncertainty and inexperience making it difficult to see the eventual role clearly. Now we can review some of the changes to our fundamental thinking.

Who should be an associate nurse?

Experience of the associate nurse role is a prerequisite to becoming a primary nurse. The potential for personal and professional development is great and, I feel, vital in preparing a primary nurse.

Most of our associate nurses are newly registered or part-time qualified nurses, but student nurses may fill this role as long as they have appropriate supervision. It should also be remembered that the associate nurse may be another primary nurse in the team who is providing cover during a colleague's absence.

Hierarchy

The hierarchical structures which supported our traditional nursing practice have had to be dismantled where they were found to be inhibiting us. For example, our communication network previously meant that the associate nurses discussed nursing care issues with the sister or nurse in charge, who would then decide whether to take the issue to the nurse specialist, doctor or other professional. This inhibited the development of the associate nurses' confidence and creativity. To combat this all had to work hard to promote and support direct communication, so the associate nurses can initiate discussion with any professionals. We have found the role of sister has become one of advisor on clinical issues rather than major decision-maker.

We have tried to transfer the values and beliefs about the relationship with clients to our relationships with each other. These hinge on the nature of the relationship between the nurse and client – it must be a close partnership, with each party able to identify the other – the notion of 'my nurse' or 'my patient' as Manthey (1970) puts it.

The freedom and comfort required to develop the partnership can be inhibited by an hierarchical nursing team, but an open atmosphere of mutual trust and respect helps partnerships to flourish. It is important to recognise, however, that this is not the whole answer – individual nurses must want to develop these relationships. For many nurses this is uncharted territory and can be perceived as very threatening.

Part of the willingness to participate comes from each member feeling valued as part of the team, a feeling which is very much influenced by the ward sister. Manthey (1970) suggests that the ability of the ward sister to change her role and allow open and free staff relationships to develop is crucial to the overall implementation of a primary nursing system. Regular ward meetings, sometimes with the ward sister disclosing her own fears, worries and triumphs encourage an atmosphere in which other nurses feel able to disclose and share feelings. This open interest in and care of each other is new for many nurses. It is important that all members of the team work to develop an atmosphere in which individuals feel comfortable disclosing their feelings without fear of ridicule or retribution.

Smaller teams

One way of promoting this working relationship is to break the large nursing team into smaller teams. Headed by one or more primary nurses, the rest of the small team is composed of associate nurses. These teams look after a small group of patients within the ward or department, allowing all staff continuity of care – that is looking after the same patients each time they are on duty. Without a team approach, an associate nurse who acts exclusively in that role can find herself looking after one primary nurse's patients one day and another's the next, so she herself does not experience continuity of care.

One associate nurse described this as feeling like a foster mother. Having worked hard at developing a good relationship with one group of clients she had to hand them back to the primary nurse feeling very much as a foster mother might feel when returning a child to its natural mother. Using a team approach means the associate nurse looks after the same group of patients whenever she is on duty.

The diagrams illustrate examples of team membership. In Figure 1,

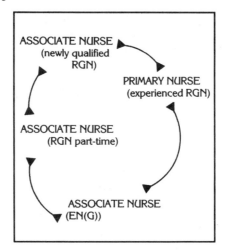

Figure 1. The primary nurse is responsible for nursing care in this team, helped by the associate nurses.

meeting clients' nursing care needs is the responsibility of the primary nurse. The associate nurses assist in carrying out this care, especially when the primary nurse is off duty. Clarification of care can be elicited from the care plan, but as the associate nurses can have as much continuous contact with the clients as the primary nurse, communication is generally easier, more effective and less open to error or breakdown. Figure 2 illustrates that where there is more than one primary nurse in a team each will 'associate' for the other when she or he is off duty, thus acting in both roles on one shift. The associate nurse will 'associate' for both primary nurses in their joint absence.

The feeling of belonging gained from the team approach, of contributing to the care of a group of clients, of receiving

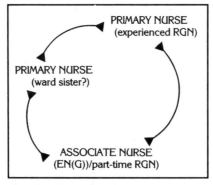

Figure 2. When the team has more than one primary nurse, they will 'associate' for each other, both helped by the associate nurse.

acknowledgement of one's endeavours all reflect Maslow's hierarchy of needs. The stage is then set for the creative contributions of the associate nurse in giving highly personalised nursing care.

Guidelines

For individual nurses to reach this point, some guidelines are necessary. Up-to-date job descriptions and standards help clarify what is and what is not expected, but it is important that individual nurses feel that acknowledgement is made of past experience and special abilities. Setting personal targets from job performance reviews is helpful in this area, which is ripe for development by ward sisters.

Associate nurses are essential members of the nursing team within a primary nursing system. They are accountable for their own practices, and their contribution to clients' care is active rather than passive. They are trained to use professional judgement in their clients' interests, and to evaluate their own practice. The level of decision-making expected from associate nurses can vary, but all team members should be clear about it. They, and nurse managers, must also acknowledge that some associate nurses may have extensive experience and expertise.

If the associate nurse role is to emerge as a positive and valued role within a primary nursing system, all members of the team need to examine all aspects of their behaviour which might inhibit freedom of speech and action in other team members. Otherwise the associate nurse will merely be the primary nurses' handmaiden.

References
Manthey, M. (1970) A return to the concept of my nurse and my patient. *Nursing Forum,* **9,** 1, 65-83.
Manthey, M. (1980) The Practice of Primary Nursing. Blackwell Scientific, New York.
Maslow, A. (1970) Motivation and Personality (2nd Ed.) Harper Row, New York.

38

Primary nursing – an individual approach to patient allocation

Andrew Gibbs, RMN
Nurse Teacher, Wycombe Health Authority

When our acute psychiatric ward implemented a system of primary nursing, it replaced a workbook, in which tasks to be undertaken that day were listed, along with the names of nurses allocated those tasks. This was intended to give ward activity a measure of preplanning to allow nurses to organise their day effectively.

The system reflected a task-oriented approach to care, focusing on the complexity of the task rather than the patient's needs. Accountability was for task completion, with responsibility for decision-making resting with the ward sister or nurse in charge. It was decided to implement a system of team nursing, which would focus on the patients' total needs.

A team of nurses were given responsibility for the planning and implementation of care for a group of patients. However, problems soon became apparent with the new system. There was constant swapping of patients between teams, in an effort to maintain balanced workloads, and overall responsibility still seemed to rest with the team leader or nurse in charge. Care became fragmented, complex channels of communication were needed and it was unclear who had responsibility for patients.

Dissatisfaction with team nursing in Minnesota (Manthey, 1980) brought about the original development of primary nursing systems, which are advocated as effective organisational frameworks (Castledine, 1982; Lee, 1975; Ellis, 1982; Ashley, 1986; Tutton, 1986). It is particularly seen to enhance the nurse–patient relationship in psychiatry (Ritter, 1987) and said to minimise the institutionalising effects of hospitalisation (Armitage, 1985).

We decided to implement a primary nursing system which addressed the four elements of responsibility, communication, care giver as care planner and patient allocation (Tutton, 1986). I will concentrate on patient allocation, as the development of such a framework within a traditional hospital service often produces difficulties which seem insurmountable – so much so that the term 'primary nursing' is occasionally used to describe a modified team approach (Green, 1983,

Cavill, 1981). The distinction between team and primary nursing is important, as there is evidence to suggest that in some circumstances team nursing may deteriorate into task allocation with its attendant limitations (Manthey, 1980).

Patient allocation problems

Staff organisation and the distribution of responsibilities within a nursing team is an issue raised by the Nursing Process Evaluation Working Group (1987). They see the nature of patient allocation as an important facet of ward organisation, a means by which nurses can make the transition from task-centred work to patient-centred care.

This type of patient-centred approach has been apparent for some time and was developing prior to the widespread introduction of the nursing process. In 1975, Mathews, in an extensive study of patient allocation described benefits for both nurses and patients. Patients felt their relationship with individual nurses had improved, giving them a greater feeling of safety and less anxiety, which in turn gave them more time to rest. Nursing staff felt that their care became more patient-centred rather than ward-centred, which produced more cohesive care delivery. As individual needs became more apparent, procedures such as drug administration became more meaningful, rather then dull routines. This greater involvement produced a feeling of improved systems of information with an appropriate emphasis on management techniques.

Patient allocation and the nursing process are complementary. Many authors have described their versions of patient allocation when implementing individualised care. Generally this has involved sub-dividing patients and staff into small groups (Jones, 1982; Green, 1983; Cavill, 1981). Each group has a team leader who coordinates patient care and supervises standards of care within the group.

The charge nurse or sister takes a supervisory and organisational role directing the workload and monitoring the results. The nurse in charge needs to constantly check and monitor learners' and untrained staff's activities and written work (Wright, 1985), and closely supervise those staff whose allocation to patients demands care skills beyond their experience (Jones, 1982). Another responsibility is to allocate workload to team members (Cavill, 1981). This situation, where the nurse in charge is the focus of communication, control and accountability seemed unsatisfactory within a primary nursing system.

Organisational problems

Further problems we were encountering in the team approach were reflected in nursing articles on the topic. There was a tendency to resort to task allocation when organisational problems arose, such as staff shortages or too few experienced staff on duty (Wright, 1985). It was also difficult to include night staff in the system (Mathews, 1975). The heavily structured format appeared to minimise the scope for self-development of nursing staff, as group needs took priority over individual learning needs. The off-duty was also organised so that one member of each of the teams was on duty each shift. This complex planning led to less overall flexibility within the staff group.

Far from the nursing staff becoming responsible and accountable for their own work, it appeared that our efforts had created a structure which produced such a need for conformity within it that patients' needs could not be met effectively. We had wanted to develop a system of individualised care that emphasised individual nurses' responsibility, decision making capabilities, and desire to consolidate existing skills and develop further through therapeutic relationships with patients. Our difficulties were:

- Centralised responsibility.
- Focus on structure rather than patients' needs.
- Undesirable conformity.
- Lack of recognition of the nurse as an individual.
- Lack of clarity regarding day to day responsibility for care planning.
- Uncertainty about change of role.

Selective allocation

We decided to devise a more satisfactory system. Smaller groups would meet to brainstorm ideas which would be bought to larger group meetings twice weekly. This seemed an effective way of generating new ideas and ensuring all staff were consulted and involved. Finally, we agreed that our system of primary nursing would involve only first level nurses as primary nurses, which seemed to be in accord with rule 18 of Nurses, Midwives and Health Visitors Act (1983).

As staff had differing experience and expertise, we decided that the primary nurses would take responsibility for assessment, care planning and evaluation at all times; be responsible for implementing care while on duty and ensuring effective implementation while off duty. They would do this by providing clearly written care plans which would act as nursing prescriptions in their absence.

Nursing staff would be allocated to patients on two levels – long term and day-to-day. The primary nurses would allocate themselves to patients on their admission to the ward. They would then act as primary nurse throughout that patient's stay on the ward, supported by an associate carer who had also selected the patient. The associate carer could be a first or second level nurse or a nursing auxiliary. The relationship with the primary nurse would be educational with a mutual sharing of ideas and experience, rather than a deputising role in the absence of the primary nurse.

Selecting patients

When selecting patients staff were asked to pay attention to their current workload and that of their colleagues, their relationship with the patient and the potential to apply existing skills or develop new ones. The selection process allowed them to regulate their workload and control their learning needs, while the negotiable aspects of the system encouraged sharing by discussion, with potential to practise skills in assertiveness, compromise and confrontation. There was also scope for staff of differing experiences, status and outlook to work together. This increased the potential for learning through role modelling and stimulated nurse–patient relationships based on interest and self-motivation rather than imposition and direction.

1. Each nurse selects a number of patients with whom to act as primary nurse.		
2. Each member of staff selects a number of patients with whom to act as carer.		
Patient's Name	**Primary Nurse**	**Assoc. Carer**
A	Jones	Clarke
B	Smith	Robinson
C	Robinson	Smith
D	Clarke	Jones
E	Jones	Clarke
F	Smith	Robinson

These selections should be made with regard to:
a) Current workload of self.
b) Current workload of others.
c) Dependency of patient.
d) Nurse's relationship with patient.

Figure 1. Patients were allocated a nurse and associate carer.

On a day-to-day basis, primary nurses allocated themselves to their own patients. In their absence the associate carer stepped in to implement care for that shift (Figure 1). If neither were on duty, another member of staff allocated themselves to the patient. To clarify the allocations made on any day, a chart was compiled showing patients' names, the date and shifts as shown in Figure 2. Signing their name next to a patient's for a shift indicated acceptance of responsibility for the implementation of care for that shift. The allocation list for each shift, when completed, was displayed where patients could see it. Staff were also expected to introduce themselves to their allocated patients at the beginning of each shift to generate a plan of action. Any change considered significant was reported to the primary nurse via daily progress notes, with the onus resting with the primary nurse to seek further information relevant to the patients' future care.

Supervision and management
On each shift a registered nurse acted as a coordinator, enabling the daily activity to run smoothly, dealing with general enquiries (or directing them to the relevant primary nurse), offering support to staff either by discussing specific incidents or giving practical help such as assistance with lifting and the administration of medication.

Selective Allocation.
Day by Day Nursing Interventions.
A chart is compiled as follows:

Patient	1st Jan. am	pm	n	2nd Jan. am	pm	n	3rd Jan. am	pm	n	4th Jan. am	pm	n	
A													H
B													I
C													G H
D													L
E													O
F													W

Nurses select the patients for whom they wish to implement care for that shift. Signing their name next to a patient for a shift indicates an acceptance of overall responsibility for the implementation of care for that shift and to meet any contingencies. They must also communicate significant changes to the primary nurse. In this way there is record of responsibility for all patients at all times.
Primary nurses must always select their own patients when on duty. In the absence of primary nurses, assoc. carers must always select their own patients when on duty.

Figure 2. A chart showed patients' names, dates and shift.

In this way a record was kept of responsibility and accountability throughout the patient's stay in hospital. The system's flexibility made it operable over a 24 hour period regardless of the number of staff on duty. Staff also retained their individuality and the right to request an off-duty pattern which suited their needs.

The nurse in charge of the ward was free from organisational activities such as directing and regulating workloads. The off-duty rota was easier and could be delegated to others and the initiative for decision making and learning was with individual staff, which allowed the nurse in charge more time to act as a clinical resource who could monitor and supervise standards of practice. Monitoring the selective allocation system allowed the nurse in charge to review patterns of allocation, highlighting areas of expertise or avoidance. This information was helpful in identifying relevant teaching input.

Selective allocation explicitly states individual responsibility, allowing nurses to practise and continually develop new skills. Their learning and workload were now shared in a planned way and both were able to link even in times of staff shortage.

Evaluating the system
The system was evaluated in an informal, subjective way, which, while it may be a disadvantage, was welcomed by both staff and patients. Doctors said they found it mildly annoying that they had to seek out different nurses to discuss different patients, and that this could be time consuming. However, the system seemed to enable proactive rather than reactive care planning, and appeared particularly useful in the care

of quiet, withdrawn patients who receive only minimal care under traditional systems (Altschul, 1978). Patients who are often labelled 'demanding' found it helpful to have a designated nurse to approach who was more likely to deal with the factors motivating the demanding behaviour rather than treat the patient as unpopular (Stockwell, 1976). Overall, it was easier for the nurse in charge to identify 'unpopular' patients and discuss the staff dynamics that may contribute to their demanding behaviour. Patients also soon identified 'their' nurse.

Despite these positive comments, the system had many problems. The night staff refused to become involved, for reasons which are unclear, and competition to take on more work became, at times, quite destructive. Some nurses felt that others were 'not pulling their weight'.

Staff shortage
An acute staff shortage highlighted the fact that when staff were brought in from another ward or an agency, the system enabled them to play an effective part in giving care. However, the shortage led to a deterioration in long term allocation and reduced flexibility in off-duty planning. When the senior nurse left, the system collapsed completely, but 18 months later, a slightly modified selective allocation system has been re-introduced.

I feel the positive aspects of the system outweigh the negative and that more effective management of change may have enhanced the possibilities of the system's success. The two essential components of the system are: flexible management who can cope with devolved responsibility, and a balanced skill mix. If these are present, I believe the system may enhance delivery of care in any environment.

References
Altschul, A. (1972) Patient Nurse Interaction. Churchill Livingstone, Edinburgh.
Armitage, P, (1985) Primary care. *Nursing Times,* **81,** 38, 36-7.
Ashley, J. (1985) From team nursing to individual care. *Nursing Mirror,* **160,** 18, 20-21.
Castledene, G. (1985) Defending the all rounder. *Nursing Times,* **81,** 84.
Cavill, C. and Johnson N. (1977) Steps towards the process. *Nursing Times,* 2091.
DHSS (1987) Report of the nursing process evaluation working group. HMSO, London.
Ellis, E. (1982) The nurse's accountability. *Nursing Times,* **154,** 21, 33-35.
Green, B. (1983) Primary nursing in psychiatry. *Nursing Times,* **79,** 3, 25.
Jones, J. (1982) The nursing process in psychiatry. *Nursing Times,* **78,** 30, 1273-75.
Lee, M. (1979) Towards better care. *Nursing Times,* **75,** 51, 133-6.
Manthey, M. (1980) A theoretical framework for primary nursing. *Journal of Nursing Administration,* **10,** 6, 11-15.
Mathews, A. (1975) Patient allocation. *Nursing Times,* **71,** 29, 65-8.
Ritter, S. (1987) Primary nursing in mental illness. *Nursing Mirror,* **160,** 17, 20-21.
Stockwell, F. (1976) The Unpopular Patient. RCN, London.
Tutton, L. (1986) What is primary nursing? *The Professional Nurse,* **2,** 39-41.
Wright, S. (1985) Special assignment. *Nursing Times,* **81,** 36-7.

Legal and Ethical
Issues

39
Confidentiality

Elizabeth M. Horne, MA
Editorial Director, The Professional Nurse

The Code of Professional Conduct (UKCC, 1984) states that: registered nurses, midwives and health visitors shall: "Respect confidential information obtained in the course of professional practice and refrain from disclosing such information without the consent of the patient/client, or a person entitled to act on his/her behalf, except where disclosure is required by law or by the order of a court, or is necessary in the public interest."

Conflicts in practice

Isolated from practice, this statement may seem reasonable, but practitioners are daily faced with decisions based on the application of these principles in situations which may contain inherent conflicts of interest. They need confident, working definitions of the elements involved, and to establish clear priorities between the expectations of their patients and those of a wider public. Not so easy when, for example, a sister in a psychiatric day hospital finds a patient in possession of large quantities of controlled drugs that he cannot have obtained legally, or an occupational health nurse is asked by her manager for information about an employee. These examples are cited by the UKCC in a new advisory paper on confidentiality (UKCC, 1987), which suggests that the most difficult problem for practitioners is identifying and establishing the boundary between clients' expectations that information will not be disclosed, and the expectations of the public that they will not be unreasonably put at risk.

Confidentiality is important for effective communication

The knowledge that confidentiality will be respected is important for effective communication. There is much information people would not discuss with anyone unless they knew the recipient was completely trustworthy in their offer of confidentiality. Without this trust they may choose to keep quiet, which could affect their health.

Standards of confidentiality should be made clear to clients

It is not practicable to obtain clients' consent every time information needs to be shared with other health professionals, so it should be made known to all clients what standards of confidentiality are maintained.

The practitioner who holds the information must ensure, as far as possible, that it is imparted in strict professional confidence and for a specific purpose serving interests of the client. An individual practitioner is responsible for deciding when it is necessary to obtain the explicit consent of a patient or client.

Practitioners must be familiar with how record systems are used, who has access to them and what are the risks to confidentiality associated with their use. Where students, or those involved in research, require access to records, the same principles of confidentiality apply, and the patient's consent must be sought where appropriate, and the use of the records closely supervised.

Breaches of confidentiality

The principle of confidentiality must be the rule, and breaches of it exceptional; the practitioner must be sure that the best interests of theclient, or thoseof confidential information. The interests of the community may, occasionally, take precedence over those of an individual.

The withholding or disclosing of confidential information may have serious consequences, and the practitioner's decision can be extremely difficult. However, the responsibility cannot be delegated. The individual practitioner must make the decision, and must be able to justify it. It may be helpful to make a written note of the decision and reasons for it on the file for future reference. Situations of this nature can be very stressful, and if other practitioners are aware of them, it may be helpful to discuss the problems. However it is still the responsibility of the individual practitioner, and he or she must ultimately make their own decision.

The UKCC Advisory Paper on Confidentiality is available from: UKCC, 23 Portland Place, London W1N 3AF (send a S.A.E.). It discusses the responsibility of individual practitioners for confidentiality, and the everyday implications for practice, the ownership and care of information, and some of the issues which arise when confidentiality is deliberately breached.

References

United Kingdom Central Council for Nursing, Midwifery and Health Visiting, (1984). Code of Professional Conduct for the Nurse, Midwife and Health Visitor. Second Edition. UKCC, London.

United Kingdom Central Council for Nursing, Midwifery and Health Visiting, (1987). Confidentiality: A UKCC Advisory Paper, UKCC, London.

40

Informed consent: a patient's right?

Alison Kennett, RGN, Cert. Onc
Research Sister, Royal Marsden Hospital, Surrey

Nurses involved in patient education all face the decision of what information should and should not be disclosed. The boundaries of patient advocacy are unclear and nursing ethics must play a part in providing guidelines for what is divulged. In areas such as oncology nursing, the issue of informed consent is particularly important and should be discussed.

Research has shown that the more knowledge patients have about their disease and its subsequent treatment, the more they are able to participate in their own care and the better they feel, both mentally and physically (Hayward, 1973). This research is related specifically to postoperative patients but from my experience in oncology this statement is still most relevant. Indeed it is used on the inside cover of the Royal Marsden Hospital patient education booklet series on all subjects relating to cancer. But the problems arise when we consider who should tell patients, what they should be told, when it should be told and also where it should be told.

Before a patient receives any care it is essential to obtain an informed consent. Failure to do so can give rise to both civil and criminal proceedings (Martin, 1977).

What is informed consent?
A doctrine of informed consent has evolved and patients' rights, as established in the doctrine, have direct implications for the nursing profession collectively and individually. By law, no diagnostic or therapeutic procedure can be performed on a patient without him having been told the risks of the procedure and the alternatives to it prior to giving his consent (Bucklin, 1975). As far back as 1914 Judge Cardozo declared that "every human being of adult years and sound mind has a right to determine what should be done with his or her own body". The principle of informed consent is derived from Anglo-American law which holds that an individual is master over his own body and, if mentally competent, may choose to refuse even life-saving treatment. The United States has much published material on the whole issue of informed consent, whereas English sources are much less abundant. No doubt this is due to the fact

that America has substantial legislation in this area, particularly the Patients' Bill of Rights which includes many of the elements listed below.

Elements of informed consent   The essential elements of informed consent should include:

- a full explanation of the proposed treatment involving important incidental procedures;
- information in a manner intelligible to the patient involving as little jargon as possible;
- explanation of inherent risks and benefits;
- alternatives to proposed treatment;
- adequate time to allow the patient to question the proposals, to ensure the patient realises he has the option to withdraw consent from the treatment or procedure whenever he likes — indeed he has the right to refuse any treatment initially.

Obtaining informed consent

There appear three difficult areas in obtaining a meaningful consent:

i)who should give the information?

ii)what information should be disclosed?

iii)where should the information be given?

Both Miller (1980) and Bucklin (1975) state that it is the doctor's responsibility to provide enough information to his patients so that an intelligent decision about the procedure can be made. Barkes (1978) also says that disclosure for consent should be regarded as the doctor's prerogative as he is the one to perform the procedure and his is the ultimate responsibility for the communication of facts. In most cases it is the doctor who obtains the consent but in some incidences it may be the senior nurse who obtains the signature on the form after the doctor has explained the procedure.

Besch (1979) in investigating the possible barriers to obtaining a meaningful consent, found that the doctor-patient relationship appeared to interfere with patient autonomy. The patient tended to trust the doctor's recommendation completely and many did not understand that it was a choice that was being asked of them and not complete compliance. Comments such as these illustrate this: "I guess the doctor knows best." "I wasn't going to argue with him, he knows what he is doing." "If that's what you think I should do, doctor."

Surely, by virtue of this authoritative role, the physician may, inadvertently, introduce an element of coercion into the consent procedure, thus preventing the patient from making a voluntary decision. "Coercion nullifies consent" (Meissel, 1977).

Effective communication

"Doctors often find it difficult to relax with patients who have incurable cancer and this impairs their ability to communicate effectively with them"

(Hanks, 1983). It must be here that the creation of a patient advocate position would be enormously beneficial to ensure the patient's comprehension of the medical information before making a decision. The nurse can amplify, clarify and encourage questioning if the doctor has used jargon-laden phrases and shrouded the true message sufficiently to render a patient unclear as to what the doctor is actually explaining. I feel that it is the nurse who may be more skilled and more aware of non-verbal cues and other communication techniques. She is constantly at hand to answer any subsequent questions that may be posed by the patient, whereas the doctor is likely to be off the ward most of the time and only contactable by going through the time consuming bleep system.

The nurse herself has to be well informed and perceptive in order to assess the extent of the patient's comprehension. This will only come as a result of an established rapport with the patient with whom the nurse has had most contact and who, I suggest, has the patient's wishes foremost in her mind.

What to disclose

Wells (1979) stated that "In the treatment of malignant disease it is often at diagnosis that a catalogue of deceit and half-truths begins, when those whose responsibility it is fail to be honest with the patient and the members of the health care team become entangled with the complicated task of keeping information from the patient."

This makes a mockery of obtaining subsequent informed consent for necessary procedures. Another problem is that explanation is time consuming and some physicians would argue that full explanations produce unwarranted anxiety. It is known, however, that explicit information prior to a procedure can lead to a substantially improved prognosis. "Is it then ethical or fair to decide without the patient's knowledge what he should or should not know about his own life? Is it right to assess a personality, and its potential, without knowledge of its strengths and weaknesses, after a brief contact arranged for an entirely different purpose? The position is rather similar to knowing that an individual is going to have to perform a task requiring considerable fortitude and endurance. The individual is kept in ignorance of the true nature of the task on the grounds that it is best not to anticipate an unpleasant experience, so that the individual is shocked and unprepared for what then transpires" (Goldie, 1982).

Alternative treatments

Alternative treatments may not be proposed to the patient, who remains unaware of the options. Interestingly, a nurse who was practising in the United States of America, where there is a Patients' Bill of Rights ensuring that they have the right of self determination, chose to explain to a patient alternative methods of treatment available which a doctor had not, and was found guilty of professional misconduct — a decision against which she is now appealing. Here an ethical argument arises; the nurse, acting as informer of the alternative treatment, presents an ethical dilemma involving her in the actual decision for the planned treatment whereas the doctor is more removed from the emotional aspect of the decision-making.

Where the information is given The circumstances in which information is presented are often overwhelming — the patient is usually in hospital, in unfamiliar surroundings with strangers around, being confronted with procedures to undergo and invasions of privacy. Often the information is given implying that the decision is required immediately and the patient does not appear to have an opportunity to discuss the proposals. Nurses are rarely present when surgeons or physicians explain the reasons for, and what is involved in surgical and medical procedures. This ''right hand not knowing what the left hand is doing'' syndrome confuses both nurses and patients and may have a disastrous impact on the patient's overall trust in the caring team. While it would be wrong to suggest many forms of consent are obtained without the patient being fully aware of his illness and its likely outcome, it would be equally wrong to pretend it does not happen.

''It is in situations such as these that a nurse is required to support her colleagues and assure the patient. Can the nurse be expected to support the decision that a patient is to have further surgery in the hope of curing what is known to all except the patient to be an incurable disease?'' (Wells, 1982).

The values of effective communication between patient and carer seem easy to state but difficult to put into action. It involves a commitment to patients' rights to decide what happens to their own bodies. To uphold such views health professionals, especially doctors, must learn to become more communicative and less paternalistic and they must accept that informed consent is an essential part of the doctor-patient-nurse relationship and of proper patient care. The nurse's role as patient intermediary requires knowledge and a commitment to this concept of assisting patients in making an intelligent, educated decision; that is in ensuring patient autonomy.

As nurses we should not be regarded as a threat by our medical colleagues, but rather recognised as a source of support and information that has yet to be harnessed to improve the overall care for the patient.

References
Ashworth, P. (1984) Accounting for ethics. *Nursing Mirror,* **158,** 10, 34-6.
Barkes, P. (1979) Bioethics and informed consent in American health care delivery. *Journal of Advanced Nursing,* **4,** 23-38.
Besch, L. (1979) Informed consent: A patient's right. *Nursing Outlook,* January, 32-35.
Bucklin, R. (1975) Informed consent: past present and future. *Legal Medical Annual,* 203-214.
Ferguson, V. (1981) Informed consent: given the facts. *Nursing Mirror,* **155,** 35.
Goldie, L. (1982) The ethics of telling the patient. *Journal of Medical Ethics,* 8, 128-133.

Hanks, G. (1983) Management of symptoms in advanced cancer. *Postgraduate Update,* 1691-1702.

Hayward, J. (1973) Information – a prescription against pain. RCN, London.

Kennedy, I. (1980) Medical ethics are not separate from but part of other ethics. Reith Lecture, *The Listener,* 27 November.

MacDonald, M. and Mever, K. (1976) Medicolegal notes: informed consent. *The Mount Sinai Journal of Medicine,* **43,** 104-107.

Marks, M. A Patient's guide to Chemotherapy – Your Questions Answered. Royal Marsden Hospital Patient Guide series.

Martin, A.J. (1977) Consent to treatment. *Nursing Times,* **73,** 810-11.

Meisel, A. (1975) Informed consent – the rebuttal. *Journal of American Medical Association,* **234,** 6, 615.

Miller, L. (1980) Informed Consent. *Journal of American Medical Association,* **24,** 2661-2662.

Wells, R. (1979) Who, what and when to tell. *Nursing Mirror,* **75,** 22-3.

41

Balancing public concern and patients' rights in HIV testing

Ann Shuttleworth, BA
Editor, The Professional Nurse

The issue of HIV testing gained further controversy recently with the news that doctors are being asked to take blood for tests from patients who have not given informed consent. The British Medical Association said insurance companies have been asking doctors to take the blood from people who have applied for life insurance. The doctors are then asked to send the samples to a laboratory who will inform the insurance company of the result. The first indication people have that they are HIV positive could be the refusal of their application for insurance.

The BMA argue that the standard letter issued to applicants, briefly outlining the test with an attached consent form does not constitute informed consent. They insist counselling is essential before a test is given and then after for the result to be followed up correctly. This view is shared by the DHSS (1986).

Implications for nurses

The whole issue of HIV testing has wide implications for nurses, who often take the blood samples. If they do so without the full consent of the patient, they could find themselves defending civil actions for damages or criminal actions on charges of battery. If they knowingly collude with a doctor in taking such a specimen they may face charges of aiding and abetting an assault, while they also risk being struck off their professional register if they mislead patients about the reason for taking blood samples.

In a circular on professional conduct, the UKCC emphasise that nurses must especially heed the first two clauses of their Code of Professional Conduct with respect to people with or suspected of having HIV infection. These state that they must always act in such a way as to promote and safeguard the wellbeing and interests of patients, and ensure that no action or omission on their part or within their sphere of influence is detrimental to the condition or safety of patients.

Sherrard and Gatt (1987), defining informed consent, say that it must be genuine, and not obtained by misrepresentation, fraud, deceit or duress. Surely the prospect of not being allowed life insurance, and therefore a mortgage, could be construed as duress? The law may interpret a test taken in such a situation as being taken without informed consent.

More generally, practitioners taking blood for HIV tests must take account of the patient's 'right of bodily integrity' – the right to determine what is to be done with his or her own body. Sherrard and Gatt say the far reaching implications of a positive result for the patient would probably make implied consent insufficient from a legal point of view. It is not good enough to take a blood sample 'to run a few tests' and assume the patient realises an HIV test will be among them, and consents to this. The patient must explicitly consent to an HIV test. Obviously nurses should beware of taking blood for HIV tests without the explicit consent of the patient. But does anyone benefit from HIV testing anyway – apart from the insurance companies?

Those responsible for planning and allocating services for AIDS sufferers would certainly be grateful for more information on how many people are HIV positive and therefore likely to contract AIDS. Such information is currently in short supply. Nor is there much information on how far HIV infection has spread into the heterosexual community.

The more people who have HIV tests, the more information will be available on the epidemiology of the virus. This would enable services to be more efficiently planned before a situation arises, rather than when it has reached crisis proportions. This is assuming such action would really be taken, which is by no means certain.

Who should be tested?

While mandatory testing of the entire population is logistically impractical and undesirable from the aspect of individual rights, the voluntary testing of certain groups may be beneficial. Pregnant women are one important group, for two reasons. Pregnancy has been shown to make HIV positive women more likely to develop AIDS because the functioning of mother's immune system is lowered so that her body does not reject the foetus (ACHCEW, 1988). This is thought to give the HIV virus more chance to gain ascendancy. Half of HIV positive mothers can also be expected to pass on HIV to their children either during pregnancy or at birth. Testing would give them the option of having an abortion.

Pregnant women could also be epidemiologically extremely valuable. Brain (1988) said that midwives and antenatal women would be unwise to oppose the routine screening of all pregnant women if they are the only group who would give a clue to the spread of the disease into the heterosexual community. She recommended that testing be voluntary and that the women know its full implications. She also expressed concern at reports that a group of antenatal women had been tested without their consent.

The Government is to decide whether or not pregnant women should be tested anonymously – and whether this should be with or without their consent – when it receives a report on surveillance and monitoring for the Expert Advisory Group. However, Britain's Chief Medical Officers recently refused to support a call for such anonymous screening without the women's consent. They were criticised by Black et al (RSM, 1988), who said anonymous testing would be easy to administer, using blood left over from that taken for routine tests, and would provide a sensitive index of the rate at which the disease is entering the heterosexual community. Women could be told their results if they wished, the rest of the samples would be sent to a central laboratory.

The question of who should be tested and under what circumstances is an emotive one which many nurses will feel strongly about. They have their safety and that of patients and colleagues to consider but must also protect their patients' rights, which may be compromised in the quest for information.

Testing certain groups would not only provide epidemiological information and give pregnant women the chance to have an abortion, say Masters, Johnson and Kolodny (1988). Infected people who were unaware of their status could be identified and counselled to modify their behaviour and avoid infecting others.

As well as pregnant women, they recommend testing all people admitted to hospital between the ages of 15 and 60. Again, the epidemiological information would be valuable. The results would also ensure that staff were aware of the hazard of contact with biological fluid from seropositive patients, and that immunocompromised people were not put at unnecessary risk by exposure to contagious illnesses.

How reliable are the tests?

However, there are other factors in the debate about HIV testing. While the tests currently used are highly reliable compared with many other routine medical tests, some errors are made.

The main test used is the enzyme-linked immunosorbent assay (ELISA), which works by mixing serum with protein pieces of HIV in the presence of chemical reagents. These cause a colour reaction if the HIV antibody is present. ELISA is relatively cheap to administer, and under ideal conditions will detect 98-99 per cent of samples correctly. However, high sensitivity means it occasionally registers false positive results, especially in people who have had numerous blood transfusions and women who have had numerous pegnancies.

The effect of a false positive test on a person could be almost as catastrophic as a true positive. They will suffer the same stigmatisation and emotional trauma as if they were infected, and from a practical point of view, are unlikely to be able to get life insurance or a mortgage among other things. While they may not have the same health problems as a seropositive person, the stress of believing themselves to be infected would be likely to have a detrimental effect on their health. ELISA also shows a small percentage of false negative readings.

To guard against a high number of false positive test results, readings are only considered positive if they are consistent with a repeated ELISA and confirmed by a more specific test like the Western blot. This test is carried out only on samples which have given positive readings with ELISA, because it is much more expensive and requires a higher degree of technical skill to administer. This means false negative readings are not retested. The two tests give a high degree of accuracy, but they are not infallible, or free of the possibility of human error.

Compulsory testing

Compulsory testing of either the whole population or certain groups, usually those who are at high risk of infection, is a subject raised from time to time. At present, however, the question is really academic. The purpose of such screening would be to discover all those who are infected with HIV, and presumably to take steps to ensure that they do not spread the infection. The time lapse between infection with HIV and the body producing the antibodies to the virus can be anything from two months to over a year, so even screening the entire population would not give an accurate picture of who was infected. Until a test is devised which isolates the virus itself, rather than the antibodies, the compulsory testing lobby is unlikely to get very far. If such a test does become available, however, nurses may have to defend their patients' right to bodily integrity from more sustained and vociferous campaigns.

The arguments about HIV testing are bound to continue, but common sense on the part of health care professionals can do much to protect both those afraid of infection with HIV and those already infected. For example, nursing care should not change if a person is diagnosed seropositive – body fluids from seronegative patients may contain other biohazards and should be treated as potentially hazardous. This weakens the argument for compulsory testing – why bother if the same precautions are necessary for seronegative and seropositive people?

The case for voluntary testing, either anonymously or otherwise, is probably the strongest. The information such a programme, properly conducted, could yield would be invaluable if it were used to plan services and public education programmes, and full patient confidentiality were retained. If it were simply used to whip up hysteria against minority groups, however, it would be worse than useless. In such a case it would merely deflect attention from the real issue of how to care for people with AIDS effectively and prevent other people from infection. It would discourage people from going for the test, and make the already catastrophic personal situation of being HIV positive much worse. Any testing programme must be carefully conducted.

How nurses can help

By remaining calm and giving effective education to those who need it nurses can help people take reasonable steps to protect themselves from infection and overcome any unreasonable fears they may have. Hopefully they will also be able to ensure that HIV testing is never used in a negative way against those who are infected with the virus.

Nurses have a huge part to play in protecting both their patients' health and their rights. The medical establishment has expressed its voice in the public debate – albeit often in a contradictory fashion. Nurses are often at the 'coal face' in these issues. It is time the nursing profession made itself heard as well.

References

ACHEW (1988) AIDS and HIV Infection (Health News Briefing). Association of Community Health Councils for England and Wales, London.

Brain, M. (1988) President's address to the 1988 RCM annual conference.

DHSS (1983) AIDS. Booklet 3. DHSS, London.

Masters, H., Johnson, V.E., Kolodny, R.C. (1988) Crisis – Heterosexual Behaviour in the Age of AIDS. Grafton, London.

RSM (1988) Anonymous testing for HIV. *The AIDS Letter*, **1**, 5, 7.

Sherrard, M. and Gatt, I. (1987) Human immunodeficiency (HIV) virus antibody testing. *British Medical Journal*, **295**, 911-2.

UKCC (1987) AIDS – testing, treatment and care. Circular PC/87/02. UKCC, London.

42

The ethics of brain death

Douglas Allan, RGN, RMN, RNT

Nurse Teacher in Continuing Education, South College of Nursing, Glasgow

Nothing in life has a greater finality than death, and nurses and other health care providers have had to learn to cope with dealing with it as part of their normal working practice. To many people outside the caring professions, death is a simple concept. Nurses will testify differently, having witnessed the different ways in which people can die. This chapter explores one of the rarer processes of death, that of brain stem death and all its ethical implications.

Brain stem death accounts for approximately 4,000 deaths per annum in the UK (less than one per cent of all deaths). Half of these occur as a result of head injury and another 30 per cent as the result of an intracranial vascular problem such as spontaneous haemorrhage (Jennett and Hessett, 1981). It is important to clarify terminology; brain death or cerebral death are terms often used, although a stricter description would be that of brain stem death. This is based on physiological reasoning and is outlined in the UK criteria, which sets out the practicalities of diagnosing brain stem death. However, all three terms appear to be readily interchanged in the literature; this is probably not that important provided that the reader has a sound understanding of the concept itself.

Historical perspective

Brain stem death is nothing new. The first description of this phenomenon was published in 1959 by Mollaret and Goulon in their classic work. Before this, attention was focused on the heart as a measuring stick for life; as long ago as 1740, a report determined that a sure sign of death was putrefaction (Jennett, 1981). Jennett continues by stating that the invention of the mechanical lung ventilator and its increasingly widespread use during two polio epidemics in 1952 and 1953, further complicated the situation.

In 1968 the World Medical Assembly declared that the point of death in various cells was not as important as the certainty of irreversibility (Gilder, 1968). During the same year the Ad Hoc Committee of the Harvard Medical School (1968) produced a set of criteria, using the term 'irreversible coma', which, in hindsight, was unfortunate as this led to confusion with the phenomenon of the vegetative state (Pallis, 1983). However, despite this, the report was hailed as a watershed in the attempt to clarify the situation.

The Harvard group was the first to state that its criteria was not the 'be all and end all' and that further modifications would take place as knowledge improved. Indeed, within 12 months of the issue of the report, the group acknowledged that the iso-electric electro-encephalogram was unnecessary, while retaining the opinion that it could constitute valuable supporting data (Beecher, 1969). Other aspects of the Harvard criteria remain an essential and indisputable part of present day criteria, such as the presence of apnoea and the notion of repeating the tests in their entirety to eliminate observer error.

In 1971 the notion of irreversible damage to the brain stem as the point of no return and the idea that a diagnosis could be based on clinical judgement was introduced by Mohandas and Chou. It was also at this stage that the existence of preconditions emerged. Twenty of the 25 patients in the study had sustained a head injury, a diagnosis found in at least half of the patients at present.

British criteria

After much deliberation and discussion among anaesthetists, neurologists, neurosurgeons and physiologists, the British criteria appeared in 1976 (Conference of Medical Royal Colleges and their Faculties, 1976). Following a further year of discussion, and in the absence of any adverse comment, copies of the guidelines were then distributed to hospital doctors for use in diagnosing brain death (Figure 1). (For details of these guidelines see Allan, 1987).

The UK guidelines in particular rely upon the presence of apnoea, an interval between testing, preconditions, the idea of irreversibility and a clinical diagnosis of brain stem death. Essentially, this is a combination of all the available data and was subsequently imitated in other parts of the world. Despite the publication of the Harvard criteria as long ago as 1968, it was not until 1981 that national guidelines were published in America (Report to the President's Commission, 1981), and it was possible to be declared dead in one state and not in another.

However, two years before this in the UK, a number of allegations were made in a Panorama television programme in October 1980. The programme, entitled Transplants – Are the Donors Really Dead?, focused on three particular issues. First, that brain death was a new concept introduced without prior consultation or discussion. Second, that it was created to satisfy organ transplantation demands and, finally, that the criteria were unreliable. The crux of the unreliability argument centred around the existence of two patients who had apparently survived, despite fulfilling the brain death criteria. This allegation was subsequently withdrawn (Paul, 1981). A relationship between the development of brain death criteria and organ transplantation was also proven not to exist. The brain death criteria had existed long before the ability to perform successful transplants and, indeed, if all organ transplants were stopped, it would still be necessary to diagnose patients

Diagnosis to be made by two doctors, one a Consultant and the other a Consultant or Senior Registrar.

Diagnosis should not be considered until at least 6 hours after the onset of Coma; 12-24 hours will be more usual.

Name .... **Unit No** ....

Pre-conditions Nature of irremediable brain damage		Time of event leading to coma
Dr A		....
Dr B		....
Do you consider that apnoeic coma is due to:	Dr A	Dr B
Depressant drugs		
Neuromuscular blocking (relaxant) drugs		
Hypothermia		
Metabolic or endocrine disturbances?		

Tests for absence of brain stem function		
Is there evidence of:	Dr A	Dr B
Pupil reaction to light		
Corneal reflex		
Eye movements with Cold Caloric Test		
Cranial Nerve Motor Responses		
Gag Reflex		
Respiratory movements on disconnection from Ventilator to allow adequate rise in $PaCo_2$?		

Date and time of first testing ....
Date and time of second testing ....

Dr A	**Dr B**
Signature	Signature ....
Status	Status ....

Figure 1. Criteria for diagnosis of brain death.

as clinically brain dead.

In the few months following the programme, much was written in both the general and medical press, debates took place and a mass of evidence emerged from various sources in the light of further experience.

In a small way, the Panorama programme did focus the general public's attention on the necessity of having brain death criteria, although at the time many individuals discarded their transplant cards.

Implications for nurses

Throughout the development of the brain death criteria, nurses have had little or no involvement in the formulation and performance of the criteria. Although not advocating that nurses are the appropriate people to diagnose patients as brain dead, it is unfortunate that they were not more closely involved during the early discussions in order that a nursing perspective could have been applied at the beginning.

Several fleeting references are made in the medical and nursing literature about the bad effect on the morale of nursing staff who are looking after brain-dead patients on a regular basis (Allan, 1984; Jennet, 1981; Pallis, 1983). Pallis (1983) in particular emphasises the damaging effect on the morale of highly trained nursing staff asked to clean the mouths or treat the pressure areas of patients who are already dead. He continues by recounting the plight of relatives who became emotional hostages to uncomprehending machines in the days of ventilating to asystole. Given the close relationship between the nurses and relatives of such patients, this must have had an enormous impact on the nurses.

Rudy (1982), commenting in an American nursing journal, states that in the concern for proper medical and legal determination of brain death, the very important role of nursing is neglected. She continues that it is imperative that nurses have a mechanism for making their feelings and views known. The same author outlines the additional difficulties faced by nursing staff where children or neonates are involved, and the particular problems posed by the family of the patient.

Nursing involvement with brain-dead patients can be considered under the following headings: physical care of the patient; psychological care of the patient and family; and psychological care of the nursing staff.

Physical care of the patient   Physical nursing care of any critically ill patient will aim, initially, toward supporting and maintaining failing body systems. However, in some instances the priorities change. The goal in the nursing care of the brain-dead patient becomes one of facilitating a dignified death and, if organ transplantation is a possibility, the preservation of the remaining functioning body systems (Daly, 1982).

The nature of the patient's condition demands the use of critical care facilities and the highest possible standard of basic nursing care. The brain-dead patient is perhaps the ultimate example of total dependence upon nursing staff to deal with the physical needs of the patient as they arise. This implies a rigorous assessment of the patient's needs and meticulous application of effective nursing care, coupled with an ongoing evaluation process to deal with changing priorities. The nurse will need to assist in the tests for the absence of brain stem function.

Psychological care of the patient and his family Any care plan must include the patient's family and significant others, and it is an emotionally traumatic and upsetting time for them. Many relatives show signs of the grieving process before the actual withdrawal of support from the patient. Daly (1982) suggests that it is helpful if the nurse is aware of the different stages of the grieving process and the ways in which these may be manifested in individuals, in order to enhance understanding of the needs of the relatives.

The patient is likely to be surrounded by technical machinery and it is imperative that the relatives sense that he or she is treated as a person and that the nurse demonstrates a humane, caring attitude in the performance of her care and interaction with the relatives. To reinforce this notion, the relatives are encouraged to touch the patient and there is no reason why they cannot perform simple nursing tasks. The nurse is usually the first person to make contact with the relatives and will certainly become their most consistent contact in the hospital.

It is important that the nurse is aware of the extent of the relative's knowledge with regard to the patient's condition so that any new information or reinforcement of existing information is carried out consistently. For example, a nurse could be present when the doctor speaks to relatives. To accommodate this, proper facilities must be provided whereby the family is afforded some privacy and time to make what are very personal major decisions. Involvement of others in the care of the relatives should be initiated, if appropriate. These may include a social worker or religious adviser.

Psychological care of the nursing staff This aspect of caring for the brain-dead patient can be easily missed. Few nurses can fail to be affected in some way by their dealings with even one brain-dead patient. Several aspects are involved here, and this paper does not and cannot provide the answers to all the questions that are raised. With the close interaction which is inherent in any nurse–critically ill patient relationship, the nurse will often be the first person to notice the patient's deterioration. While undertaking routine nursing procedures, such as suctioning, the nurse may notice that the patient's gag reflex is weakened or absent or that the corneal reflex is weakened or absent, as would be observed during routine eye care.

Some nurses may have difficulties dealing with their own feelings and emotions in this situation. Rudy (1982) suggests that good communication between medical and nursing staff and peer support can help to alleviate or minimise these problems, but does not elaborate on how to achieve this. An understanding of the criteria and the medico-legal requirements would contribute to the avoidance of any possible misunderstandings, which might lead to difficulties for some nurses.

Difficulties do not end with the nurse directly responsible involved with the patient. This author can recall, as a charge nurse, wrestling with a quite separate set of problems. How to explain to a relative why the ECG monitor still has a 'heartbeat'? How to allow the mother of a brain-dead child to lift the child up in her arms when he is attached to a ventilator, monitoring machines and infusion pumps? What to do about the relative who insists on sitting at the bedside 24 hours a day, neglecting her family and her own health? How to allocate hard-pressed resources, both staff and equipment? Many readers can probably add other problems to the list.

This is undoubtedly an area of nursing practice which merits further attention. Some of the unanswered questions which demand closer examination might include:

- Can we identify the difficulties/problems/needs of nurses involved in caring for the brain-dead patient?

- What can we do to help?

- How can we help the ward manager deal with the managerial nursing problems?

Only with further research can we begin to address these issues.

Bibliography
Pallis, C. (1983) ABC of Brain Stem Death. British Medical Association, London.
   A comprehensive series of articles from the *British Medical Journal* which examines brain death from historical, medical, ethical and legal standpoints. Does not contain any nursing aspects.
Rudy, E. (1982) Brain death. *Dimensions of Critical Care Nursing,* 1, 3, 178.
   One of the few articles available which examines for nurses the ethical and legal issues of brain death for nurses. Written for the American nurse, some parts of the paper are not applicable to British practice but it is still worth reading.

Reference
Allan, D. (1987) Criteria for brain stem death. *The Professional Nurse,* 2, 357-90.
Beecher, H.K. (1969) After the definition of irreversible coma. *New England Journal of Medicine,* 281, 1070.
Conference of Medical Royal Colleges and their Faculties in the UK (1976) Diagnosis of brain death. *British Medical Journal,* 2, 1187.
Daly, K. (1982) The diagnosis of brain death; an overview of the neurosurgical nursing repsonsibilities. *Journal of Neurosurgical Nursing,* 14, 2, 85.
Gilder, S.S.B. (1968) Twenty-second World Medical Assembly. *British Medical Journal,* 3, 493.
Jennett, W.B. (1981) Brain death, *British Journal of Anaesthesia,* 53, 11, 1111.
Jennett, W.B. and Hessett, C. (1981) Brain death in Britain as reflected in renal donors. *British Medical Journal* 283, 359.
Mohandas, A. and Chou, S.N. (1971) Brain death – a clinical and pathological study. *Journal of Neurosurgery,* 35, 211.
Mollaret, P. and Goulon, M. (1959) Le coma depasse. *Revue Neurologique,* 101, 3.
Pallis, C. (1982) From brain death to brain stem death. *British Mecical Journal,* 258, 1487.
Pallis, C. (1983) ABC of Brain Stem Death. British Medical Association, London.
Paul, R. (1981) Survival after brain death: withdrawal of allegation. *The Lancet,* 1, 677.
Report of the Ad Hoc Committee of the Harvard Medical School (1968) Examination of the definiton of irreversible coma. *Journal of the American Medical Association,* 205, 85.
Report to the President's Commission (1981) Guidelines for the determination of brain death. *Journal of the American Medical Association,* 246, 2184.
Rudy, E. (1982) Brain death. *Dimensions of Critical Care Nursing,* 1, 3, 178.

43

Labelling: attitudes, beliefs and customs

Gillian James, RNMH, RGN, RCNT, FE Teacher Cert

Nurse Teacher, Department of Continuing Education, Brent House, Hatton, Warwickshire and also Vice Chairman, RCN Society of Mental Handicap Nurses

In 1986 at the Annual Meeting of the Royal College of Nursing Representative Body, a resolution was passed by a large majority asking RCN Council to take appropriate action to raise the level of public awareness about the special needs of people with mental or physical handicap. The labelling theory was used in support of the argument and it was emphasised that real effort should be made to avoid over-professionalism and to develop a more appropriate image for this group of people who are, after all, our fellow citizens and entitled to be treated as such.

Following the debate, I felt there was a need to increase not only *public* awareness but awareness within the nursing profession about the whole concept of labelling, how it is used and what effects it has.

Attitudes to labelling

In her book, Shearer (1981) says it is the inability of people which leads to labelling. Everyone has setbacks, she asserts, but disablement means having to face problems every day. She questions what makes them the disabled population. Is it where they live? Where they go to school? Where they spend their adult life? Do others set up special requirements and laws for them? If so, does this make their disability more conspicuous? Does it mean that they cannot cope with the term 'normal life'? Are we tolerant enough of human weaknesses? As the health of the general population improves, do we view any deformity, however small, with contempt or intolerance?

Spencer (1977) looks at terminology and says terms "reflect the hopes and fears, the precepts, prejudices, ignorance, arrogance, optimism and pessimism".

Myers and Heron (1985) state: "It is the way in which and the extent to which the needs of the intellectually impaired and thereby disabled person are or are not met that determines the degree to which he or she is handicapped." They go on to say that the perception of people with intellectual disability as being capable of learning may not be held by those in society who have a major say in providing resources. The disabled person may develop a poor self-image and show incompetence in several areas of development. The problem is mostly one of attitudes.

A person with a mental handicap who, for instance, has shown severe behaviour disorder, has often been segregated or even moved to a more secure place. If they have committed an offence they will be relabelled, for example, under a section of the 1983 Mental Health Act as being mentally handicapped, having a behaviour problem and needing control under the law. The restriction placed on them may accord even more prejudiced attitudes upon that person.

Does this mean that the consequences of labelling and blame for the existence of subculture lies with those who have the power to control and are agents of change within the social framework of the nation? What are the consequences of labelling, how does it happen and how can it be avoided?

The labelling theory

According to theorists who have studied labelling, it is the labelling of a person which ensures his behaviour. The label not only does this but also reinforces his behaviour until it becomes an identifiable and perhaps permanent feature of that person. In the medical sense it is the punitive labelling to which society reacts and defines the unacceptable behaviour as 'deviant'. The label defines that person as being of a particular kind and the tendency is to interpret what he does in terms of the label.

Labelling is also class-linked. Members of lower status groups appear to have a lower resistance to particular stigmatising labels. Attitudes to the same behaviour in two different social groups will be treated in two different ways. For example, a group of youngsters seen fighting in lower income groups would be interpreted as being of low intellectual level. The same situation in a wealthy area would be treated as high spiritedness. Race is also often used in a similar way as a social labelling device (Rack, 1982).

Stigma

Some groups have the power to make labels stick, namely the professional groups; the police, the courts, teachers, social workers and nurses, for example. The labelling of a person or a group does not remain neutral; it overrides any other status that person has. Others may respond to him in terms of that particular label and not to him as an individual. Stigma probably also reinforces what would otherwise have been a short-lived behaviour, people tend to have expectations of that person's behaviour and so label him.

The label will then encapsulate the total condition in the eyes of others and identify that person or group, often to the detriment of other areas in their total make-up. The person is then classed as a 'deviant' and is socially sanctioned or treated as such with the label concerned with the negative definition of him.

Any behaviour which is not socially accepted is then selected for special attention and even highlighted because a person has a stigmatising label. The same behaviour may well go unnoticed or overlooked in the rest of society, but the labelled person may be punished or penalised (Haralambos, 1985). The label may often deny that person the right to live an ordinary life, a right which is open to most people.

Because of this, a subculture develops and within this the attitudes, values and beliefs identifying the group justify its existence and support its activities. In fact, those within that subculture often act within the terms of the concept of the group, and society itself applies pressure to the group or individual to be treated as they are labelled. The label may well be retained well into adulthood and the individual qualities of that person overlooked because of the clinical diagnosis of his condition which defines how he will function.

Irreversible

Owens and Birchenall (1979) described labelling as a "global one and once a person becomes labelled it is often almost always irreversible. Labelling affects a person's self-esteem. Some may even adopt a 'cover' story in order to cope with it.

"A labelled person can be defined in some way as standing in opposition to the normal society (placed outside and made to feel 'strange').

"Stigmatisation is an important aspect of labelling as people will often react to differences in speech, sight, hearing or physical features; this will become uppermost in their mind and they will react by either being able to interact with them or retreating.

"This reaction will often be dependent on that person's exposure to the disability and by how much experience they have had in the past. Labelling has sometimes been thought of in the past as being in the best interests of the disabled person, often when it has then been required to have treatment, special care or training."

Trying to solve the issue of labelling

If labelling comes about because our beliefs and attitudes colour the way we see situations that present problems, we must carefully judge our attitudes as professionals. Do patients admitted to hospital adopt the role required of them because of the function of that place? Are institutions both within and outside the NHS equal to regulations, bureaucracy, conformity, uniformity (Hockey, 1981)?

Does society highlight the disabilities by having special declarations of rights, Ministers for the Disabled, Mental Health Acts and special categories within the welfare system?

In its leaflet, the Campaign for People with a Mental Handicap (CMH)

(1987) lists commonplace misconceptions of mental handicap:
- Mental handicap is hereditary.
- Mental handicap is the same as being mentally ill.
- People with a mental handicap cannot speak for themselves.
- They cannot look after themselves.
- They can be violent, dangerous and unpredictable.
- There will always be some who need to live in hospital
- They prefer to be with their own kind.
- People do not want those with a mental handicap in their street... anyway it lowers the property values...

Community care

When developing community care and looking at, for example, strategies for coping with different types of handicapping conditions, any changes need to be done with a great deal of sensitivity. The public reaction to handicapping conditions may well reduce the chances of that service succeeding. Prejudices and therefore rejection are often a result of a lack of knowledge and understanding.

Terminology often does not help and the use of words such as 'mental patient' often describes quite wrongly and inappropriately those who have been in hospitals or institutions perhaps for many years, when in fact they do not require hospital treatment.

When providing community care for those who have lived in institutional settings with their rules and regulations, a great deal of re-education has to take place both for the resident and the general public. Being labelled an ex-patient often makes re-entry into the community quite difficult. Do disabled people, and in particular people with a mental handicap, fit into the community as a member of that society? Are they accepted or does the stigma of having once lived in an institution follow them into the new setting?

One way of solving the problem and stopping the stereotyping may well be to accept the label but change the negative association of it to a positive one, and not allow it to colour other statuses that person may have. If the label is accepted then perhaps some of the presenting features of the condition may also be accepted.

Nursing staff can play an important role in all aspects of disablement and handicaps. It is essential that reactions of members of a family into which a handicapped child is born are very carefully responded to by the professionals, particularly the nurses who are involved in the delivery and early part of that child's life.

The responses by the parents must be fully understood in order that they are coped with expertly; nurses play an important part in supporting that family through each crisis. If the physical features of a person are part of the label, they may identify a specific condition, syndrome or diagnosis but this may also suggest, for example, a life expectancy which causes a great deal of anxiety for the parents.

We need to look at the disabled person not as someone with a physical or mental affliction but as a whole person with individual needs, and to build up their self-esteem. A change in terminology could help but "if real advances are to be made, community programmes need to include a more 'normal' living environment" (Owens and Birchenall, 1979). Everyone should be a valued member of society. This can only be achieved if people with a mental handicap are seen as part of the local community. For this to happen, adequate services and resources are essential to give them the opportunities other people take for granted.

Bibliography
Craft, M. et al (1985) Mental handicap – A Multidisciplinary Approach. Bailliere Tindall, Eastbourne.
An excellent textbook on mental handicap.
Heron, A. and Myers, M. (1983) Intellectual Impairment – the Battle Against Handicap. Academic Press, London.
These co-authors are well known within all disciplines in mental handicap.
Parrish, A. (1987) Essentials of Nursing – Mental handicap. Macmillan Education, Basingstoke.
A new book in the series.
Parsons, T. (1951) The Social System. Free Press of Glencoe, New York.
The author is a well known, often quoted sociologist.
Scheff, T. (1966) Being Mentally Ill – a Sociological Theory. Aldine Press, Chicago.
This broadens the discussion to include mental illness.
Sugden, J. (1985) Labelling theory. *Nursing*, **2**, 35, 1021.
A good article, specifically on labelling.
University of Kent (1987) (PSSRU) People First. Care in Community Newletter, 7, 11.
The Personal Social Services Research Unit is currently studying mental handicap relocation projects.
Warnock Committee Report (1978) Special educational needs. Cmnd 7212, HMSO, London.
This report recommends 'special' education for children regarding labelling.

References
CMH (1987) Campaigning for valued futures with people who have learning difficulties: Fact and fallacies. CMH, London.
Haralambos, M. (1985) Sociology – Themes and Perspectives. University Tutorial Press, Slough.
Hockey, L. (1981) Current Issues in Nursing. Churchill Livingstone, Edinburgh.
Mental Health Act (1983) HMSO, DHSS.
Myers, M. and Heron, A. (1985) Concepts about Mental Handicap. *Physiotherapy*, **71**, 3, 102-4.
Owens, G. and Birchenall, P. (1979) Mental Handicap – the Social Dimensions. Pitman Medical Publications, Tunbridge Wells.
Rack, P. (1982) Race, Culture and Mental Disorder. Tavistock Press, London.
Shearer, A. (1981) Disability – Whose Handicap? Blackwell, Oxford.
Spencer, D.A. (1977) What's in a name? *Apex*, **5**, 1, 102.

44

Negligence: defining responsibility

David Carson, LLB

Senior Lecturer, Faculty of law, University of Southampton

The six tests

When dealing with cases of alleged negligence in nursing, the courts do not just ask "Was the behaviour negligent?" They go through a series of separate tests which, together, make up the law of negligence. It is most easily understood as six questions.

1. Did the nurse owe a duty of care to the injured person?
2. Did the nurse break the appropriate standard of care in the circumstances?
3. Did that breach of the standard cause the injuries?
4. Are the injuries of a kind that the courts compensate?
5. Were the injuries reasonably forseeable?
6. Did the injured person contribute to the happening of, or the extent of, the injuries?

Questions 1 to 5 must be answered "Yes." If not there is no legal liability. If question 6 is answered "Yes" then there has been contributory negligence, which means that the injured person's compensation will be reduced.

Court decisions are illustrative but it is dangerous to generalise from the facts rather than the law. Injecting a patient in the wrong place may break the standard of care in one case but not in another where, for example, there are special reasons such as an emergency.

The duty of care

Nurses only owe a duty of care to certain people, certainly to their patients and colleagues. But how do the courts decide who else nurses legally owe a duty of care? In *Towers v. Cambridgeshire Area Health Authority & Others* (unreported, March 9, 1982) an ambulanceman injured his back lifting a heavy patient. Anticipating a difficult lift, his colleague asked, two or three times, for help. One nurse took a drip but otherwise his requests were ignored. They began to lift. The colleague lost his grip and Mr Towers had to take the patient's weight. His back was injured.

Did the nurses owe the ambulance officers a duty of care? The trial judge said that nurses were not "primarily carriers" and there might be other claims upon their attention. So it did not matter how unreasonable or bad the nurses' behaviour was; they were not liable because they had no duty of care to the ambulance officers. The Court of Appeal disagreed. The trial judge had confused the second question about the standard of care with the first question about the duty of care. If a nurse had something more important to do then he or she would not be in breach of the *standard* but could still owe a *duty* of care to the ambulance officer.

The courts say we owe duties of care to our 'neighbours', people whom it is reasonably foreseeable may be affected by our actions and inactions. On this occasion it was reasonably foreseeable that these ambulance officers would have been affected by these nurses' behaviour. It may not be possible to imagine some of the people nurses owe duties to. Discharge a patient early and the relatives may harm themselves in trying to cope. Is that reasonably foreseeable? Is it reasonably foreseeable that a head injury patient will suffer further if not told to seek immediate attention if he or she begins to vomit? Many things are foreseeable. But it must be reasonable, not fanciful.

The standard of care

The judges decide who is owed a duty of care but the profession invariably decides the standard of care. The essential question is whether the nurse acted in a way that reasonably competent nurses would have done in those circumstances?

In *Walker v. South West Surrey D.H.A.* (unreported, June 17, 1982) a woman was giving birth. She said that she was injected with pethidine in the inner side of her right thigh. That fact was disputed, though both sides agreed that if it was true then it broke the standard of care. "No careful nurse or doctor would give an injection at that point unless there was some compelling reason to do so."

The standard is not what the best nurse or what most nurses or the average nurse would have done. It is about the reasonably competent nurse in that, if any, specialty. Expert witnesses may be called. They will be asked whether reasonably competent nurses would have done that. The test is not what the witness would have done. The test depends upon and reinforces professional standards. Certainly the courts reserve the right to declare professional practices and standards too low but that is a rarely applied reserve power.

The test recognises that standards should keep improving. What was reasonably competent once, say not knowing about adverse reactions to a new drug, will soon become unreasonable. The role of journals in spreading information about new standards can be crucial. Failure to read a journal could be the breach of standard.

"The test is the standard of the ordinary skilled man exercising and professing to have that skill. A man need not possess the highest expert skill: it is well established law that it is sufficient if he exercises the ordinary skill of an ordinary competent man exercising that particular art." That is known as the *Bolam* test. *(Bolam v. Friern H.M.C.* [1957] 1 W.L.R. 582,

586.) It has been restated many times by many courts. While it involved a doctor, the same principles would apply to a nurse. The test recognises differences of professional opinion. Provided a responsible body of professional opinion would support the action, the standard is met. Without differences of opinion there is no progress.

Causation

A patient in a psychiatric hospital had florid delusions about Christ, snakes, fires and said she had to die. She was diagnosed as having a ''depressive illness with some paranoid features''. She was to be nursed on the ward but not subjected to constant observation. She was noted as being potentially suicidal and likely to abscond. One day her husband gave a nurse a box of matches. He explained that his wife had given them to him saying that she might otherwise set fire to herself. This was not noted in the nursing records. The patient had periods of being very disturbed, shouted about fires, escaped from the ward but returned voluntarily. Her consultant concluded that she was in a psychotic state. He did not alter the nursing instructions. Then one day she seemed calmer, agreed to join in some activities but first went to the toilet, alone. There she set fire to her tee-shirt and burnt herself badly.

The patient claimed that both the doctors and the nurse were negligent. The doctors should have required constant observation. The nurse ought to have recorded the incident with the box of matches. The trial judge decided that the doctors were not negligent; reasonably competent doctors in that position would not have required constant observation. The matchbox incident, however, should have been recorded. Thus the nurse owed a duty of care to the patient and the standard of care had been broken. The nurse was therefore negligent, the trial court decided.

The Court of Appeal disagreed. (*Gauntlett v. Northampton Health Authority*, unreported, December 12, 1985.) The trial judge had confused the separate questions about breach of the standard of care and causation. The evidence was that if the consultant had known of the matchbox incident he would still not have required constant observation. The injuries would still have happened. The nurse may have behaved improperly but that did not cause the injuries. Many would link the matchbox incident and the subsequent burning but it is the effect on the decision-makers that counts; ''. . professional experience of dealing with people with disordered minds gives it a much less literal significance, as an indication of possible, or probable, future acts by the patient.''

The causation rule in the law of negligence requires us to think twice. If the injuries would have happened anyway then some apparent causes might not be causes at all. (But disciplinary action could still be taken for the breach of the standard of care which, luckily, did not cause injury.) But this point must not be overstated. That several people cause somebody's injuries simply means that each is liable and the court will settle how much each should pay.

If the injuries would still have happened, but not so soon or so extensively, then those have been caused. In *Sutton v. Population Services Planning Programme Ltd.* (unreported, October 31, 1981) a nurse was working in a well-woman centre. When a patient complained of a lump in a breast she was supposed, it was agreed, to refer her to a doctor at the centre. She did not, and the patient subsequently had a mastectomy. Thus there was a duty of care and a breach of the standard of care. But, it was accepted, the doctor would not have found the lump, even with a mammograph. Did the nurse's breach cause the loss? The Court examined the steps likely to have been taken. The doctor would have referred to a specialist. The specialist would not have found anything but told the GP. The patient would have returned and repeated her complaint. The GP would have sent her to a specialist. The specialist would have found the lump, with or without a mammograph, and operated a few days later. The operation would have taken place about 10 weeks before it actually did take place and caught the cancer at an early stage. The patient would then have had a greater chance of survival for longer. Thus the nurse's breach of the proper standard did cause the loss.

Foreseeable losses
The courts will only compensate certain kinds of loss. This certainly includes injuries to the person and their finances. Pain, suffering and loss of amenities are covered. They will compensate recognised psychiatric disorders but are reluctant to compensate experiences such as sorrow and upset and not just because of problems of proof.

Recognised loss
A recognised loss or injury might nevertheless go uncompensated because the way it occurred was not reasonably foreseeable. This point is unlikely to arise frequently in nursing cases but it is possible. Say a mentally disordered patient leaves a hospital, through a nurse's breach of standard of care, and causes problems for a relative. Presuming the nurse owes a duty of care to the relative, he or she is unlikely to be liable if the loss or injury was, for example, to the relative's investment portfolio. That could be regarded as not reasonably foreseeable.

Contributory negligence
It is the plaintiff, the patient, who might be guilty of contributory negligence. If he or she is guilty, then the compensation will be reduced by the proportion by which the court thinks he or she is to blame. It includes both contributing to the cause or happening of the accident and contributing to the amount or extent of the injuries or losses by, for example, not seeking medical attention or disregarding advice. In *Patel v. Adyha* (unreported, April 2, 1985) a patient consulted her GP about back pains. His examination broke the standard of care. He should have discovered symptoms which would have led him to refer the patient to

a specialist who would have diagnosed a tubercular condition with kyphosis. She deteriorated and, according to the judgement, her spine 'collapsed'. The doctor's lawyer argued that she should have sought further medical attention when her problems would have been noted and treated in time. But the Court of Appeal decided that it was perfectly understandable that she did not return to her doctor when she had been led to believe that there was nothing that could be done. However, if she had been "inviting disaster," if she had not acted as a reasonable person in her condition would have acted then, the Court implied, she would have been contributorily negligent.

45

Taking risks with patients – your assessment strategy

David Carson, LLB
Senior Lecturer in Law, University of Southampton

Nurses make judgements, decisions. Nurses take risks. An elderly patient may be allowed matches in his bed despite the risk of fire. A mentally disordered patient may commit suicide while allowed the freedom of the hospital grounds. A patient discharged early may be unable to cope. There is a dignity and individuality in being able and allowed to take risks. In fact, taking risks is often a highly valued activity. But, despite the hope for and expectation of success, there is a risk of harm for the patient – and a risk of litigation, disciplinary action or professional inquiry for the nurse. Although risks may be frightening and worrying, risk-taking can be the essence of professional responsibility. This chapter outlines a way of assessing risks. It encourages risk-taking after careful analysis of the risk and, properly used, should prevent legal liability and professional censure if things should go wrong.

Making decisions

The method outlined below describes an approach to risk-taking. It does not take the decision away from nurses, nor provide easy solutions for individual cases. It does not tell nurses *what* to decide, rather it suggests a *way* of deciding. In view of the increasing pressure on resources and new care philosophies which encourage risk-taking and patients' rights, this framework could help in making decisions. Indeed, it might be used as the basis of a risk-taking policy which health authorities could adopt with a promise to support those staff who follow it. The framework is as follows:

1. Analyse whether the proposed action is best described as a gamble, a risk or a dilemma.

2. List all the possible kinds of benefits, for the patient, of acting.

3. List all the possible kinds of benefits, and knock-on benefits, for other people.

4. Analyse the likelihood of each of these benefits occurring.

5. Manipulate the risk by taking steps to make the benefits more likely to occur.

6. List all the possible kinds of harm, to the patient, of acting.

7. List all the possible kinds of harm, and knock-on harms, to other people.

8. Analyse the likelihood of each of these harms occurring.

9. Manipulate the risk by taking steps to reduce the likelihood of the harms occurring.

10. List any duties to risk.

11. Obtain the patient's informed consent.

12. Obtain the informed agreement of colleagues.

13. Assess whether 'the risk' should be taken.

Gamble, risk or dilemma?

Consider three different activities; gambling, taking a risk and facing up to a dilemma. Which is it that nurses do? Gambling is something that *may* be done (it does not have to be done) to gain a benefit where the act of gambling is often pleasurable. Taking risks involves deciding that the potential benefits of a proposed act outweigh the potential drawbacks. You may take risks because the potential benefits make it desirable. In contrast, facing a dilemma involves *having to act*, having to choose between options – each of which carries both potential benefits and potential harm. When facing a dilemma, something has to be done; doing nothing is, or soon will be, harmful.

Nurses' actions will often be better described as facing up to a dilemma rather than taking a risk. Merely calling it risk-taking is a disservice to both the nurses and their judges. Besides giving more credit and greater respect, we expect less and apply a lower standard when we know that a dilemma is involved. A situation requires quick thinking and action in the face of a dilemma. Who would argue with the questions: "We took a risk; can you say our decision was wrong?" and "We faced a dilemma; can you say our decision was wrong?"

Analysing decisions into gambles, risks and dilemmas is being truthful and honest, and fair judgements can be made. However, this article will refer to 'risk-taking' to avoid being repetitive.

The two sides to a risk

A risk can be divided into the *consequence* – the gain or loss, the benefit or injury that might occur – and the *likelihood* – the odds, the chance, the possibility, that it might occur. For example, there is a 10:1 risk (likelihood) the horse will win. There is a risk (consequence) I might lose £10 and a risk (consequence) I might win £100. Both senses of the word should be considered.

When the risk is of a dramatic injury or loss, like a patient's death or lifelong paralysis, we – quite naturally – get worried. But that is only one part of the risk. It is very easy to suggest that death is possible; it is possible every time we cross a road. A proper analysis of risk must consider the likelihood of each suggested outcome. A risk-taking scheme should ensure that the likelihood of each possible outcome is assessed separately. Epidemiological data may sometimes be used to describe statistically the chance but, if unavailable, words and concepts of possibility can be used. Precision may be impossible but that does not prevent clear thinking.

Benefits and losses

Another understandable tendency when taking risks is to concentrate on harms, injuries and losses. We tend to stress what may go wrong rather than what may succeed. When a child is returned from local authority care to its parents who then abuse it again, the press and media will concentrate on the risk of such abuse occurring. Little attention will be paid to the reasons for taking that risk, to the objectives of the exercise. However, if the decision was actually taken in terms of 'seeing if we can get away with it', then those who took that risk deserve the censure. The reasons or the objectives of taking risks should be clear and easily stated. Risks should be taken to achieve specific goals in the light of possible harms occurring: "We were trying to achieve . . . although, yes, we realised that these harms might occur."

Having goals and objectives for a patient or client is surely a central part of the nursing task. Some might argue that it is enough to justify the risk after the event, if and when it goes wrong. This is unwise. The reasons may show that it was a wise decision and that the same decision would be made again. That could be enough to show that the risk-taking did not cause, in legal terms, the loss suffered. (See the section on causation in the previous chapter on the law of negligence. But it could show enough carelessness to justify disciplinary proceedings. When a court or tribunal assesses the quality of a risk-taking decision, it can only consider the information and reasons that were actually available at the time to the decision-maker. Disciplinary action should be concerned with poor decisions whether or not harm results.

The range of benefits and losses

A patient gets his wish to return home quickly. That is a benefit to consider in assessing the risk of early discharge. But it should not be limited to that. There could be benefits to other members of his family. It is not just the patient or client who may benefit or be harmed, but relatives and others. And it is not just the return home itself, but what it may lead to; for example, a reconciled marriage, preserved employment, pets not destroyed, skills maintained, accommodation retained. Risk-taking schemes should consider both the range of people who may be affected and the ways in which they may be affected. It should also consider the 'knock-on' effects. Somebody else may be able to use the bed. Funds may be allocated to another desirable activity.

A duty to risk?

A reason for early discharge, for example, may be pressure on beds. The reason for allowing a client sharp tools may be a belief in the right to take risks or the need to show trust. These are not disreputable reasons. There are pressures on nurses from the government to make best use of scarce resources. There are care philosophies, such as normalisation, suggesting how nurses should behave and patients should be regarded. So, to an extent, nurses are being told or encouraged to take risks. Community care is a policy full of risks, although highly desirable. These duties should be acknowledged in risk-taking schemes and decisions. They are an important dimension affecting behaviour. Indeed, they may demonstrate that it is a dilemma rather than a risk. Judges should consider the duties to act in particular ways.

Sometimes care policies or goals sound empty or vague: "We believe our patients have a right to individuality, respect and a valued environment." But who doesn't? That policy may actually be empty, or there may be a series of documents or models which show what those proud goals mean in actual daily life. The more that these goals and policies can be converted into statements of what people will actually be doing, then the easier it will be to get them accepted as genuine and important duties in the risk assessment.

Manipulating risks

Risks do not exist in a vacuum. They can be manipulated. The risks involved in not asking a doctor to arrange an admission to hospital can be reduced by ensuring that the patient or an informal carer has a relevant telephone number and knows what signs to look for and how to respond. Just as the amount or likelihood of the harms can be reduced, so can the amount and likelihood of the benefits be maximised. Instead of having a vague objective for a patient of living in an ordinary house in the community, *specific* objectives could be cooking, washing and shopping for himself. The more things that could go right, the more justifiable the decision to risk.

It also becomes possible to re-analyse a risk as a dilemma. Moving someone from a large, rundown institution into an unfamiliar community is facing up to a dilemma. Nurses must do something. Staying there is not good enough, something must be done. Government or health authority policies, scarce resources, professional standards – all can make a risk better analysed as a dilemma.

Informed consent

Getting the patient's informed consent is good practice and it helps to show that the decision to risk was wise. The patient stands to gain or lose, and agrees with the decision. Similarly, colleagues' opinions would help to show that it was not just an individual's opinion and this would add further support.

The decision

No help can be given with the final decision. That is for the individual case and the individual nurse. But any decision to risk should be presented as a decision to obtain certain goals, for certain reasons, in the knowledge of the possibility of (and being prepared for) some harms.

Although this strategy does not solve individual cases, it could encourage more risk-taking. It emphasises the importance of accurately representing the risk and the benefits that could come from it. It discourages the overdramatising which may result from concentration on what might go wrong. It can lead to risk decisions being taken proudly rather than with a measure of shame and regret.

But, it may be objected, this long and detailed approach cannot be used every time a nurse has to decide whether a patient can, for example, go to the toilet unaided. Very true: it could often be impractical. It is an aid to decision-making, not a substitute. But, even if not used in detail, it could aid thinking about risks. What are the advantages of letting the patient go unaided? It encourages thought and responsibility. It justifies drawing the line when insufficient potential benefits can be demonstrated. It can help justify judgements when nurses are pressed to take decisions with which they disapprove. And it should encourage self-esteem through nurses realising the number of risk-taking judgements they make (Carson, 1988).

References

Carson, D. (1987) Negligence: defining responsibility. *The Professional Nurse,* **2,** 141-30.
Carson, D. (1988) Risk-taking policies. *Journal of Social Welfare Law,* 328-332.

46

What are the legal implications of extended nursing roles?

Susannah Derrick, RGN

Senior Staff Nurse, Intensive and Coronary Care Unit, Northwick Park Hospital and Clinical Research Centre

Recent advances in medical technology have led to constant demands being made on both the knowledge and skills of nurses. This is highlighted in 'high tech' areas of nursing such as intensive care and renal units.

Nurses have a complex role in these areas. It requires not only competence in providing basic care, support and education to patient and family, but also a high level of theoretical knowledge and practical skill to understand and contribute to treatment. The role of the specialist nurse encompasses many procedures which have previously been considered within the medical domain, such as venepuncture and emergency defibrillation.

The legal issues

I would suggest that nurses working in these areas extend their role willingly. However, although they are trained for practice, they may not fully appreciate the legal issues surrounding it.

A research case study carried out using RGNs in an intensive/cardiac care unit as a sample population supports this suggestion and has provided factual information on the degree of knowledge and appreciation of the legal implications of the extended role held by this specific population (Derrick, 1987). The study also presents a reasonable overview of the RGN population as a whole, as it demonstrated the broad background and wide range of hospitals and health authorities in which the sample had previously worked.

What is an extended role?

An extended role can be described as one which is not included in basic training. They have developed for various reasons; the most obvious is development of new technology and treatment. However, economic factors can not be overlooked – nursing manpower is cheaper than medical.

In the light of the change and extension of the nursing role the DHSS, medical and nursing professional organisations attempted to clarify the situation. The DHSS issued a circular in 1977 explaining the legal implications and training requirements (DHSS, 1977), and this was supported by a publication from the RCN and BMA (1978). These documents set out some clear guidelines for the management of extended roles for nurses, and are summarised by Rowden (1987.)

The guidelines stress the need for joint discussions, mutual trust and respect between professions and state that extension of role must be in the interests of patient care. An opinion often aired is that on a busy ward where staffing levels are low, skilled nurses should not be using precious time administering intravenous drugs.

The circular also states that 'Work which has hitherto been carried out by doctors ought therefore to be delegated to nurses only when:-
a) The nurse has been specifically and adequately trained for the performance of the new task and she agrees to undertake it;
b) this training has been recognised as satisfactory by the employing Authority;
c) the new task has been recognised by the professions and by the employing Authority as a task which may be properly delegated to a nurse;
d) the delegating doctor has been assured of the competence of the individual nurse concerned.'

It also states:- 'In order to be successful and safe such delegation should be in the context of a clearly defined policy . . . and it should be made known in writing to all staff who are likely to by involved.'

Certification
A certificate of competence is issued for some extended role procedures. Unlike the administration of intravenous drugs (Breckenbridge, 1976) many procedures do not require certification in some authorities but do in others. Certification is not a legal requirement, but it does serve a worthwhile purpose, not just as is sometimes flippantly suggested 'to reassure the nurse'.

Each individual nurse has a choice whether or not to extend her or his role. It can be generally accepted that any nurse choosing to work in specialised fields expects, and is willing to undertake an extended role, and with adequate training should be fully aware of the medical and nursing implications of her or his actions. Comment is rarely made, however, about the importance and need for training to enable nurses to appreciate the legal implications of their actions. This knowledge is surely necessary, and if Derrick's research is representative, it is seriously lacking among the practising nursing profession.

Law and the nurse
Accountability   "Each registered nurse, midwife and health visitor is accountable for his or her practice" (UKCC, 1987). Accountability means

being answerable for work, decisions about work and being professionally responsible for the standard of practice. Nurses are first and foremost legally responsible for each and every nursing action undertaken or omitted, and must practise in accordance with the standard of care of a reasonably prudent nurse practising under the same or similar circumstances. *Primary liability* is held by the individual nurse for her or his own actions.

It is possible for nurses to be persuaded or pressurised into carrying out treatment or procedures – extending their role – either to be helpful or 'to keep the peace', particularly when wards are busy or staffing levels are low. In such instances both medical and nursing staff should have the consequences of the unauthorised practise brought to their attention. Protecting one another from primary liability is a duty everyone should adopt, and be thanked for, albeit as an afterthought.

Negligence   Negligence is divided into three main components (Rea, 1987):
• **The duty of care** The legal duty of care encompasses the professional, moral, ethical and sociological duties of care within which nursing operates. It is what the nurse is required to do under the terms of her contract of employment. Deviation from this in any way is negligence.
• **The breach of the duty**   This is the alleged wrongdoing.
• **The resultant damage** The damage to the patient must be the result of the breach of the duty of care.

The law relating to negligence principally seeks to identify conduct which does not reach an acceptable professional standard. If injury results from such conduct the possibility of an action for damages (compensation) arises. Liability to pay damages may be shouldered individually, covered by an insurance company or by membership of a professional organisation which offers legal liability insurance to its members.

Vicarious liability

In the DHSS circular (1977), and in law, it is made clear that any role extension *must* be approved officially by the employing authority. In the United Kingdom (Master-Servant Statutes) "the law takes the view that the master will accept responsibility for the actions of servants, where the servant is working in accordance with the policies agreed by master and servant" (Rowden, 1987). Within the NHS the employing authority is the master and the nurse the servant. It is normally accepted that the senior nurse will act on behalf of the authority.

In discussion with legal advisers at regional health authority level and advisers at the RCN, two particular issues were highlighted as examples of nurses being asked to carry out procedures they were not trained to do. First, nurses can be persuaded or pressurised into carrying out treatments or procedures – extending their role – either to be helpful or 'to keep the peace', particularly when wards are busy or staffing levels are low. In such instances both medical and nursing staff should have the consequences of the unauthorised practice brought to their attention. Protecting one another from primary liability is a duty everyone should adopt, and be thanked for, albeit as an afterthought.

Second, it is suggested that the insistence of some authorities that nurses hold extended role certificates is good practice. This is not only from the patient's point of view by maintaining standards of care, but of paramount importance to the nurse from the legal standpoint. The health authority will accept responsibility for the actions of nurses when they are working within policies agreed by both parties and officially recorded. If a certificate is not required and the procedure is not recorded in a policy or procedural document, the health authority is *not* aware of the action, so the nurse performing it will hold all responsibility. In the extended role a certificate is proof not only of competence but of the authority's knowledge and agreement for the nurse to practise (Derrick, 1987).

If the authority/employer is to accept legal liability for the action of the

Certificates of competence can protect nurse against liability.

nurse/employee, it is necessary that the authority should know exactly the role being practised and agree to it. This is known as *vicarious liability* (sometimes called secondary liability). Although not a legal requirement, extended role certification is proof of competence and demonstrates the health authority's agreement for the nurse to practise.

It is essential to confirm in writing any extension of role. It is too easy for confusion to arise or a convenient 'lapse of memory' to occur where verbal agreements are concerned. How many times has a doctor been heard to say 'I will cover you'? The number of nurses willing to accept 'cover' in such a way and the belief (perhaps by both parties) in the cover is alarming (Derrick, 1987). Doctors are *not* permitted by their defence organisations to take responsibility for the actions of nurses. When errors occur, for whatever reason, it's every man for himself, with responsibility being tossed from doctor to nurse like a hot potato.

Documenting the extent and boundaries of an extended role may seem tedious and bureaucratic, but it is in the interests of practitioners and patients alike.

Ensuring knowledge

Facilities must be provided within individual health authorities to promote interest in and provide knowledge on the legal side of nursing. Research has highlighted the need to achieve a dramatic improvement in nurses' appreciation and understanding of the implications of the extended role, and with this in mind, and the ever increasing expectation that all nurses at all levels extend their role further, I would make the following recommendations:

- Individuals and management must be alerted to the need for more education.

- The teaching of the legal aspects of nursing should be incorporated into basic training on a formal and mandatory basis and all nurses should be encouraged to question their own knowledge and safeguard their own practise. More effective teaching would result in knowledge being retained.

- Incorporation of the legal implications in the criteria of certification for an extended role procedure would ensure awareness of the policy and requirements of the issuing health authority/employer.

- Attempts should be made to find time and finance to increase the number of study days, teaching sessions, workshops and discussions available.

Each registered nurse, midwife and health visitor is accountable for his or her practice. It is every nurse's individual responsibility to understand the legal implications underlying that accountability. Do you?

References
Derrick, S.M. (1987) Unpublished case study on nurses' appreciation of the legal implications of taking an extended role.
DHSS (1977) The extending role of the clinical nurse – legal implications and training requirements. DHSS, London.
RCN/BMA (1978) The Duties and Position of the Nurse. RCN, London.
Rea, K. (1987) negligence. *Nursing*, **3**, 533.
Rowden, R. (1978) The extended role of the nurse. *Nursing*, **3**, 576.
UKCC (1978) Code of Professional Conduct for the Nurse, Midwife and Health Visitor. UKCC, London.

Your Teaching Role

47

Ward sister: teacher and practitioner?

Sarah Cullingford, RSCN, SRN, PNT
Paediatric Ward Sister

Joan Juniper, SRN, PNT
Sister, Accident Centre, both at Royal Surrey County Hospital Guildford

Juliet Joseph, SRN, SCM, PNT
Midwifery Sister

Maureen Englefield, SRN, SCM, PNT
Clinical Nurse, Community Midwifery

Selvamalar Ratnasingham, SRN, SCM, PNT
Sister Midwifery Unit at St Luke's Hospital, Guildford

Wright (1985) likened the ward sister to a "superhuman personality with dynamic abilities" but recognised that we must be realistic in our expectations.

The ward sister/charge nurse is a key role, having clinical, managerial and teaching responsibilities. Ward based assessment and staff development programmes all make demands on the ward sister as the facilitator of learning, a role which is increasingly emphasised. She has a particularly important part to play with learners: clinical experience enables the learner to develop clinical judgement and expertise.

The exciting feature of the combined responsibility of the ward sister is the inter-action necessary between her clinical expertise and her skills as a teacher or facilitator of learning. As Jarvis and Gibson (1985) point out the teacher/practitioner uses her professional clinical knowledge and skill for the benefit of her patients, and also to help learners prepare for their occupation. To succeed in both roles, she must be both an expert clinician and an expert teacher.

Lack of support

Ironically, the ward sister often lacks support in her teaching role. Ogier (1981), Runciman (1983) and Marson (1984) have suggested competing priorities, lack of time, lack of expert help, difficulty in assessing learners and lack of preparation as factors contributing to the ward sister's difficulties in fulfilling this role.

The English National Board (1985) have stressed their belief that the "further integration of teaching and practice is essential in the future preparation of nurses" and have recommended that all ward sisters complete the National Board Clinical Course 998 — Teaching and

Assessing in Clinical Practice. The Welsh, Scottish and Northern Ireland Boards support the idea that all ward sisters should have this experience.

At the University of Surrey, the Department of Educational Studies is running a course for field work teachers, practical work teachers and ward sisters. We attended the first course open to qualified ward sisters in 1985.

Figure 1. Elements of the course.

The course had a core programme shared by all groups and separate sessions for individual groups in which course tutors examined relationships with practice, requirements of the syllabus, examinations and their application in practice. Three two-week blocks were based at the university and included micro-teaching sessions, development of teaching aids and construction of research proposals. The teaching aids were particularly imaginative and many ideas were exchanged by colleagues:

- Photographs to illustrate child development
- Flip chart
- Tape recordings for use by individuals
- Video to illustrate admitting a patient

Time away from the ward

Time and self confidence are factors that often inhibit ward sisters from getting involved in updating activities. The course offered the opportunity to take time out of the ward, to think clearly, and have this acknowledged as a "respectable" activity. The opportunity to develop understanding between the staff of the school of nursing, the university and the clinical situation was valuable in offering continued support.

Learning can be a passive activity: ward sisters can take a positive role in enabling learners to be more active in their learning. A team approach to this is useful and a 'resource' centre with booklists, relevant articles and other sources can stimulate both learners and colleagues alike.

Ward sisters are often assumed to be able to 'cope' and respond to the various demands made of them. The course acknowledged ward sisters' need for the opportunity to learn and in so doing made them less isolated. Knowledge of counselling skills and coping with unusual or threatening situations gave more confidence in dealing with daily situations. And most important: we grasped how to make the most out of every potential learning opportunity.

References
Wright, E. (1985) Taking Charge: a newly appointed ward sister, *The Professional Nurse*, **1**, 7-9.
Runciman, P. (1983) Ward Sisters at Work. Churchill Livingstone Edinburgh.
Ogier, M. (1981) Ward sisters and their influence upon nurse learners. *Nursing Times* Occasional Paper 77, No.11.
Marson, S. (1984) Developing the 'teaching' role of the ward sister. *Nurse Education Today*, **4**, 1.
Jarvis, P. and Gibson, S. (1985) Teacher Practitioner in Nursing, Midwifery and Health Visiting. Croom Helm, Beckenham.
English National Board (1985) Professional Education Training Course (Consultative Paper) English National Board, London.

The significance of including ward sisters in the course

Rosemary Bryant, SRN, RNT, MSc.,
Director of Nurse Education, St. Luke's Hospital, Guildford

In the last 10 to 15 years a number of developments have increased ward sisters' involvement in the training of student nurses. Obvious examples are ward based assessments; the identification of ward learning objectives; module/units of learning relating theory and practice and plans for continuing assessment. But all too often the ward sister has not been actively involved in these curriculum developments largely because she continues to feel unprepared. (Farnish, 1983, Bryant, 1985).

Present changes in basic and continuing nurse education make a closer working partnership between nurse teachers and nurse practitioners even more necessary. The devolved arrangements for the qualifying examinations are one opportunity to use the experience of those who are now practical examiners in contributing to the larger picture of assessment. More and more schools of nursing are moving towards a pattern of continuing assessment, (ENB, 1986). This involves both the ward sister and experienced staff nurses.

Courses for clinical teachers cease   A further significant move is the discontinuation of courses to prepare clinical nurse teachers. It has been argued that clinical nurse teachers are ''bridging the gap which doubtless should not have been created'', (GNC, 1975). Closing this gap between theory and practice surely depends on tutors who have an integrated plan of learning for both clinical areas and classroom. It also depends on sisters who are suitably prepared to form a partnership with teachers in developing an integrated curriculum. This is why sisters and charge nurses have been included in the Teacher Practitioner Course at the University of Surrey. The teacher practitioner is building on existing teaching skills and exploring the context in which his/her contribution to student learning takes place. Sisters already have considerable responsibilities for the learning of student nurses which, it is argued, now need to be matched with appropriate preparation and support through a partnership with nurse teachers.

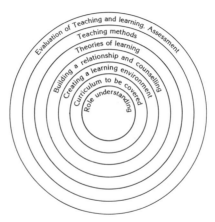

Figure 1. Curriculum Model.

Figure 1 shows the curriculum model underpinning the course with the central pivot being role understanding. The theoretical aspects of the course build on this fundamental analysis of the role of the ward sister.

Confidence in confronting situations   The Teacher Practitioner Course gives ward sisters greater understanding of students' needs. They have more knowledge of counselling and coping with confronting situations which will give them confidence in dealing with unusual situations in future. They are far better able to join in a dialogue with nurse teachers regarding the curriculum and particularly in the linking of theory and practice.

Due to the success of Teacher Practitioner course, we expect sisters and charge nurses in all training wards and departments to attend. The ENB award a Statement of Attendance, as for Course 998 (Teaching and

Assessing in Clinical Practice). However, the Teacher Practitioner course covers 30 days, with assessed course work and supervised teaching practice. The requirements thus equate with those for Practical Work and Fieldwork Teachers' Certificates awarded by the ENB.

References

Bryant, R. (1985) The Role and Preparation of the Ward Sister involved in Nurse Training. Unpublished MSc dissertation. University of Surrey.

English National Board (1986) Continuing Assessment and the Present Position Regarding the Final Written Examination. Circular 1986 (16) ERBD March 1986.

General Nursing Council. Teachers of Nursing 1975 as appendix to circular 78/38/A. Teachers of Nursing 1976.

Farnish, S. (1983) Preparation of Ward Sisters; a Survey in Three Hospitals. Nursing Education Research Unit Dept Nusing Studies, Chelsea College, University of London.

48

Promoting self-directed enquiry

Janice Hoover, BScN, RN, SRN
Nurse Teacher, Combined Training Institute, South Glamorgan

Much of student nurses' learning is passive, the mere ingestion of facts to be regurgitated at a later date to obtain a grade in an exam. It is not uncommon to hear student nurses asking qualified nurses to impart their textbook knowledge to them: ''Teach me about congestive cardiac failure''. How do nurses learn and develop once they become qualified, when to ask such questions is unacceptable? Besides, who would the qualified nurse ask?

Ward sister role
In March, 1986, at a study day organised by the King's Fund Centre in London, my nurse manager, ward nursing tutor and myself (then a ward sister) were asked as a 'triad' from Llandough Hospital, South Glamorgan Health Authority, to consider one aspect of 'The developing role of the ward sister'. Interested in attacking this problem of passivity in nurse learning and in finding a way to encourage staff members to assist themselves to learn, we chose to examine the ward sister's role as an educator. So we began the 'nursing care conferences' on our ward (an acute 30-bed medical/geriatric ward).

In 1968, Knowles popularised the word "andragogy" which describes an emerging science of adult learning. The greatest learning experiences are believed to result from methods which involves the learner intensely in self-directed enquiry. Adult learning is thought to be a process which occurs within the individual (Rosendahl, 1974).

The educator does not merely transmit knowledge, but facilitates another person's learning through self-directed enquiry. This is what we set out to achieve, with the nursing care conferences.

It was planned to ask a qualified nurse or two or three learners to present a nursing article, nursing care plan or topic of nursing interest to the rest of the ward nursing team for group consideration and discussion. Each presentation was to last from 30 to 40 minutes. We hoped that this would be a first step towards stimulating a life long habit of self-directed enquiry.

We devised a questionnaire to measure nurses' attitudes and behaviour related to the self-directed learning process. We wanted to measure these variables before and after participation in the project to determine the project's success and, to discover any correlation between different nursing grades and initiative in self-learning. However, due to our questionnaire's small sample size, we felt that to do so would have threatened the anonymity of everyone completing the questionnaire. Also, any correlation which we might have found using such a small sample would not have been particularly significant. The pre-project questionnaire results, however, did provide us with the ward nurses' overall support for our project. Most were "keen" or "very keen" to participate and thought that they would learn more by presenting a topic for discussion rather than by listening to topics presented by others.

Change, no matter how well supported, can lead to staff resistance, so we attempted to establish as much favour for the project as possible. The following techniques (New and Couillard, 1981) were used:

Presentation

● **Education** Six weeks before the project started, it was explained to the staff that a great deal could be learned by sharing their different nursing interests, knowledge and experience with each other. Current good patient care on the ward could only stand to improve further from such an exchange. It was also explained in detail how the project was to be implemented and what would be expected of both the presenters and the rest of the group.

● **Gradual introduction** Introducing the project well in advance, gave the staff time and opportunity to realise the benefits of the change. The ward sister presented the first conference to demonstrate what was expected. They were held once a fortnight to allow individuals time to adapt to the idea. Each nurse was given her presentation date at least one month in advance to give her time to prepare.

● **Supportive behaviour** To assist anyone with any difficulties in selecting or presenting their topic of interest, the ward sister offered herself as a resource person (with the stipulation that she be given 'reasonable' notification of any help required). It was stressed that the project was not a competition though it was hoped that individuals would be spurred on by each other's interesting presentations to do their best.

● **Incentives** With a schedule of fortnightly conferences, each individual was called on to present a topic approximately only once every eight months. It was stressed that the rest of the time one was free to enjoy listening to others' presentations.

● **Participation** While the design and implementation of the project had already been decided, an enthusiastic senior staff nurse was asked to promote the most positive aspects of the project to the others.

Expectations

Two further techniques were employed to lessen resistance to change. First, the more enthusiastic individuals were selected to present topics first in the hope that they might generate enthusiasm in the others. Second, high expectations of the presentations going ahead as scheduled were set by the ward sister. Postponements because of difficulties in completing work on time were not considered without a strong suggestion that more efficient organisation of time could get the job done. It was hoped that if people were tacitly 'expected' to complete a task, they would feel an onus on them to do so.

Once the nursing care conferences began in July, 1986, it became the ward sister's responsibility to ask the group questions and to stimulate thoughtful creative discussion relevant to the group's area of practice (Plummer, 1974).

This focusing on the specific problems of everyday practice was vital in making the conferences interesting and valuable as a learning experience for everyone. Praise and encouragement were given to presenters and the non-presenters when merited to reinforce individuals' positive feeling about themselves and their abilities and accomplishments. At the time of writing it was not possible to measure the project's success because not everyone had presented their first topic.

Staff perceptions

More than half the nurses (of all grades) commented that they thought that the conferences were a good idea, in that they helped to keep them up-to-date. They viewed this as very important and, were keen to apply new knowledge which they acquired from the sessions. The more relevant and interesting they perceived the topics and related discussions to be, the more actively and enthusiatically they participated in the conferences.

Motivation

The conferences provided the motivating environment now thought necessary for learning (Gordon 1982). They were a channel, throught which individual enquiry (coupled with group discussion) into topics of each individual's own nursing interests was directed. With the ward sister's help as a conference leader, staff confidence in presenting their findings to the rest of the ward nursing team expanded. Staff development and education were facilitated with minimal extra resources and it is hoped that a broad foundation was laid for a life-time of learning.

Bibliography
United Kingdom Central Council for Nursing Midwifery and Health Visiting, Educational Policy Advisory Committee, (1986) 'Project 2000, A New Preparation for Practice'. Proposals for the education of nurses in Great Britain by the year 2000.

References

Gordon, G.K. (1982) Motivating staff: A look at assumptions. *The Journal of Nursing Administration,* **12,** 11, 28.

New, J.R. et al, (1981) Guidelines for introducing change. *The Journal of Nursing Administration,* **11,** 3, 18-20.

Plummer, E.m. (1974) The clinical conference discussion leader. *Nursing Forum,* **13,** 1, 94 and 103.

Rosendahl, P. (1974) Self-direction for learners: an andragogical approach to nursing education. *Nursing Forum,* **13,** 2, 138.

N.B. In our initial literature search we uncovered 150 journal articles of potential interest to our project. Of these, we selected 25 of what we felt would be the most relevant articles to read through. The above references comprise those articles which we ultimately found to be the most significant for our purposes. An additional bibliography of the remaining 21 articles is available upon request from Janice Hoover, Nurse Teacher, Combined Training Institute, Heath Park, Cardiff, CF4 4XW.

49

The age gap: teaching students about health education for the elderly

Beverley Holloway, RGN, Cert Ed

Nurse Tutor, The Portsmouth District School of Nursing, Portsmouth, formerly at Chichester and Graylingwell School of Nursing

Evidence shows that the average age of the UK's population is increasing (Phillipson, 1985). With continuing general improvements in healthcare helping people to live longer, the elderly are an increasingly large group of the hospital population. Student nurses will therefore be exposed to large numbers of elderly people throughout their training and future careers, so it is important that aspects of caring for the elderly well, rather than simply the elderly sick are considered.

When teaching student nurses about the health education needs of the elderly, the teacher is confronted with the same problems that have made the appropriate and effective provision of health education for elderly people so difficult. This in itself can provide a powerful experiential tool with which to examine the issues surrounding this area of health promotion. These problems include ageism stereotyping and a difference between normative and expressed needs.

The students reach their care of the elderly module at the end of the first year. At this stage, each has experienced three clinical placements: a basic care ward – which may be medical, surgical, or elderly nursing, – followed by medical and surgical placements. Consequently, some will have already come into contact with elderly people.

Students' attitudes

A useful starting point when teaching student nurses about health promotion in elderly people is to encourage exploration of their own attitudes to them. Despite the fact that many are familiar with elderly people on a personal level, or have worked in nursing and rest homes, and claim an affection for them, accurate analysis of perceptions often reveals issues which need to be discussed and clarified. Skeet (1985), claims that: "Looming over all these major issues is ageism – the deeply rooted discrimination against the elderly . . . one source of this prejudice is the fear among young and middle-aged people of joining the ranks of the ignored and the dispensable. . ." To allow student nurses to function with elderly people they must be given the opportunity, through discussion, to free themselves from the constraints of an ageist approach. This does not detract from the effect of the attitudes of the elderly themselves, and students need to be made aware of the often fatalistic view adopted by the elderly: Muir-Gray (1983) found that some elderly patients felt they should avoid exercise as 'the body will wear out'.

Students are asked to write down their feelings about being old, and how they imagine they will be when they reach old age. Responses vary; some students openly admit they are frightened by the prospect of being old and alone; others feel they would be frustrated by not being able to do things they wanted. Overwhelmingly however, students find it almost impossible to imagine what it is like to be elderly, and it is generally found enlightening to discuss what effects this inability to imagine has on the care given to the elderly.

A further productive exercise is to ask students to describe elderly stereotypes; these frequently resemble those cited by Brearley (1975) "the rigid, inflexible, dogmatic elder or the charitable, loyal, upright figure." A recent addition to this list was described by one student nurse as "a

cantankerous old so-and-so". The effects of stereotyping can then be discussed, for as Brearley points out "it is a small step from the acceptance of the stereotype to the adoption of it personally."

Thus, attitudes and images, particularly in the negative sense with ageism and stereotyping, can be raised as important influences in health promotion for the elderly. Comparing different perceptions of needs of the elderly appears to generate interest and concern for them in the students. They are asked to determine what they see as the health education needs of the elderly. They are then asked to examine either normative needs or felt and expressed needs. Various methods of data collection are used, as the students feel appropriate, and this will usually include interviews with professionals and elderly people, literature reviews, and amassing available health education or promotion material.

Role play
An alternative method, depending on time availability, involves dividing the students into small groups, and asking them to imagine that they are either a group of elderly people or nurses working in a care of the elderly unit. They are then asked what they feel the health education needs of the elderly might be. Each group can be carefully selected depending on their responses to how they feel about becoming old themselves. The exercise appears to work well in that each group tends to identify different aspects of health education.

Students are usually surprised to discover a gulf between normative needs and expressed needs of the elderly. Their own beliefs are frequently similar to those of health professionals, such as emphasis on hypothermia or the need for mobility. The greatest impact, however, occurs when the students analyse the responses of the well elderly people they have interviewed (where possible), and discover the elderly themselves are less concerned with physical or even specific aspects of health, but see social and psychological health as most important. Overwhelmingly the elderly articulate their problems in financial terms, expressing particular needs such as assistance with telephone installation and bills. The lack of awareness regarding the services and schemes that are available to assist them financially enforces the sometimes inadequate or inappropriate provision of health education or promotion. To simply criticise existing provision would not only be a negative exercise, but would also deny the valuable contribution made by many groups, organisations and individuals concerned with caring and providing for the health of the elderly.

The next activity requires the students to find out what exists in terms of health education, and who is making the provision. They are asked to find examples from each tier of the national framework which exists to meet the needs of the elderly. At central government level they can explore provision made by the Department of Health, and that of Social Security, at a local level how the NHS and local authorities provide for their elderly, and – importantly – the work of the voluntary organisations. This latter group is particularly welcoming, encouraging students to look at their work. Age Concern West Sussex has developed an especially close liaison with the local nurse students; the group, and in particular their health education adviser (jointly appointed with three health authorities), are keen for the students to become involved in the awareness of health education problems affecting the elderly.

Purpose-made materials

Apart from a global view of how organisations work, students are encouraged to examine specifically produced materials for the elderly, such as 'Helping Yourself to Health', a resource pack produced as part of the Pensioners' Link Health Education Project (1987). Our district health authority's education department is extremely helpful in allowing students to explore the resources they have on offer for groups and individuals within the district. With this information, the students can identify and piece together a picture of what material is available locally for health professionals to use when providing elderly people with health education. At this point it is useful to look at the disciplines involved, and it is important to air feelings about other professional groups, as this may uncover negative attitudes. An understanding and acceptance of contributions made by all the different groups and individuals encountering the elderly is desirable to maximise and coordinate efforts. Nurses, working in a variety of settings, form one of the many groups, and the student nurses are asked to think about their possible contribution, before going on to list other groups whom they believe contribute to the health education of the elderly.

Planning to meet needs

As a final exercise the students are divided into groups of three or four and asked to draw up a plan to meet the health education needs of the elderly. They are asked to look at what provision is required nationally, locally and individually and to say how they feel this could be best achieved. The students are also asked to think about how they could provide health education for those already in hospital. It is encouraging that by this stage they usually state the importance of listening to what the patient says. Having shared their ideas, the session closes with a look at the work of Brocklehurst (1976) and Phillipson (1985) whose contributions to this field have been significant.

While these exercises have been designed to be carried out in the classroom-based setting, they are readily adaptable for use in clinical placements, be it in hospital or the community. Caring for the elderly has historically been seen as lacking both appeal and glamour. However, more recently there has been a thrust towards promoting interest and a positive image in this field. It is hoped that by teaching today's students about this vital area and by facilitating their confrontation of the issues

254   *Your Teaching Role*

surrounding the elderly, they will be able to competently make useful contributions to an already committed team.

Bibliography

The following sources of information are recommended to those wishing to further explore this subject.

Garrett, G. (1983) Health Needs of the Elderly. Macmillan, London.

An extremely readable book, this would be an excellent place to start for anyone wanting to gain an overview of the health needs of the elderly.

McClymont, M., Thomas S., Denham, M. (1986) Health Visiting and the Elderly. Churchill Livingstone, Edinburgh.

A useful book, not only for health visitors, but for any health professional wanting to understand more about the application of health education theory to practice with the elderly.

Muir-Gray, J. and McKenzie, H. (1986) Caring for Older People. Penguin, Harmondsworth.

A comprehensive, practical book, focusing clearly on the health needs of the elderly. The information is useful to professionals, families with elderly members, and the elderly themselves.

Tinker, A. (1986) The Elderly in Modern Society. Longman, Harlow.

A background of how the elderly have come to be in their present position in society. The book not only presents information clearly, but looks at existing literature and relevant research.

For further resources, or specific information the reader is advised to contact their local Health Education Department, local voluntary organisation such as Age Concern or the Health Education Authority.

References

Brearley, C.P. (1975) Social Work, Ageing and Society. Routledge and Kegan Paul Ltd., London.

Brocklehurst, J.C. (1976) Health education in the elderly. *Journal of the Institute of Health Education,* **14,** 4, 115-20.

Muir-Gray, J. (1983) Beliefs and attitudes – the ageing process (2), August 17, *Nursing Mirror.* 36-37.

Pensioners' Link Health Education Project (1987) 'Helping Yourself To Health' Pensioners Link.

Phillipson, C. (1985) Developing a health education strategy with older people. *Journal of the Institute of Education,* **23,** 3, 184-87.

Skeet, M. (1985) 'Some international concepts of old age'. *Nursing,* **41.**

50

Building confidence: a development programme for newly qualified staff nurses

Sue Thame, BA
Independent Management Trainer, Pinner, Middlesex

When you first qualified as a staff nurse, would you have welcomed yet more training? The findings of a review conducted by Hillingdon Health Authority (1986) clearly showed that one of the major causes of dissatisfaction among nurses was the lack of training and education immediately after qualification. The authority therefore made it a priority to pioneer a development programme for newly qualified staff nurses.

Setting up the programme

In June 1987 Barbara Baker, an experienced nursing tutor, was appointed Senior Nurse Professional Development, with a remit to create a programme for newly qualified staff nurses. The key purpose was to prepare a more confident and skilled staff nurse for the future, and help with retention and recruitment.

The programme outline suggested a two year course (later amended to 12 months) and newly qualified staff nurses would be recruited both internally and nationally. They would be offered an attractive package: five days off-the-job training in management and interpersonal skills; three-monthly study days in their own selected subject areas; on-the-job support and counselling from a full-time nursing tutor; on-going written assignments; and planned four-monthly rotations between different wards. The nurses' individual development would be based on their own assessments of their areas of greatest need, drawn from a broad spectrum of learning objectives. Their choices would be made in consultation with the nurse tutor and their nurse managers. The heart of the programme was to be the on-the-job counselling and support. This programme outline has been fully implemented.

My involvement in this project came about by invitation from Barbara Baker. I was already working with Hillingdon on an extended programme for nurses to improve their communication skills. Mounting such a major project within tight deadlines could have been more than just a headache – it could have spelt disaster. The coordination and communication required was extensive – not least finding, within a year,

30 nurse managers who would enthusiastically accept and train a revolving nursing staff. The Authority, however, organised itself efficiently by establishing a steering group that could be effective across the district, co-opting people who were enthusiastic, believed in the basic concept and could communicate across the hospital complex. The steering group had to influence people with hard facts and persuasive argument to obtain the resources and commitments required.

Since the new programme was to be based on findings of Rogers and Lawrence (1987) it was essential that all those involved agreed the basic rationale behind it. There were also all the politics of organisational life that must be attended to, in order to manage an innovation like this successfully. Too often, the power games for managing innovation are dealt with *sotto voce*, as if it is not quite 'naice' to speak and think the politics of a situation through clearly. The steering group's composition ensured the delicacies of diplomacy would be addressed. Each hospital and the community was represented on the group by a senior nursing manager. There was a senior representative from the nurse planning committee, a tutor from post basic education and Barbara Baker herself.

The programme

The first programme began in February 1988 and we now have some measure of the impact on the initial five participants, all of whom have found the programme a positive experience. Perhaps the most noticeable strength of the programme is its clear learning objectives. For the first time there is a full picture of what kinds of development a newly qualified staff nurse requires, with real support in attaining those aims.

At the start of the course the nurses are given a 20 page document on guidelines and objectives of the course (Baker, 1987). Daunting? Perhaps – until they see and understand the treasures it offers. It is their route to learner-centred development, and to taking charge of their own development. There is a comprehensive description of the aims and structure of the course and a full listing of the range of learning objectives they can choose to pursue for themselves (Table 1). Later they receive a profiling instrument to help them assess their starting point across all the learning objectives – to select their priorities for development. The evaluation forms, which enable the nurses to monitor their own progress, are used at the end of their ward allocations.

This comprehensive documentation ensouls the philosophy being pioneered at Hillingdon, and if my reading of the literature is correct, they are pioneers within the NHS as a whole too. At the core of their approach is the belief, from their own experience, that an effective hospital service must be based on a workforce constantly aware of the need to learn and change. Responsibility of this kind must be shared between employer and employee, because neither, alone, can know what is best. Both sides must interact to identify individual and group learning needs and to meet those needs. Nurses have traditionally been spoon-fed their basic

Six Key Aims

1. Interpersonal skills
At the end of the course the nurse will have an appreciation of the factors involved in good communications and an increased awareness of self and others.
Four specific objectives are listed eg, use a problem solving approach
: thinking skills
: transactional analysis

2. Management of patient care
At the end of the course the nurse will understand the principles of clinical management and the role and responsibility of the staff nurse.
The nurse will be able to draw up and administer the individual nursing care plans based on the nursing process following the pattern of assessing needs, planning nursing care programmes, delivery of the care and evaluation.
Seven specific objectives are listed eg, identify features of stress and anxiety in patients and relatives
: signs of stress
: symptoms of stress
: stress in hospitals

3. Teaching and assessing
The nurses will have an understanding of the learning process and a basic knowledge and skill in teaching and assessing.
Fourteen specific objectives are listed eg, identify the factors which stimulate and sustain motivation in learners
: needs, drives, motives
: need to achieve and fear of failure
: rewards and punishment
: nature and necessity of feedback
And so on with   Aim Four – Ward Management
Aim Five – Personnel Management
Aim Six – Nursing Research

The 'B' Model (O'Neill, unpublished).
The Colours Model (Rhodes and Thame, 1988).
Transactional Analysis (Harris, 1973).
Temperaments Model for Stress (Thame, unpublished).
Maslow's Hierarchy of Needs (1954).
Theory X and Y (McGregor, 1960)
Hygiene and Motivation Factors (Herzberg, 1966).

Table 1. Staff nurse development aims and learning objectives.

Table 2. Models used in the staff development programme.

training in an authoritarian teaching environment that ill-prepares them for the dynamic responsibilities they have to face on the ward. Their further education has been conspicuously neglected. Now, when their demands for more training are being heard, the time is also right for them to collaborate in shaping their own further development.

Shifting into this mode of joint-responsibility requires a bit of a helping hand from those who have more experience and the will to show the way. Practical tools are also needed, like the guidelines given to participants, which show nurses how to start assessing themselves, start discussing their progress with other more senior people and making judgements for themselves on what to pursue for their own development.

The Hillingdon programme of self-development is supported by an off-the-job programme in which the nurses attend a five-day course with an emphasis on raising their self-awareness. This involves profiles, questionnaires and exercises which introduce them to different models and languages for understanding their thinking style and behavioural styles (Table 2). The nurses find the introduction to this approach exciting because for most of them psychology is a new world – and this approach involves the psychology of health and self-confidence through self-awareness, rather than the psychology of illness.

Underlying the variety of approaches is a common thread – the unravelling of the processes of management and communication. The key to development, as we see it, is systems learning; recognising patterns within different kinds of data, so that knowledge from one situation can be transferred to the next. Although this is central to the nursing process, many nurses find it difficult to understand and apply. This is a special field of research and study by our consultancy (Rhodes and Thame, 1988), so our knowhow fitted well with the aims set out in the staff development programme.

Self-confidence
The first week of the programme devotes a lot of time to issues of self-confidence. On the fourth day there is a major exercise originally devised for salesmen, which involves a brain-storm in which the nurses generate lists of adjectives to describe their personalities to one another. They sort and categorise the listings into positive and negative attributes, based on observed behaviours during the course, then identify how each individual can work to capitalise on their strengths and improve on their weaknesses. Handling this kind of exercise must be done skillfully to ensure the individuals can work together honestly and supportively – its successful completion gives the nurses a real insight into the subtleties of self-assessment and leads to self-evaluation later in this programme.

The final day of the first week focuses on identifying key objectives for each nurse to work on. Although this is a detailed piece of work which involves considering many learning objectives, it is rewarding for the nurses because it sets the path for the kinds of tasks each must keep in the forefront of their mind. The week finishes with a visit to their new wards.

On-job learning
During their first months on the job the nurses are asked to keep a

personal diary to encourage them in the processes of inner reflection. It is suggested that they write notes on their thoughts and feelings, what upsets them, what gives them pleasure, who they learn from, who makes difficulties, and so on. They are then asked to complete written assignments from the diaries, applying the behavioural models to real life happenings on the ward. This encourages them to look more objectively at situations which may have upset them at the time.

Throughout these weeks on the ward the nurses are visited and encouraged by the programme's nurse tutor, David Richards. Since this is David's first tutoring post, he has had to find his way, like the young nurses in the wards. This is especially exciting because it demonstrates the best qualities of joint development. David understands the ward situation, and his caring approach means the nurses have someone to turn to who knows the difficulties they face. At the same time, he can view their development not as their direct manager but indirectly, working with managers to enhance the nurses' learning opportunities.

Our first study day, held in May 1988, produced encouraging developments. We began by reviewing the nurses' assignments, and heard some moving accounts of how they had tackled difficult situations using the behaviour models to help them analyse other people's intentions and shape their own responses. One particularly moving account told how one of the nurses encountered a desperately ill female patient who appeared to be showing aggression. Other nurses were struggling to restrain her, and the scene was violent and distressing. The nurse looked beyond the appearances, and recognised that the woman was terrified. A loving and calming hand was stretched out to her, soothed her and she became peaceful. A short while later she died. The nurse felt glad to have brought peace at the end.

The next activity was a series of role-plays through which the nurses could prepare for their next assignments. This involved their interviewing a senior member of staff to obtain information about a subject area they particularly wanted to investigate, linked to one of their learning objectives. For example, if they wished to extend their understanding of manpower management, they would interview a senior personnel officer. The nurses' first reactions were fear – they do not have much contact with senior people's roles, but after we had finished the role-plays they felt confident and excited at the prospects.

These assignments began in May 1988, and the first few months' progress caused great enthusiasm among the nurses. Later they attended the ENB 998 Teaching and Assessing course, and did a variety of assignments based around their six weekly off-the-job study days.

The nurses who joined the first programme have now graduated, and some plan to pursue their professional development through the Diploma in Nursing. The reports of their work have all been excellent and they have developed their confidence and skills in both practical nursing and communications. Due to the programme's good reputation, nurses are applying for the three annual intakes from within Hillingdon, though the district is maintaining national advertising to attract new people. The programme is a progressive and successful approach to staff development.

References

Baker, B. (1987) Guidelines of Course and Objectives. Hillingdon Health Authority, London.

Harris, T. (1973) I'm OK, You're OK. Pan, London.

Herzberg, F. (1966) Work and the Nature of Man. World Publishing, Cleveland, Ohio.

McGregor, D. (1960) The Human Side of Enterprise. McGraw-Hill, New York.

Maslow, A.H. (1954) Motivation and Personality. Harper and Row, New York.

O'Neill, H. (Unpublished) The 'B' Model. Research for London Borough of Hillingdon.

Rhodes, J. and Thame, S. (1988) The Colours of Your Mind. Collins, London.

Rogers, J. and Lawrence, J. (1987) Continuing Professional Education for Qualified Nurses, Midwives and Health Visitors. Ashdale Press and Austen Cornish Publishers, London.

Thame, S. (Unpublished) Temperament Model For Stress.

51

Participation in a curriculum committee

Patricia M. Stephenson, MSc, Dip.Curr.Dev, RGN, RNT, DN, OND
Lecturer in Nursing, University of Manchester

The busy ward sister or charge nurse may view an invitation to sit on a curriculum committee as a mixed blessing. Their reaction may be "Great, I'd like to be involved because clinical staff should have a major input into what students are taught". A simultaneous reaction might be "Help! Can I cope with all the extra work? What will be expected of me and what do I need to know?" These reactions are understandable so this article offers some suggestions which may help in preparing for and working on a curriculum committee.

Prior to commencing work on a committee new members will need to know what definition for the term 'curriculum' is being used by colleagues, and may need access to sources of information on the curriculum, about colleagues' expectations of them and about facilitation of curriculum planning.

Sources of information

Clinical members of curriculum committees are usually appointed because of their expertise in their present area of practice, so they are expected to be knowledgeable about current trends and developments in practice and curricula in the specialty. Specialty experts usually exchange ideas about educational programmes, innovations, research

- Minutes of previous meetings.
- A set of National Board for Nursing, Midwifery and Health Visiting circulars related to the course.
- District Health Authority policy documents which may have relevance for course design.
- A copy of the present curriculum which is to be developed or replaced.
- Clinical allocation information, eg clinical areas approved by the National Board, areas in current use, present levels of trained staff.

Figure 1. Documents for new curriculum committee members.

and practice through meetings and specialty journals. A visit to another course centre may provide an opportunity to see a curriculum of similar type and may suggest alternative approaches to learning and teaching.

A visit to the allocation officer in the school of nursing may yield many benefits in helping the new member to make sense of the clinical allocation system in current use for the course being developed. Graphic plans of the size, sequence and 'flow' of groups of students through clinical areas may be much easier to understand than raw computer print-outs, so it is useful to ask to see different presentations of allocation material. Systems may be perfectly clear to the person who designed them, but may fail to give a clear message to the noninitiated. A clearly presented plan containing a comprehensive key to its symbols is a great asset to the new committee member. Some curriculum committees facilitate new members' orientation by giving them an initial set of documents as listed in Figure 1.

Representing colleagues

When being appointed to a committee, it is important for new members to establish whether they are there to represent their colleagues or as an individual who will give their own opinions. If they are to represent, for example, sisters or students, a clear network of communications should be established with the following aims:

- to seek the views of as many colleagues as possible on issues to be discussed and decided at meetings;
- to feed back information to colleagues on curriculum decisions;
- to discover colleagues' reactions to decisions;
- to identify problems related to the introduction of change;
- to feedback information to the curriculum committee from the colleagues represented.

This network can consist of seeing each colleague individually and explaining the issues, but this can be time consuming and is not advisable for most issues. There are however occasions where only one-to-one, face-to-face discussion will accomplish a task to the satisfaction of both individuals.

In most communication tasks related to canvassing and disseminating information, opinions and reactions to curriculum proposals, group discussions with all the colleagues represented is recommended. Change theories indicate that people who will be affected by a change are more likely to help in its implementation if they have participated at all stages in the planning of the change (Miller and Mauksch, 1982; Lancaster and Lancaster, 1983). It may be expedient to arrange a meeting with colleagues after each curriculum meeting so that information can be imparted about development of the curriculum so far and ideas, proposals and responses to items on the agenda for the next meeting obtained. It would also be an opportunity for seeking colleagues' advice on planning matters related to any sub-committee work which is being undertaken such as planning an aspect of the curriculum.

When there are contentious issues to be debated and eventually decided upon in the curriculum committee, the case presented by the member will be stronger and likely to be given more consideration if it can be stated to be the unanimous view of all sisters on a unit who discussed the matter at a recent meeting and made their recommendations. If a person is acting in committee as a representative of a group of colleagues it is expected that they will indicate when they are giving their personal views and when they are presenting the views of the group represented.

Facilitating curriculum planning

Knowledge of curriculum theory and research aids understanding, the quality of debate and decision making in curriculum meetings, so senior staff in many schools of nursing have organised curriculum workshops which are attended by all committee members. The workshops are sometimes shared by staff from other schools of nursing, midwifery or paramedical professions, so that there can be a 'cross fertilisation' of ideas, and experiences and problems may be shared. An example of topics included in many curriculum workshops is included in Figure 2.

- The nature of nursing and educational knowledge.
- Curriculum theory and planning.
- Management of educational innovation and change.
- Curriculum process and evaluation.
- Assessment and examination – theory and practice.

Figure 2. Topics for a curriculum workshop.

A lead lecture may provide information, issues for discussion and act as a catalyst for group work by participants. Meaningful learning and new ways of looking at many practices can originate from the group discussions in the workshop, and this is facilitated by the use of learning resources such as handouts, books and journals which are usually provided by the librarian for reference.

The scope of this article does not allow for discussion about how to design or develop curricula, but Figure 3 contains a sample of articles and books which could act as starting points for learning and exploring areas of curriculum theory and design.

Structure and function of the committee

Membership of a nursing curriculum committee may consist of students, nurse educationalists, practitioners, managers, general educationalists and other professionals. The contributions of doctors, physiotherapists,

Topics	Authors
Introduction to designing nursing curricula.	Heath (1982)
Models of nursing.	Kershaw and Salvage (1986)
Models of nursing in curriculum development.	Vaughan (1986)
Models of curriculum. Designing a learning programme. Teachers' roles. Assessing students' work.	Jarvis and Gibson (1986)
A research based method of selecting curriculum content.	Stephenson (1985)

Figure 3. References related to curriculum development.

speech therapists and others are important but the range of professions represented on a committee will depend on the type and level of course being planned. General educationalists from higher education are usually included to give expert educational advice and they can also present a consumer's view on issues. A member of the District Health Authority (DHA) or Community Health Council (CHC) may also be invited to join the committee as an official representative of consumers.

Knowing who the committee members are, where they come from and what work they do is essential in establishing effective working relationships. It also aids understanding of the context from which they will make suggestions or proposals in meetings. Knowing the professional background and interests of other members can also be useful when the new member is asked to choose which working group of the committee they wish to join. Working groups usually meet more frequently than the committee, and have a task to accomplish and a report to make to the committee. It is important that the terms of reference and the objectives of the group are clear and that the time scale for completion of the work is defined.

The committee will usually have regular committee meetings with the dates published well in advance. Agendas for meetings and minutes of meetings are usually circulated; which ensures that members who have missed a meeting can come to the next meeting knowing about any decisions which were made. It can be frustrating if a member who was absent from a meeting insists on rediscussing issues which have been fully explored and decided upon in their absence.

How groups work

The process of group dynamics is fascinating in curriculum meetings. The new member is well advised to be a good listener during the first few meetings to assess the professional orientations, knowledge, personalities and value positions of fellow members. For example, some members are the ideas people with lots of new and creative suggestions to make and plans to propose, while others have the ideas but become unstuck when feasible planning suggestions are required. Some will weigh up information and discussion in a meeting, jot down points and only after they have heard all sides of the argument will they offer their point of view in a succinct and balanced way and others will present 'red herrings' and 'go off at a tangent' from the issue being discussed. Much time can be wasted if the chairman does not redirect the discussion to its central theme. As many members pursue 'red herrings' at some time, no-one should feel aggrieved when the chairman has to tactfully move the discussion away from the speaker.

Other actions of committee members can include persistently introducing a topic into every agenda item, regardless of its relevance to the issue. It may be a value or position which they wish to promote or they may wish to emphasise their view of the superiority of their specialty over others, but whatever the reason or the topic, members can become irritated with and unsympathetic toward the proposer. Nonverbal cues and tone of voice of other members will usually indicate to a speaker when they should drop a topic from the discussion.

There will usually be people proposing and opposing change in the committee, but as its task is to develop an existing curriculum or design a new one, change will be inevitable. This can be unsettling and uncomfortable especially when introduced at an inappropriate time such as when staff morale is low, or stress levels are high. If staff are not given an opportunity to learn about a change and practise the relevant skills, they are more likely to resist it. New and Couillard (1981) stated that resistance to change results from:

- threatened self-interest;
- inaccurate perceptions;
- objective disagreement;
- psychological resistance;
- low tolerance for change.

The behaviour of either committee members or the group involved in implementing change may indicate if they have one of these attitudes. The committee members may act as change agents and be directly involved in the educative process in preparation for change. They should ideally participate in the day-to-day efforts to make the change work – theorising about change without having any responsibility for its enactment is not the best way of persuading people that the change is beneficial.

Members of a curriculum committee will at some time have a conflict of ideas and be on different sides of a debate. This can usually be handled in a mature way if the members recognise that it is not them personally who are being opposed, but the idea they are presenting. A heated debate can ensue followed by both members going out to lunch together. Mutual respect, tolerance of others' idiosyncrasies in the hope that they will tolerate ours and respect of opinions we do not share tends to develop as the committee works and grows together.

Presenting a proposal

A working group may be set a task of designing the learning objectives, content, teaching methods, clinical experience and evaluation for a unit of the course. The person elected by the group to present their proposal will usually be required to prepare a paper setting out the plan in detail. A copy should be sent to the committee secretary in plenty of time for it to be distributed to members before the meeting at which it is to be discussed. The person who prepares the paper usually speaks on it at the committee meeting.

The paper usually contains an outline of the reasons why change was necessary and any problem or changes in the learning environment. The proposed plan for the unit of learning with diagrams to aid communication is often included. The disadvantages and advantages of the plan may be enumerated – listing the advantages last will end the paper on a positive note.

The composition of members attending the committee at which the proposal is presented is crucial, the presence or absence of one vocal member may determine the 'sway' of the decision to accept, defer or reject the proposal. It is beneficial if all members of the working group can be present when the paper is presented to support the presenter. It may also be helpful to view the contents of the paper as proposals for discussion and not the final result of the work.

The time and energy spent on preparing for and working in a curriculum committee can be immensely rewarding in many dimensions. The students can benefit by having current expert practitioners involved in selecting content of courses and in influencing the curriculum process. The patients can benefit from the high quality of nursing practice which students can be facilitated to provide and the committee member may find that 'spin offs' from the committee work may enhance their professional development and job satisfaction. So the challenge and hard work involved in curriculum development activities can have tangible rewards and contribute to the quality of student learning and patient care.

References
Heath, J. (1982) Curriculum Design in Nursing. NHS Learning Resources Unit, Sheffield.

Jarvis, P. and Gibson, S. (1985) The Teacher Practitioner in Nursing, Midwifery and Health Visiting. Croom Helm, London.

Kershaw, B. and Salvage, J. (1986) Models for Nursing. Wiley, Chichester.

Lancaster, J. and Lancaster, W. (Ed.) (1982) Concepts for Advanced Nursing Practice; The Nurse as Change Agent. Mosby, St. Louis.

Mauksch, I.G. and Miller, M.H. (1981) Implementing Change in Nursing. Mosby, St. Louis.

New, J.R. and Couillard, N.A. (1981) Guidelines for introducing change. *Journal of Nursing Administration*, **2**, 3, 17-21.

Stephenson, P.M. (1985) A research based method of selecting curriculum content. *Journal of Advanced Nursing*, **10**, 3-13.

Vaughan, B. (1986) Models in Curriculum Development. In: Kershaw, B. and Salvage, J. (Eds.) Models for Nursing. Wiley, Chichester.

52

Effective use of health education skills

Jill Macleod-Clark, PhD, BSc, SRN
Senior Lecturer in Nursing Studies, King's College, University of London

Sally Kendall, BSc, RGN, HV
Lecturer in Nursing Studies, Bucks College of Higher Education

Sheila Haverty, BA, RGN
Research Officer, Department of Nursing Studies, King's College, University of London

The importance of developing the nurse health education role is now well recognised. The need for a shift in emphasis has been accepted by the profession (UKCC,1983). Project 2000 proposals, for restructuring nurse education reflect this acceptance by recommending that health concepts and issues underpin the first eighteen months of nurse education programmes (UKCC, 1986). Similar recommendations have also been made in the Judge Report (1985) and the Cumberlege Report (1986).

There is thus a growing awareness in nursing of the need to move away from the medical model and ensure that the focus of care directed towards enhancing health. This conflict of philosophies often makes it difficult for nurses to be health educators – they are trained to care for the sick and dying by following doctors' orders not to take on a more autonomous role based on promoting or maximising health.

Previous work has shown that nurses need to develop both their knowledge and their interpersonal skills in order to become effective health educators (Faulkner and Ward, 1983; Macleod-Clark et al, 1985). It is also important that nurses have the ability to recognise opportunities for health education. Kendall has examined the opportunities nurses have in relation to smoking education (Kendall, 1986).

Smoking continues to be the largest cause of preventable disease in the UK. One in 4 of all smokers will die from a smoking related disease such as lung cancer, heart disease or chronic destructive lung disease (Doll and Peto 1981). Smoking therefore provides and excellent example of an area where nurses can develop and use their skills effectively in health education. Hopefully, it can be seen that the approach suggested is equally applicable to many other areas of health education such as nutrition and exercise.

Framework for health education

Recent research by the authors (in press) has demonstrated that health education by nurses can be effective if it is structured and skillful. The suggested framework is based on the nursing process approach since health education should be individualised like all aspects of nursing care. The long-term aim in this case is that the client stops smoking.

Assessment   This involves assessing the smoker in terms of:
● Motivation to give up;
● Health beliefs and worries about smoking;
● Level of knowledge about smoking and health;
● Factors influencing smoking behaviour, eg family circumstances;
● Factual information, eg number smoked per day.

   Using interpersonal skills effectively in the assessment stage is more likely to lead to an eventual successful outcome. The skills necessary for effective assessment will be discussed and illustrated with extracts from real conversations between nurses and their clients which have been recorded by the authors in the course of their research.

Questioning skills   Any kind of nursing assessment requires questioning in order to gather information and to build up a complete picture of the client in terms of health and social needs. There are many ways of questioning people but two which can be most usefully employed in assessment are *open* questions and *closed* questions. Open questions usually commence with how, what, where, when, who or why. They allow the respondent to answer in their own words without limitations.

Example 1
N: How keen are you to give up?
C: Well, I know I should give up and I
     know I would like to. Its just — I
     think it would be difficult.

Open question

In Example 1 the nurse has asked an open question in order to establish the client's level of motivation. It is important to do this in the early stages as an unmotivated client is unlikely to respond positively to any health education intervention. If the client is not motivated then the intervention should focus more on increasing motivation than changing behaviour.

   Open questions are also used to find out about the client's belief system. Efforts at health education will be unsuccessful if the nurse and the client have different beliefs and values about health. If the nurse can establish what the client's beliefs are she can work within that client's frame of reference. It cannot be assumed, for example, that everybody is worried about getting lung cancer — many are not.

   In Example 2 the nurse is now aware that the client is worried about breathlessness and heart disease. She could now expand on these areas

Example 2
N: What worries you about continuing to smoke?
C: Only that, you know, you can't breathe properly.
N: Mmm
C: . . . and some people get, you know, something wrong with their heart.

but keep the focus of her intervention on what is relevant to the client. It is equally important to establish the worries people may have about giving up smoking.

Example 3
N: What concerns you about giving up smoking?
C: I would really worry about putting on weight, there's no way I would want to do that.
N: Yes, a lot of women are very worried about that.

By asking an open question the nurse has established the client's fear of weight gain (Example 3). Obviously, this kind of information about the client is essential before any sort of plan can be formulated. This client will not feel committed to giving up smoking if she is not also given some guidance and support regarding diet and weight maintenance.

Open questions can also be used to gather factual information which will be central to the planning stage, eg "How long have you been smoking?", "How many do you smoke a day?".

Closed questions

Closed questions limit the type of response that can be given — usually to "yes" or "no". In a nursing assessment they are most useful for gathering facts quickly but should not be used to the exclusion of open questions since they do not provide the depth of information required to make a satisfactory assessment.

Example 4
N: Have you ever tried to stop smoking before?
C: No.

In Example 4 a simple fact has been established which may have some influence on the outcome of the intervention. For example, it is known that ex-smokers have often made several attempts to stop before they are finally successful so it would be reasonable not to expect that this client will be successful first time.

Listening and encouraging skills   Some of the most powerful skills apparently require very little effort from the nurse. However, it is more difficult than at first appears to both develop these skills and recognise their potential in assessment. Listening means more than just hearing, it means being able to interpret and make use of what is being said. In every day conversation we tend to interupt and talk over each other instead of listening. Traditionally in nursing the nurse has been very much in control of the patient which usually means she has done most of the talking. When helping people to make decisions about their lifestyle and health they should be encouraged to do the majority of the talking so that the assessment made is accurate and client-centered. Encouraging people to talk more usually only requires the nurse to give her full attention and to say things like ''uh-uh'' or ''go on''.

Example 5
N: What sort of ways have you thought about giving up smoking?
C: I've tried several times, um, and I've always stopped for about a week.
N: Mmm
C: But I get this really empty feeling inside my stomach.
N: Mmm
C: I get really moody.
N: Uh-uh
C: And I've been thinking recently, that instead of just thinking about it, I thought I'm going to set a date.
N: Mmm
C: Its best not to think about it.

As in Example 5, open questioning and encouragement often go together. By listening to this client the nurse can focus her intervention on the information she has learned.

Responding to cues   Cues are hints that the client may give as to real worries not openly expressed. A skillful listener will pick up these cues and encourage the client to talk more about them. Frequently, they may be areas of concern which the client wished to discuss but was unable to — perhaps through fear, anxiety or embarrassment.

In Example 6, the nurse picks up on the client's nervousness by echoing back what the client is telling her. This technique also encourages the

Example 6
C: Um, I've been trying to cut down since I was pregnant.
N: Mmm
C: But I haven't thought about stopping altogether because it calms my nerves.
N: Mmm
C: I've been very nervous during this pregnancy.
N: You're nervous?

client to say more about the underlying cause of the nervousness so that the nurse can focus her smoking education around this, ie explore other ways of coping with anxiety.

Cues will frequently be non-verbal and it is just as important to observe and interpret these signs of anxiety and restlessness such as clock-watching or tearing up a paper handkerchief. An inattentive or worried client will not be able to respond fully to the intervention.

Giving information During the assessment it may become apparent that there are some areas in which the client needs or requests information. Information given appropriately can enhance the client's understanding of the problem. Information given will refer back to the clients beliefs and worries and should be contained within the client's frame of reference.

Example 7

C: I think with lung cancer, I mean if your lungs pack up you have more or less had it haven't you?

N: Mmm. Yes.

C: I think that's the one that really worries me.

N: Mmm. Women are increasingly getting lung cancer because more women are smoking now. At one time, women used to think it didn't affect them and that more men die. In fact, the statistics are going up for women so it is a definite health risk.

The information given in Example 7 is appropriate because it responds to the client's worry and is given at the client's own level, avoiding jargon. Compare this with the following extract:

N : I'll just explain to you that when you smoke, carbon monoxide attaches itself to the red corpuscles that are in the blood. Blood goes to every tissue in the body so carbon monoxide, which is poison, is being sent everywhere. So what it tends to do to your hands and feet is make them tingle. Do you ever feel tingling?

C : No.

N : You don't?

C : No, never.

N : Well, this is one of the sort of circulatory problems which taken to its end is gangrene, fingers falling off and things like that.

The nurse has saturated this client with unsolicited and inappropriate information. She has used technical terms which may mean nothing to the client and has resorted to terror tactics to gain her client's attention. It is not necessary to tell every client everything you know about smoking.

Where information is given it is often useful to back it up with written material so that the client has a chance to absorb the information quietly

It is often useful to back up information with written material such as this HEA leaflet.

later on. There are many leaflets and booklets freely available on smoking and other subjects from health education units.

In summary, the initial assessment involves the skills of questioning, listening, encouraging, responding to cues and giving appropriate information. The aim of the assessment is to build up a picture of the client, enabling the nurse to focus her intervention within the client's frame of reference.

Planning

When formulating a plan the overall aim should be kept in sight, ie cessation of smoking. However, before a total behaviour change is achieved there may be other short term goals to be met. Such short term goals should be realistic and mutually agreed between the client and the nurse. Frequently, the client may be pleased to accept the nurse's guidance as she will have practical suggestions and access to methods of cessation (see Kendall, 1986) previously unavailable or unknown to the client. However, a plan conceived and imposed by the nurse alone is unlikely to be successful. Some short term goals which may be useful to consider are:

- Create no-smoking areas in the home/car;
- Keep a smoking diary for one week, ie write down how many cigarettes are smoked, when and why;
- Reduce smoking by half within one week;
- Find out where the nearest smokers clinic is.

The overall plan and the short term goals should be based on the needs and beliefs established during the assessment. For example, if a client smokes as a way of relieving stress then the plan should be based on alternative methods of coping with stress. Asking questions such as "How do you think you could go about giving up?" may be useful in giving some initial direction to the plan and in helping the client to feel that she is participating in the lifestyle changes she is making.

Clients often feel that a behaviour such as smoking is outside their control and that the risks of smoking are on a par with the risks of nuclear war for example. Clients should be helped to see that they can control their own behaviour and setting realistic goals often helps to put the behaviour into perspective.

Implementation

Once the client and the nurse have established the "giving up" plan in which there are agreed goals and objectives it is up to the client to implement it. Many smokers will say "It is only me that can do it". This is true, but the client can be helped by offering support. This could be done in the form of leaving a telephone number on which the nurse could be contacted (eg on the ward or health centre) or could be more formalised with future meetings being planned. If it is inappropriate for the nurse herself to offer support (ward-based nurses may find this difficult) then support could be sought from within the family or friendship network. For example, partners may find it helpful to give up together. Some clients might be attracted to group support and in this case a stop smoking group may be appropriate. Whatever form the support takes it must suit both the client and the nurse.

Evaluation

Whenever possible, following an intervention the nurse should arrange to see the client again at least once. This could take place in the home, in the antenatal clinic, outpatients clinic or wherever is most appropriate to the nurse's field of work. This follow-up has a dual purpose. It gives the client something to work towards and allows priorities to be reorganised and goals reset.

If, by the time of the agreed follow-up, there has been no demonstrable change in behaviour, the nurse should not regard her intervention as a complete failure. Many ex-smokers make several attempts before finally giving up and a change in motivation is as successful as a change in behaviour. It may be that the continued interest and support of the nurse will give the smoker the required impetus to give up eventually.

However, a reassessment of the previous intervention will give guidance for tackling problems and setting new short-term goals. If the original plan was unsuccessful it may be necessary to make adjustments or formulate a new one. If the client is successful in giving up smoking then she should be encouraged to continue and where possible continued support offered if required.

In summary, this framework requires the nurse to assess her client, make a plan of action with the client, support and encourage the client in its implementation and evaluate the intervention.

It may at first appear that the framework is complicated and time consuming. However, in their research the authors have found that with practice, it is possible to assess and plan in five to 10 minutes. The framework aims to be flexible and adaptable to various work settings. For example, if ward based nurses find the idea of giving continued support unrealistic due to high turnover of patients then they could either give the client their ward telephone number or refer her/him to one of their community colleagues. Health visitors and district nurses will have more prolonged contact with their clients and may decide to spread the assessment and planning over two visits and they will be more able to offer support over a period of time.

The framework is not rigid and if nurses of all disciplines could adapt it and use it in their every day practise there is potential for a considerable impact on attaining the WHO target of health for all by the year 2000.

References

Cumberlege, J. et al (1986) Neighbourhood nursing – a focus for care. Report of the Community Nursing Review. HMSO. London.

Doll, R. and Peto, R. (1981) The Causes of Cancer. Oxford University Press.

Faulkner, A and Ward L (1983) Nurses as health educators in relation to smoking, *Nursing Times*, Occasional Paper 8, **79**, 15, 47-48.

Kendall, S. (1986) Helping people to stop smoking. *The Professional Nurse*, **1**, 5, 120-123.

Macleod-Clark, J. Elliot, K. Haverty, S. and Kendall, S. (1985) Helping people to stop smoking – the nurse's role. Phase 1. Health Education Council, London.

Macleod-Clark, J. Haverty, S. and Kendall, S. (1987) Helping people to stop smoking – the nurse's role. Research Report No.19.

Judge, H. et al (1985) Commission on nurse education. RCN, London.

United Kingdom Central Council for Nurses, Midwives and Health Visitors. (1986) Project 2000, UKCC.

World Health Organisation (1978) Report of an international conference on primary health care Alma-Ata, USSR. WHO, Geneva.

Research Awareness

53

Research awareness: Its importance in practice

Elisabeth Clark, PhD

Lecturer, Distance Learning Centre, Polytechnic of the South Bank

Interest in research has been growing steadily for 20 years. An increasing number of nurses are becoming personally involved in research projects, and an even larger number find themselves working in situations in which research is being undertaken. Research-based knowledge has the potential to affect virtually every aspect of professional practice and all nurses — whether clinicians, teachers or managers. Nursing should, therefore, become research-based. (Report of the Committee on Nursing, 1972; Report on the Royal Commission of the Health Service, 1979).

Mystique?

Unfortunately, however, research is frequently regarded with suspicion by practitioners. It is seen as a complex academic activity that is time-consuming and difficult to understand. For many, the mystique creates a barrier to understanding that urgently needs to be removed. There is, therefore, a need for nurses to become 'research minded' (RCN, 1982), and for trained researchers to become more practice oriented. Despite this ideal, bridges between research and practice have not always been built, (Hunt, 1984; Hockey, 1986). This problem can only be resolved if a true partnership can be developed between researchers and practitioners based on mutual respect and recognition of each other's skills. There is a real danger that the role of the research-aware nurse is seen as rushing round doing research projects or as altering practice on the basis of the findings of a single small-scale survey.

Role of research-aware nurse

There are a number of roles for the 'research-aware' nurse, which can easily be integrated within existing practice. They are:
- raising problems and questions for research;
- cooperating with researchers in an informed way;
- seeking out and critically evaluating published research studies;
- using research findings;
- communicating with others and sharing the task of keeping abreast of new developments.

Although there are several different approaches to research and a variety of research techniques, a logical sequence of steps, the research process, underlies all research activity:

- identification of a researchable problem;
- critical review of existing literature in that area;
- designing the study and developing any instruments needed to collect the data;
- pilot study to assess the feasibility of the project;
- data collection;
- analysis and interpretation of data;
- dissemination of findings.

A detailed description of these steps can be found in many research textbooks, some of which are listed in the annotated bibliography at the end of the article. However, it is important to remember that these steps overlap and influence other stages of the process.

Identification

The identification of a researchable problem is a crucial first step in any research project. Ideas for research are everywhere: as a clinician you have an important role in constantly reviewing your practice and asking apparently straightforward questions such as "Why am I using this particular technique?" Challenging assumptions and accepted ways of doing things can bring to light many problems and questions. You might, for instance, wish to question differing treatments of pressure sores.

Just as researchers have to search the existing research literature to help them define their questions and plan their studies, so too do practising nurses have to find out whether their problems have already been systematically investigated.

Practitioners are well placed to initiate studies by trained researchers that are relevant to practice. In this way, collaboration is established at the outset, rather than at the end of the research process when practitioners are expected to use findings which may not appear relevant to their daily work.

Ethics committee

Once research is underway a conflict can sometimes arise between the demands of science on one hand, and the interests of clients on the other. The local ethics committee has an important role to play in safeguarding the interests of all individuals. However, practising nurses also have responsibilities, such as ensuring informed consent is obtained.

After the data have been collected and analysed, the researcher has an obligation to communicate the findings as an integral part of the research process. But unless consumers take some responsibility for disseminating information, nursing research will only accumulate dust on library shelves, and research-based knowledge will make little or no impact on the delivery of health care. Nurses must acquaint themselves with the research that is relevant to their own area of work. Local librarians are of invaluable help when trying to track down previously published studies on a specific subject.

Research findings may be used in a number of different ways:

- they can be deliberately rejected, either because they are not relevant or because of the quality of the research;
- they may be used to question practice, recognise the limitations of current knowledge or initiate further research;
- specific recommendations may be implemented in one's own work area.

Before findings can be used it must be certain that they are soundly based — a single small-scale study is not adequate. They should be tested in more than one study. These difficult judgements cannot be made by one individual and are usually the responsibility of groups such as the Nursing Standards group or the Nursing Practice Advisory group.

There are a number of areas where sufficient research has been undertaken to warrant changes in practice. For instance, there is now convincing evidence to suggest that the incidence of pressure sores can be reduced by two-hourly turning (Norton et al, 1975). Is this practised in your work area? If not, why not? There is also evidence regarding the benefits of giving information to patients preoperatively concerning pain, stress levels and recovery rates (Hayward, 1975; Boore, 1978). Yet, in 1985, the Ombudsman's report contained a number of claims of lack of such information.

Research may provide the necessary scientific evidence to justify existing practice. Wherever change is involved it is likely to be met with resistance, but change is something that cannot be avoided. Nurses are being required to make crucial decisions concerning clinical practice, nurse education and management. In an era of individual accountability, it becomes increasingly important to have access to reliable research-based knowledge on which decisions can be based. 'Accountability' implies that you are personally responsible for the outcome of your professional actions, and, according to Lewis and Batey (1982), requires you to disclose what you have done, why you did it and what the results of your actions were. If nurses are to be held accountable for clinical decisions, they must be able to justify them and they need to be based on current knowledge rather than on tradition or myth.

Brotherston (1960) summed it up very clearly when he wrote: ''. . . traditional customs are comfortable and necessary things, but they can be dangerous limitations to the search for knowledge and the improvements of methods of applying existing knowledge.''

The Code of Professional Conduct for nurses, midwives and health visitors requires ''every reasonable opportunity to maintain and improve professional knowledge and competence'' to be taken. This task cannot be undertaken alone. Colleagues in other hospitals, and in other countries may well be struggling with the same problems — communication is essential. Regularly scanning the relevant literature and passing on new information helps others to become aware of research findings, and to develop more positive attitudes to research.

There are research committees in most districts and it is worth finding out if your specialty is represented locally, and if there is a research nurse in your district. Almost certainly there will be people in your district — in management, education, clinical areas or research, available to advise on specific problems.

Resources

Once you start asking questions, you may be surprised to discover the resources already available. A manual of 44 research-based clinical nursing procedures has been produced by the Royal Marsden Hospital (Pritchard and David, 1988). The King's Fund run seminars and workshops which provide a forum for practitioners to discuss the implications for practice of research findings. These and many other resources are already available.

Research crosses traditional boundaries — for example you may find a learner has a social sciences degree and considerable research expertise, including the statistical analysis of data. Research results are important to daily nursing activity. It does not make good sense to consider it as a separate 'academic' subject or merely an optional extra, but rather within the context of professional practice. Research issues are clearly best discussed and understood in relation to patient care, where questions of knowledge, ethics and the implementation of findings are likely to be faced every day.

In the last decade a great deal has been achieved; during the next it is hoped that it will become second nature for practitioners to say "there is evidence to show that . . ." and "I am doing this because . . .". Nurses will then have recognised the importance of research for professional practice. Research awareness will have achieved the important goal of promoting professional self-awareness.

"Research is thus not a luxury for the academic, but a tool for developing the quality of nursing decisions, prescriptions and actions. Whether as clinicians, educators, managers or researchers we have a research responsibility; neglect of that responsibility could be classed as professional negligence" (McFarlane, 1984).

Bibliography
Clark, J.M. and Hockey, L. (Eds.) (1989) Further Research for Nursing: A New Guide for the Enquiring Nurse. Scutari Press, London.
Cormack, D.F.S. (1984) (ed.), The Research Process in Nursing , Blackwell Scientific Publications, Oxford.
Darling, V.H. and Rogers, J. (1986) Research for Practising Nurses, Macmillan, Basingstoke.
The management of change is discussed in: Mauksch, I.G. and Miller, M.H. (1981) Implementing Change in Nursing, C.V. Mosby, St. Louis.
Phillips, L.R.F. (1986) A Clinician's Guide to the Critique and Utilization of Nursing Research, Appleton-Century-Crofts, Norwalk, Conneticut.
(This American text provides a comprehensive account of the problems of using research

findings in practice and suggests way of overcoming them. A very expensive book that is worth borrowing through Inter-Library loan.)

Hunt, M. (1987) The process of translating research findings into nursing practice, Journal of Advanced Nursing, 12, 1, 101-10.

(This paper describes a research study involving nurse teachers, ward sisters and nurse managers in the processes of: identifying nursing practice problems, searching the literature, evaluating and synthesising existing research-based knowledge, and, finally, translating research findings into practice.)

References

Boore, J.R.P. (1978) Prescription for recovery, RCN, London.

Brotherston, J. (1960) Learning to investigate problems. Report of an international service on research in nursing, ICN, Geneva.

Hayward, J.C. (1975) Information — A prescription against pain, RCN, London.

Hockey, L. (1986) 'Nursing research in the United Kingdom: The state of the art' in S.M. Stinson and J.C. Kerr (eds.) International Issues in Nursing Research, Croom Helm, London.

Hunt, J. (1984) Why don't we use these findings? *Nursing Mirror*, **158**, 8, 29.

Lewis, F.M. and Batey, M.V. (1982) Clarifying autonomy and accountability in nursing service: Part II. *Journal of Nursing Administration*, **12**, 10, 10-15.

McFarlane, J.K. (1984) Foreword in D.F.S. Cormack (ed.) The Research Process in Nursing, Blackwell Scientific Publications, Oxford.

Norton, D., McLaren, R. and Exton-Smith, A. (reprinted 1975) An Investigation of Geriatric Nursing Problems, Churchill Livingstone, Edinburgh.

Pritchard, A.P. and David, J.A. (Eds.) (1988) The Royal Marsden Hospital Manual of Clinical Policies and Procedures, 2nd Edition. Harper and Row, London.

RCN Research Society Report (1982) Research-mindedness and nurse education, RCN, London.

Report of the Committee on Nursing (1972), Cmnd 5115, HMSO, London.

Report of the Royal Commission on the Health Service (1979), Cmnd 7615, HMSO, London.

54

Research and common sense

Elisabeth Clark, PhD, Bsc

Lecturer, Distance Learning Centre, Polytechnic of the South Bank, London

The previous chapter has already looked at the importance of research-based knowledge for professional practice, and considered some of the ways practitioners can, and should, contribute to research activities within nursing. Now is the time to explore the relationship between knowledge and understanding based on everyday and clinical experience, and that which is based on systematic investigation.

Researchers from many disciplines, including nursing, are frequently accused of wasting considerable time and energy, and thus valuable resources, 'proving' what is already known, or what may be considered common-sense knowledge. So, there are two questions to be answered: What are the differences between, on the one hand, common knowledge derived from experience, and on the other, research-based knowledge? Are these accusations justified?

What is common sense?

Before one can begin to tackle these questions, one must ask what is meant by 'common sense' – not the easiest of tasks. The word 'common' certainly suggests that something is taken for granted, that it is widely accepted and agreed upon; 'sense' implies some type of reasoning. Common sense would appear to be based largely on intuition and personal experience and on the kind of 'good sense' that does not depend on being highly educated: it is what 'sensible' people think and believe. Looked at in this way, common sense may be described as a form of accumulated wisdom; it relies on knowledge and judgement, and can, therefore, be considered as a way of thinking.

So far, considerable emphasis has been placed on the notion of agreement. However, in reality, so-called common sense ideas are not always as widely accepted as one might imagine. The fact is that people do not always agree on what action is appropriate in any particular situation. Take, for example, the question of how to bring up a child – a subject of considerable importance to health visitors and parents alike. You only have to ask a couple of friends, relatives or colleagues about their views on a subject such as toilet training, and you are likely to end up feeling rather confused by their diverse, and perhaps even contradictory, advice. In this context, individuals tend to talk about what makes sense to them and about what their own particular circumstances and necessarily limited experience has taught them.

Alternatively, you only need look at any one of the three volumes written by Newson and Newson (1963; 1968; 1976) to appreciate the diversity of beliefs and practices in the field of child-rearing. Despite these differences, many parents would claim that what they were doing was obvious, and by implication 'right', the reason being 'It's just common sense'. Common sense is not only likely to reflect what people *think* about a particular subject, but – and this is equally important – how they *feel* about it. In fact, it may reflect a person's prejudices and personal biases. Consequently, there may not be as much common understanding in 'common sense' as one might wish to assume, thus casting some doubt over the supposition that common sense is somehow 'self-evident', 'generally accepted' or universally applicable. And notice how received wisdom can change: women used to be considered too irresponsible to vote! Similarly, Luker (1986) reminds us that:

". . . It used to be common sense to think that the world was flat and this could be confirmed by 'just looking' or asking our neighbours. But, unfortunately, just looking or asking people who share our point of view, does not always provide valid conclusions."

Professional experience

Consider now professional experience. Clearly, the longer you have been a nurse, the more clinical experience you will have to draw upon. This fact was acknowledged by McFarlane (1977) when she wrote:

"We must all have been impressed at some time in our professional

lives by the wisdom of experienced ward sisters (head nurses). If we could only catch their wisdom and write it down we would have a rich feast of concepts of nursing practice."

At the same time, it also needs to be recognised that however old you are, and however long you have worked in a particular field, your experience is necessarily limited – after all, it is the experience of only one person. Experience is necessarily constrained by the situation and also by the knowledge that we bring to it. Other forms of knowledge, including research-based knowledge, may add to, or indeed modify, ideas developed initially from experience. As Hockey (1981) so rightly points out: ". . . What was thought to be knowledge may have been little more than inspired guesswork. Research can transform a 'hunch' into knowledge."

Common sense vs research-based knowledge

So, what are the important differences between common sense knowledge and research-based knowledge, apart from the obvious one that common sense is more readily available than the latter? First, common sense generally relies on past experience and draws on all the information that an individual can recall at any one time; it does not direct one to other 'external' sources of knowledge and may, therefore, lack reliable evidence to back it up. Second, common sense is not systematic but frequently rather haphazard and fallible, and there is a real risk of bias since we all tend to ignore data that do not confirm our beliefs. Of necessity, common sense restricts the user to what is familiar, and indeed it is often steeped in tradition. Consequently, it can be difficult to question or challenge other people's common sense ideas for the very reason that they make sense to them in the light of their personal experience. Ideas of this kind tend to be very resistant to education and change.

On the other hand, research makes explicit the ways in which information is collected and analysed: it is a systematic activity. Researchers collect data according to the criteria embodied in the scientific method, and those data are made public. Also, the 'rules' of research allow research findings to be challenged by others, and by new data, in a way that will never be possible for common sense knowledge.

Our professional experience equips us with a number of 'facts', many of which become so much a part of our thinking that they seem obvious and self-evident. As a result, certain assumptions and activities may go unchecked or unchallenged just because they are deemed to be 'common sense'. In fact, the closer something is to day-to-day experience, the more difficult it can be to convince people of the need to study it systematically:

"What happens at the other end of a telescope or microscope, that is the stuff of science. What happens in front of our naked eyes, that is just common knowledge . . . Yet, if we look at the history of these sciences [referring here to the physical and biological sciences], we can see that the most revolutionary advances were made when scientists sought directly to explain the obvious. Concepts like gravity, evolution, infectious disease, were all attempts to account for experiences which were familiar to scientists and non-scientists alike" (Eiser, 1980).

Ensuring relevance

Both common sense and clinical experience can provide a useful starting point for research, and may be harnessed to help ensure that nursing research is relevant to the problems facing practitioners. Research allows ideas that are taken for granted to be systematically studied and verified. Tradition, on the other hand, can make it difficult to learn from experience: it can obscure alternative ways of doing things and stifle a questioning approach to professional practice.

It must be emphasised that while it is neither appropriate nor desirable to regard intuition and common sense as if they were in opposition to a systematic research approach, they cannot be regarded as a substitute for more objective evidence. The aim of research has never been to overturn common sense, but to make precise, unambiguous and objective statements about specific topics.

Worthwhile or waste of time?

Imagine that you have just read the results of some research which merely confirm what you had always believed to be the case. How do you think you might react? Would you, for instance, feel that it had been a waste of time to read something that merely substantiated what experience had already taught you? Or, would you be pleased to find that your ideas had been endorsed by a carefully conducted piece of research? Instead of thinking 'so what?' when we next have our common sense ideas verified by research, we should recognise that intuition, endorsed by systematic evidence, is a more reliable basis for professional decisions and actions than either common sense or intuition alone.

Conversely, research findings should not be dismissed as 'rubbish' or rejected outright merely because they conflict with one's own experience or traditional beliefs. The recognition of such a conflict needs to be taken as the starting point for a careful evaluation of the precise nature and potential of both the research-based and the traditional knowledge. This is a necessary first step if your practice is to become research-based wherever appropriate.

What you think you know

A good idea when reading a research article is to work out at the start what you think and know about the particular subject so that you are better able to recognise some of the initial assumptions and ideas which will form the 'filter' through which you are likely to view and interpret the research findings. There is otherwise a real possibility that you will evaluate the research purely on the basis of its common sense value rather than from a more informed standpoint. This is when it is particularly helpful to recognise that at least some of our beliefs and assumptions may be wrong and be contradicted by valid and reliable research findings.

It is, therefore, important to be able to distinguish between knowledge based on research evidence on the one hand, and intuitive insight on the other, and recognise the interface between the two. Often, however, it is tempting to indulge one's intuition and to draw too heavily on experience. Aggleton and Chalmers (1986) express concern about the "tendency for much nursing practice to be organised around the intuitions of those involved". Similarly, as Hewitt (1985) reminds us:

"To know something is in itself not enough. There are times when it is necessary to provide a basis for knowing, otherwise we may drift into an area of subjective judgement or even the domain of feelings."

Unchallenged practice

To illustrate the difference between practice based on 'common sense' and research-based evidence, an example drawn from midwifery should help. The practice of perineal and pubic shaving before childbirth evolved when it became known that specific micro-organisms created infection under certain conditions. Harmful micro-organisms were assumed to exist in pubic hair and shaving was, therefore, introduced to reduce the risk of infection. This practice continued unchallenged for many years even though it used up valuable staff time and resources, as well as causing some discomfort to women. There is now evidence to show that there is no increase in infection if the hair is not removed (Bond, 1980; Romney, 1980). Reducing infection is, therefore, no longer an adequate justification for shaving off the hair; if the practice of routine shaving persists today, it is in defiance of the evidence – it has no scientific backing. If researchers were to accept 'self-evident' truths, fallacies such as the benefits of perineal and pubic shaving before childbirth might never have been challenged, and specific actions or beliefs would continue to be based on false premises.

The nurse who is accountable for her own decisions and actions must recognise that tradition and common sense alone, relying as they do on experience, may provide a rather limited, inadequate and unreliable basis for dealing with important and complex nursing problems. There is a further and very important consideration: as a nurse, you must take special care *not* to impose personal opinions and untested assumptions on others, particularly in the guise of 'professional advice'. Professional accountability rests on your ability to locate your practice in a recognised and reliable framework of knowledge.

"In our history we have emphasised the art of nursing. The art has been long on the use of the understanding of the common sense world;

it has included faith in the truths of past teaching and in intuitive judgements. It has been short on the constant renewal of knowledge and on an attitude of scepticism. The science of nursing in no way negates the strengths of the art of nursing" (Batey, 1975).

Clarifying intuition and experience

Research can never replace intuition and experience, but it can help to clarify them by providing a systematic means of examining whether one's hunches stand up in a variety of situations. So you can see why nurses should be aware of the need to rethink some of their unquestioned beliefs and assumptions, and look to systematic evidence to confirm, modify or, if necessary, disprove their personal beliefs developed from first-hand experience. Clearly, the nursing profession of the 1990s relies on individual nurses being able to recognise and combine the benefits of both art and science. Indeed, you might like to consider what part of *your* practice is based on research-based knowledge and what part is based on intuition and common sense.

References

Aggleton, P. and Chalmers, H. (1986) Nursing research, nursing theory and the nursing process. *Journal of Advanced Nursing*, **11**, 2, 197-202.

Batey, M.V. (1975) Research: Its dissemination and utilisation in nursing practice. *Washington State Journal of Nursing*, Winter, 6-9.

Bond, S. (1980) Shave It....or Save It? *Nursing Times, 76*, 9, 362-363.

Clark, E. (1987) Research awareness: its importance in practice. *The Professional Nurse*, **2**, 11, 371-373.

Eiser, J.R. (1980) Cognitive Social Psychology: A guidebook to theory and research. McGraw-Hill, London.

Hewitt, S. (1985) The getting of wisdom. *Nursing Times*, **81**, 50,55-58.

Hockey, L. (1981) Knowledge is a precious possession. *Nursing Mirror*, **152,** 39, 46-9.

Luker, K.A. (1986) Who's for research?, *Nursing Times*, **82,** 52, 55-6.

McFarlane, J.K. (1977) Developing a theory of nursing: The relation of theory to practice, education and research, *Journal of Advanced nursing*, **2**, 261-70.

Newson, J. and Newson, E. (1963) Infant Care in an Urban Community. Allen and Unwin, London.

Newson, J. and Newson, E. (1968) Four Years Old in an Urban Community. Allen and Unwin, London.

Newson, J. and Newson, E. (1976) Seven Years Old in the Home Environment. Allen and Unwin, London.

Romney, M.L. (1980) Pre-delivery shaving: an afterthought. *Journal Obstetrics and Gynaecology*, **1,** 33.

Managing Stress

55
Managing anxiety

Jill Birrell, MA, MSC, AFBPsS, C.Psychol
Principal Clinical Psychologist, Royal Edinburgh Hospital

What is anxiety?

- "I can't give that speech tomorrow because I'll be so nervous that I'll forget what I was going to say. Everyone will be looking at me and seeing how nervous and inadequate I am."

- "I can't go to hospital for this operation despite what the doctors say. If they give me an injection to make me unconscious I may never wake up again."

- "Every time I leave the house, my heart starts to race. I'm sure I'll have a heart attack, just like my father who died of one."

These are the sort of thoughts that sweep over people who suffer from anxiety and phobias. Anxiety is a sense of threat to one's wellbeing, either physically or psychologically. There is no useful distinction to be made between anxiety and fear.

Sometimes it is quite normal to feel anxious – going for a job interview, or going into hospital. It is only when the anxiety is out of proportion with the threat or situation that it is pathological and treatment is required. The management of the anxious person largely depends on whether or not the anxiety is judged to be appropriate or exaggerated given the situation(s) in question and whether or not performance is impaired. The relationship between anxiety and performance is given by the Yerkes-Dobson curve illustrated in Figure 1. At low levels of anxiety, an increase in anxiety usually improves performance. This is followed by a plateau phase where an increase in anxiety leads to no improvement or deterioration in performance. This is followed in turn by a rapid fall off in performance if anxiety continues to rise.

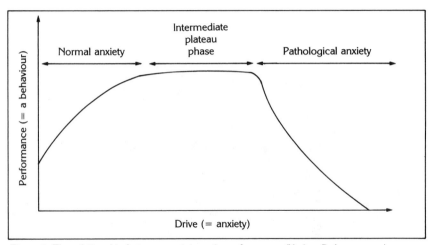

Figure 1. The relationship between anxiety and performance (Yerkes-Dobson curve).

The relationship between anxiety and performance is important in clinical management. It is unwise to treat anxiety symptoms just because a patient complains of them. A patient anxious at interview (a natural anxiety-provoking situation) may be functioning quite well outside that setting. However, if there is evidence of anxiety and impaired functioning because of it, the anxiety requires treatment.

Anxiety has both physiological and psychological manifestations. Most of the physiological symptoms result from increased activity of the autonomic nervous system and a few are the result of muscular tension (Table 1). Psychological errors in thinking can also increase anxiety; an anxious patient experiencing palpitations may think he is going to have a heart attack any minute. Such thoughts increase his anxiety further

Autonomic and Somatic	Psychological
Palpitations	Feelings of dread and threat
Difficulty in breathing	Panic
Nausea	Irritability
Dry mouth	Anxious anticipation
Muscular tension	
Dizziness	Worrying over trivia
Sweating	
Tremor	Difficulty in concentrating
Frequency of micturition	Initial insomnia
Abdominal churning	Inability to relax
Cold, clammy skin	

Table 1. Symptoms of anxiety.

and so on, and a powerful positive feedback loop is set up. It is very important to explain to the anxious patient that the symptoms being experienced are certainly unpleasant and uncomfortable but they are not dangerous. Anxiety symptoms can be tolerated and they will dissipate given appropriate treatment.

A distinction is usually made between anxiety which has no constant or predictable stimulus (so-called free floating anxiety) and anxiety that occurs only in certain situations (phobic anxiety). Anxiety states are common disorders but in most cases the anxiety is mild. Another distinction made is between acute and chronic anxiety states. Duration of symptoms is the single most important distinguishing variable. Usually acute anxiety states carry a good prognosis and rarely require specific therapy. In acute anxiety states there is alleviation by removing the stressor which is creating the anxiety, such as completion of examinations. In chronic anxiety states, the stressors may be unspecified and multiple, and usually medical and/or psychological intervention is required.

Hospital admission and surgical procedures

Admission to hospital is a stressful situation. The hospital environment is novel to patients and it involves a number of unfamiliar routines and procedures. Frequently, there is loss of privacy and loss of independence; there is separation from family, friends and work. Lucente and Fleck (1972) found that a patient's level of anxiety was determined to a greater extend by his personality and view of the hospital environment, rather than by the severity of his condition or diagnosis.

With regard to surgery, it might be thought that remaining calm at a time of threat (the operation) would be an optimum strategy for a successful postoperative recovery. However, Janis (1958, 1969) claims that the calmest patients show more emotional disturbance in the postoperative period than their more anxious counterparts. He refers to this group as those who show low anticipatory anxiety and suggests that because they remain so cheerful and optimistic prior to surgery, they have not engaged in any mental preparation as to what is to follow. Individuals who display moderate anxiety about impending surgery are least likely to show emotional disturbance postoperatively because they have sought out information about the impending surgical procedure and prepared themselves mentally for the threatening event. Finally, those with high anticipatory fear experience almost constant fear of the surgery before and afterwards and obtain only short-term relief from staff reassurance. The net result of these three preoperative attitudes is that the best postoperative emotional recovery is made by those who are moderately anxious. The curvilinear relationship between level of anxiety and postoperative recovery is shown in Figure 2.

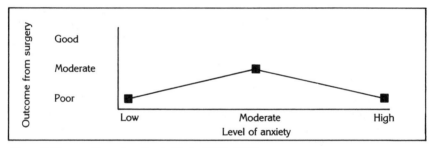

Figure 2. The curvilinear hypothesis (Janis, 1958; 1969).

A number of mechanisms may be operating which mean a highly anxious group of patients make less successful recoveries after surgery than less anxious patients. At the level of subjective reports of pain and discomfort, the patient who is highly anxious will be more concerned about his symptoms. These concerns may well take the form of numerous postoperative requests for analgesics and sedatives. In addition, medical complications after surgery may result from two sources: (1) highly anxious patients may be less likely to engage in the required exercise postoperatively because of concerns about pain and the possible ill effects of exercise; (2) some research suggests that in a very anxious individual, increased autonomic activity may lead to levels of catecholamines and corticosteroids which may retard postsurgical healing (Matthews and Ridgeway, 1981).

However, the curvilinear relationship described by Janis has not been supported by some more recent studies. Studies by Johnston and Carpenter (1980) and Sime (1976) suggest that a small linear relationship is most likely (Figure 3). Those patients showing least anxiety preoperatively were found to have the best postoperative recovery, while those with high preoperative anxiety were found to fare the worst. The debate continues.

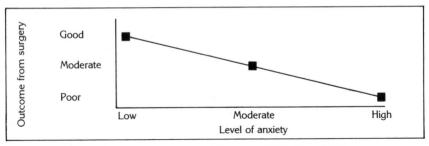

Figure 3. The linear hypothesis (Johnston and Carpenter, 1980; Sime, 1976).

Treating anxiety states

The best way to deal with anxiety is to identify the threat and then take steps to solve the problem logically, – if you are afraid of failing an exam, study more. Often, however, it is difficult to recognise the source of the problem and find a solution, and the anxious person looks for relief through therapy. There are a number of treatment approaches, which can be divided into passive and active therapies.

Passive therapy Drug treatment using the benzodiazepine group of drugs or the beta-blocker Proprandol are the most common first line of attack. Drug therapy asks no more of the patient than to take the tablets as prescribed – hence it is called a passive therapy. In the short term the use of medication to help anxiety is acceptable, but if the drug is taken for more than about a month and the threat causing the anxiety has not been dealt with, then the therapist finds that he has a patient who is anxious and 'hooked' on medication. the most commonly used

Short-acting	Long-acting
Temazepam	Diazepam
Oxazepam	Chlordiazepoxide
Lormetazepam	Medazepam
Lorazepam	Ketazolam*
	Clobazam
	Flurazepam
	Clonazepam*
	Clorazepate
	Nitrazepam
*Used primarily in the treatment of epilepsy.	

Table 2. Benzodiazepines commonly available in the UK.

benzodiazepines used in the UK are listed in Table 2.

The neuroleptic drugs such as chlorpromazine are also effective in reducing anxiety. They have the advantage of not producing dependence and may be preferred when treating patients known to be dependence-prone, eg alcoholics. A much lower dosage is required than that used for treating the major psychoses. Unfortunately, even at low dosages neuroleptic drugs carry the risk of the iatrogenic syndrome of tardive dyskinesia which is difficult to treat. There are really no drugs which can be prescribed to treat anxiety on a long-term basis: a combination of short-term drug prescription with one of the active therapies present the best line of management. A multidisciplinary approach is essential.

Another passive therapy sometimes requested by anxious patients is hypnosis but most medical hypnotists admit that only a very small number of people can be hypnotised deeply enough to accept post-hypnotic suggestion and even for these the relief obtained is relatively short lived.

Active therapy   Active therapists ask the patient to take a greater responsibility for therapy, guided by the therapist. Together they explore the difficulties and work out treatment. Most active therapies come under the umbrella of cognitive-behavioural psychotherapy. The treatment can be used to alleviate phobic anxiety (the anxiety which occurs in a well-defined situation) and generalised anxiety (anxiety which appears to have no constant or predictable stimulus). Cognitive-behavioural psychotherapy was developed by psychologists largely on the basis of learning theory, and it is psychologists and behaviour nurse therapists who still carry out the bulk of therapy. However, it is not essential to have special qualifications to use the strategies in a nursing context. Most nursing staff when acquainted with the principles of cognitive-behavioural techniques can use them to help patients, given access to a psychologist or a behaviour nurse therapist for advice and supervision.

The most widely used techniques in the alleviation of anxiety are:

1. Progressive muscular relaxation. It has been clearly demonstrated by monitoring the activity of the autonomic nervous system and muscular systems that relaxation is the direct physiological opposite of tension. Relaxation involves getting the patient to first tense up and then relax all the major muscle groups in the body one by one. When the therapist has taught the patient relaxation skills she gives him or her a prerecorded relaxation tape and suggests that the exercises be practised regularly. Relaxation skills help to reduce anxiety when the patient is faced with an anxiety-provoking situation. The aim of therapy is not to get rid of anxiety feelings altogether, as some degree of anxiety aids performance, but to remove the excess stress which inhibits functioning.

2. Systematic desensitisation.   This is the treatment of choice of phobic anxiety. The principle in therapy is that if an individual is afraid of something (eg, heights, dogs, needles, supermarkets) he or she will progressively lose that fear if the feared object or situation is faced and not avoided. A hierarchy of tasks is drawn up with each step in the hierachy moving towards facing the fear head on (eg, if the patient was afraid of injection, then the hierarchy would be composed of steps such as looking at pictures of needles, handling a needle, injecting an orange and so on). Relaxation therapy is used at the same time to reduce anxiety. It is worth remembering that it is better if the patient is not taking anxiolytic medication during treatment because the patient may wrongly attribute success in a therapy session to the tablet taken before therapy rather than recognising his or her increasing mastery of the phobic situation without recourse to drugs. A goal of therapy should be to help the patient manage anxiety without medication.

3. Biofeedback.   Biofeedback techniques enhance the awareness of the patient's reactions to anxiety, particularly muscular tension, heart rate and sweating, by recording physiological signals from the organs concerned and converting them to visual or auditory feedback. Using relaxation techniques, the patient can learn to decrease anxiety and hence the strength of the biofeedback signals. Biofeedback is usually used in combination with other therapeutic measures.

4. Cognitive therapy.   A final area of work which is still being developed by psychologists to help patient with anxiety problems is called cognitive therapy. It has been pioneered by Aaron Beck in the United States (Beck, 1976). He has demonstrated that certain thoughts or cognitions accompany the experience of anxiety. Usually, these cognitions are focused on the future: "I'll die from a heart attack if I leave the house" or "I'll faint at the sight of blood". If these thoughts are recognised and then reshaped to conform with what is most likely to happen in reality, then the anxiety is modified. The therapy is largely concerned with athe way a patient's thoughts affect emotions and behaviour. Behaviour nurse therapy courses now include some teaching on cognitive therapy, and it is likely that in the future most nurses will be able to employ the tecniques effectively with anxious patients, given adequate instruction and supervision by specialist staff.

Bibliography
Barker, P. (1982) Behaviour Therapy Nursing. Croom Helm, Kent.
Barker, P. (1985) Patient Assessment in Psychiatric Nursing. Croom Helm, Kent.
Barker, P., and Fraser, D. (1985) The Nurse as Therapist. Croom Helm, Kent.
   These three books are the most comprehensive accounts of behavioural psychotherapy written by a nurse-therapist for nurses. There is a slant towards psychiatric nursing in these books but in general medicine behavioural tecniques are becoming more popular.
Dryden, W. and Golden W. (Eds.) (1986) Cognitive-Behavioural Approaches to Psychotherapy. Harper and Row, London.

Newman, S. (1984) Anxiety, hospitalisation and surgery. In: Fitzpatrick, B. et al (eds) The Experience of Illness. Tavistiock Publications, London and New York.
This gives a good overall review of anxiety and hospitalisation friendships.

References
Beck, A.T. (1976) Cognitive Therapy and the Emotional Disorders. International Universities Press, New York.
Janis, I.N. (1958) Psychological Stress – Psychoanalytic and Behavioural Studies of Surgical Patients. Wiley, New York.
Janis, I.N. (1969) Stress and Frustration. Harcourt, Brace and Jovanovich, New York.
Johnston, M. and Carpenter, L. (1980) Relationship between preoperative anxiety and postoperative state. *Psychological Medicine*, **10,** 361-67.
Lucente, F.E. and Fleck, S. (1972) A study of hospitalisation anxiety in 408 medical and surgical patients. *Psychosomatic Medicine*, **34,** 302-12.
Matthews, A. and Ridgeway, V. (1981) Personality and surgical recovery – a review. *British Journal of Clinical Psychology*, **20,** 243-60.
Sime, M. (1976) Relationship of pre-operative fear, type of coping and information received about surgery, to recovery from surgery. *Journal of Personality and Social Psychology*, **34,** 716-24.

56

Self-help in preventing stress build-up

Rose Evison, BSc, Dip.Ed., C.Psychol, AFBPsS
Organisational Consultant and Counsellor, Sheffield

Your personal diagnostic check

This can be done on your own but it is helpful to discuss the results with colleagues so you can provide each other with extra information and support for change. Collect information over a period of time to try to catch specific symptoms and the situations which evoke them. Why not keep a stress diary for a few weeks in which you:

Destructive coping strategies

Smoking, drinking, over-eating

Destructive drug taking

Denial of problems or feelings

Grumbling, whining, sarcasm

Long-term feelings control, leading to repression and loss of awareness

Seeking arousal, adrenalin highs

Health-enhancing coping strategies

Problem-solving around reducing stress-inducing situations and acquiring skills that can help

Working from strengths

Talking through problems with a safe person, formally or informally

Getting negative feelings off your chest

Relaxation techniques

Satisfying physical recreation

Table 1. Strategies for coping with stress.

1. Note the situations in your life which you find stressful, in work and outside.

2. Note the typical stress symptoms you develop; the descriptions given above may help you here.

3. Note the coping strategies you already use, when you use them, how effective they are, and whether they have destructive effects on you or others. (See Table 1.)

The fact that nursing is a caring profession provides the first source of stress as carers are always at risk of taking on board the distresses of others and of putting their own needs last. Both of these can only be done temporarily without penalty. There are other sources of stress for nurses in the many changes that have taken place in the profession and in the NHS as a whole; change is a source of stress even when it is positive overall — and not all the changes have been. Yet a further source of stress is the ethical dilemmas of modern medicine — to abortion we can add organ transplants, life support and resuscitation, surrogate motherhood, and the choices forced by lack of resources.

Check your ideas with these points:

- **Stress is not a disease.** It arises from our natural responses to threats to our physical and psychological wellbeing. We need our protective responses like anger, grief, disgust, and fear — it is when such responses are unnecessarily prolonged that they become dangerous.
- **Stress is not an all-or-nothing state.** All average normal people will show some symptoms of stress, but the more symptoms, the less efficient the person.
- **Stress is not inevitable even when there are many stressful conditions.** People vary in their responses according to their genetic makeup, their life experiences, and the coping skills they have learned.
- **We may not be aware of suffering stress.** This may be because we can accept many symptoms as a normal part of our personality, or because we have become insensitive to our own bodies and feelings as a way of coping. However, it still takes its toll of our minds and bodies.
- **Stress is like a disease process.** This is in that it decreases our wellbeing, interferes with our skills and problem solving, and its cumulative effects can be debilitating for ourselves and damaging for our professional work.
- **Stress can be reduced in many different ways.** Each time you disrupt a symptom you will be preventing further buildup of stress. However, to reduce the incidence of symptoms you may need to change your ways of reacting which may require a long period of working on them.

Recognising stress symptoms

Inappropriate negative feelings Negative feelings are impulses to act to remove threats and automatically focus our minds and arouse our bodies. Whenever they are inappropriate they interfere and are stressful. They may be basic feelings of anger, fear, grief, disgust. They may be resentment, anxiety, helplessness, depression, which are signals of failure to master some situation and often go along with rigid maladaptive behaviours, destructive of self or others. Because feelings are impulses to action, which we control by controlling the muscles concerned, inappropriate feelings are a source of muscular tension.

Physical symptoms of muscular tension   These may be anywhere in the body but the neck and shoulders are common places. These tensions may progress to fatigue, or focused pain such as headache or backache. Tension is stressful whether caused by feelings control or poor physical skills.

Figure 1.

Repetitive negative thoughts about self or others   These may be aggressive or dismissive, or anxieties about mistakes or disasters. Such repetitive thoughts may be justifying the feelings we have or the actions we take or think should be taken. Thoughts couched in "oughts" and "shoulds" may create anxiety through guilt, and absolutes such as "always" or "never" or "I'm no good at ...", are to be distrusted.

Sometimes our responses are rigid and repetitive in all three areas and they may be accompanied by compulsive actions. Such a complex of rigid responses can be called a *block* because it blocks us from using our flexible intelligence and learning in that area of our experience.

Strategies for decreasing stress symptoms
Working from strengths   This is a crucial strategy in overcoming stress (and it is useful for helping patients). There are two elements. First, celebrating successes, strengths, skills, positive qualities, things you've learned, difficult things you've done. Celebrating positives you have had a hand in makes your strengths and skills more readily available and less easily masked by negative feelings and thoughts. Remember, all human beings are good at problem solving and learning! Associate your name with your skills; make a list on a postcard to carry around and refer to when you are feeling low.

Second, we are at our most skilled and use our minds most effectively when we are experiencing positive feelings, so working from strengths involves maximizing positive feelings. The practical strategy is focusing our attention on positive experiences as our feelings follow our focus of attention. Successful focus on positives will switch mind and body into positive feelings, unwinding and relaxing us. This can be done through music, or activities that you enjoy. Focusing on positive experiences needs practice: try and find some enjoyable experiences each day and list them, out loud or on paper (see Figure 1). Swop some with a friend or colleague.

Changing situations   Think creatively and use the following strategies to reduce the incidence of situations you find upsetting. Where you have the choice, minimize the number of new or challenging situations you are taking on — at home and work. Consider which situations at work are inevitable and which could be changed. Within working teams discuss the impact of necessary administration and systems that are not under your control and see what ideas there are for minimizing stress produced. In particular this should be done when changes are being implemented.

Find more support from others for yourself and share support with others, among your family and friends or more formally through a colleagues' support group or a women's support group. This will alter the impact of stressful situations for you. Another way of altering the impact of stressful situations is to work on clarifying your personal values. Some useful exercises called "values clarification" can be used with groups or individuals see *Meeting Yourself Halfway*, by Sid Simon).

Dealing with inappropriate negative feelings   The simplest way to unload feelings after upsetting experiences is to talk through them. If you don't talk a lot naturally, try and deliberately increase the amount you do. Talk about what's happened on the wards to friends or family, particularly new experiences. Talk through any particularly negative experiences — several times if you can. Encourage yourself to express any feelings that come up, and be willing to listen to others in return — if you don't take turns you may be increasing someone else's stress level.

To get thoughts and feelings off your chest after you've had to hold them in, express them loudly in uncensored words — when you're alone or with friends who know you are getting rid of unwanted feelings, and not rehearsing for next time you meet the people concerned.

Encourage natural emotional discharge   Laughing, crying, shaking, and storming are all natural healing processes which restore mind and body to alertness and readiness for the next task. When you can let them go, do so. Since we have all been stopped from unloading feelings under the mistaken assumption that it is childish we need to feel safe to let go. When it is inappropriate, save them until later — use positive focusing to help control them and later find someone you can trust to express your feelings to. Letting go is not only immediately freeing, it also helps disrupt blocks (see Figure 2). However, be careful that storming is not destructive. If you are hurting yourself by banging your hands on a hard surface, this is not discharge — try ripping a cardboard box instead. If someone else is being destructive, interrupt them decisively, be supportive and suggest other ways to express anger.

Figure 2.

Dealing with inappropriate negative feelings is working against stress at a fundamental level. This approach may be pursued in counselling and in those growth groups that encourage the expression of feelings; a particularly useful system is co-counselling through peer pairs.

Relaxation Loosening muscular tension helps reduce stress. Some simple natural methods can often be used on the wards. These are known as "active relaxation" and they directly interrupt muscular tensions.
- **Stretching:** Reach upwards or outwards, make it slow and flowing like a cat.
- **Yawning:** Practise making it long and deep for effective relaxation.
- **Shaking:** Shake any and all parts of your body — this is particularly useful to loosen shoulders when you are feeling tense and anxious.
- **Jaw wobbling:** Let the bottom half of your jaw hang down, then shake your head from side to side so that the jaw wobbles loosely.
- **Neck loosening:** Done in the following way this will untense many other muscles as well. Use when standing still or sitting. Check that you are balanced evenly on both feet or buttocks. Move your arms and legs if necessary so they are not crossed. Loosen the neck muscles by rocking your head *very slightly* back and forth on the top vertebra, where the spinal column enters the skull. Do not tip your chin upwards, but position your head by imagining a gentle tugging on the middle of the top and allowing it to float upwards.

Learning and practising relaxation methods regularly will help you relax anytime you need to by giving yourself an instruction. A very useful relaxation position (see Figure 3) was developed by Alexander (the Alexander technique will be described and discussed in a Factsheet as part of our series on complementary medicine) as was the neck release.

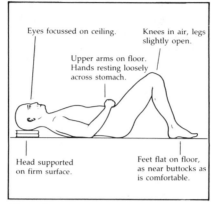

Figure 3.

Another method is progressive relaxation (Madders (1979)).

Tackle negative thoughts which produce tensions   While focusing on positive experiences can be very helpful, it is often insufficient. A generally useful everyday strategy to reduce stress by discharging tension is the use of humour. Laughter produces relaxation and reduces the likelihood of the negative thoughts being compulsive.

Thoughts or words that are aggressive to others or put-downs of yourself, can be effectively disrupted. The more serious the negative thoughts are the more effective lighthearted disruptors are. Usually laughter will result, but other forms of emotional discharge processes like crying can also occur. There are three types of suitable disruptive phrases:
Contradictions: An opposite or a contradictory phrase, for example "That was really tactful of me" after you've just been tactless.
Parody: Mockery or parody can be used as a disrupter, for instance "I'm the best mess-maker around!"
Celebrate the distress: An exaggerated phrase such as "Whoopee a mistake!" or "Hurrah, a panic!" can disrupt serious negative thoughts. All such phrases work best when you say them loudly and put energy into them. You are not trying to believe the phrases but using them to disrupt unreasonable negatives. Discuss and practise the strategy with colleagues.

Bibliography
Evison, R., and Horobin, R. (1985) How To Change Yourself & Your World: A Manual of Co-counselling Theory and Practice, 2nd edn. Co-Counselling Phoenix, Sheffield.
    This describes the peer support system and includes more information on working from strengths, discharging feelings, and disrupting negative thoughts. For information on basic classes send an sae to Co-Counselling Phoenix, 5 Victoria Road, Sheffield S10 2DJ.
Barker, S. (1978) The Alexander Technique. Bantam Books, New York.
    A practical book about the Alexander technique.
Madders, J. (1979) Stress and Relaxation in Positive Health Guide Series, Martin Dunitz, London.

Covers the practice of progressive relaxation – a method introduced by Jacobsen which concentrates on identifying muscular tension and relaxing deeply.

Meichenbaum, D. (1983) Coping with Stress Century Publishing Co., London.
A short and easily read book, this covers most areas but is short of suggestions for dealing with feelings and blocks – something also apparent in many general texts.

Simon, S. (1974) Meeting Yourself Halfway. Argus Communications, Niles, Illnois.
A series of values clarification exercises for working through individually.

57

An active role for patients in stress management

Alison Wallace, BA, RGN, CertEd

Head of School, Health Studies, Darlington College of Technology, and Stress Therapist, Netherlaw Surgery, Darlington

The debilitating aspects of stress can lead to emotional disturbances that cause people to seek help from their GP, but the character of general practice means that the needs of many patients with emotional disorders will remain unmet and their problems unresolved (McLeod, 1988). This article describes the establishing of a stress management clinic, facilitated by a nurse, in the general practice setting, which aims to promote methods of self-help for stress by developing people's personal resources which enable them to cope. The techniques can also be used by nurses themselves to reduce their own stress.

Stress and energy loss

When the body perceives danger or when an energetic response is necessary, an increase in bodily tension occurs which is normal and generally beneficial. The body makes adjustments automatically with a response that presents few problems for energy resources. The term 'stress' can be used to describe the extra demands on energy reserves caused by pressures from the internal or external environment, which overwhelm an individual's adaptive capacity at a time when obtaining sufficient rest is also threatened.

Stress is not a disturbance in behaviour itself, but the effect of stressors causing disturbances which are inappropriate and counterproductive. They may manifest themselves as symptoms ranging from discomfort or disquiet to ill health and an inability to cope.

There is a trend that patients suffering stress-related ill health become chronic attenders at GPs' surgeries and may assume that their problems can only be alleviated by pharmaceutical means (France, 1986). The concern over the widespread use of psychotropic drugs has encouraged many GPs to seek alternative treatments, but doctors are frequently too pressurised by the time constraints of the consultation to be able to offer alternative therapies for a sustained reduction of tension. In an attempt to solve this latter problem a research project, supported by the Northern Regional Health Authority, was designed to evaluate the effect of offering a stress management programme as an adjunct or alternative to other treatments for stress-related symptoms.

The research project

The study took place in one general practice over 18 months, with the stress management programme conducted by a 'therapist' with both nursing and teaching experience. Patients were referred by practice doctors having been diagnosed as suffering from problems related to, or aggravated by, stress. It was envisaged that patients would be neither too disabled nor distressed by their problems to benefit from the therapy. Table 1 shows the range of problems – most patients suffered a combination of those listed.

Problem	%
Anxiety/tension	77
Depression	27
Work-related	21
Psychosomatic symptoms	14
Phobic symptoms	11
Panic attacks	8
Hypertension/cardiovascular disease	8
Sadness	7
Bereavement	6
Other: Marital problems Insomnia Hypochondriasis Lack of assertiveness Psoriasis Asthma Drug withdrawal Unemployment	3

Table 1. Referral problems: age range 12–79 (N=109).

The management regime was aimed at explicit and clearly defined goals and offered a balanced combination of imaginative counselling, education and practical exercises. It was centred on solving current problems rather than dwelling on past history or abstract theory. The study design took into consideration the high turnover rate of people attending GPs' surgeries and the limited resources available.

It was made clear that the therapist was acting as a member of the primary care team and that the patients were totally in control of the situation and could leave the treatment programme at any point – this in itself helped to re-establish self-control and self-direction in some people. It was explained that by taking an active part in their programme, patients would become more responsible for their own health and would start to remove the negative influences of tension.

The results of the project revealed that patients who had received stress management training were more able to accept and come to terms with stress in everyday life, reduce the severity of their symptoms and plan and adapt coping strategies, compared to a control group which did not receive stress management intervention (Wallace, 1988). As the project progressed it became clear that changes in the quality of care were evolving. Patients provided encouraging feedback both during their sessions and in an evaluation questionnaire completed three months after their programme ended.

Stress management programme

Reducing inner tension requires effort and creativity, and most people develop personal strategies for coping with stress-provoking events. Those who feel overwhelmed by their problems sometimes find it difficult to believe change can occur when there are no clear routes or obvious guarantees. The nurse is in an ideal position to create a caring-trust relationship that offers total commitment, warmth, empathy and perceptiveness to help the patient see that change is possible and remain responsive to those trying to help.

> - The environment
> - Protected time
> - Assessment checklist
> - Sequence of coping skills
> - Evaluation of progress

Table 2. Areas to consider in designing a programme.

Bond (1986) emphasised that it is important to achieve a balance of coping strategies, and this must be borne in mind when designing a programme of care. Table 2 shows the main areas for consideration.

The environment

This can mean more than just physical location. The nurse must ensure a comfortable and private therapeutic setting in which the patient can feel a sense of care – if patients do not feel secure their stress-related problems may escalate. The stress management setting should be viewed as a calm oasis and not be the cause of additional stress from noise or unnecessary interruptions. The nurse must assess the need for modifications in the patient's own environment and not overlook the social, psychological and economic situations in which the patient functions, as they all influence health and must be taken into consideration when planning healthcare (Kratz, 1979).

Protected time

Sufficient time needs to be allocated for the patient to make a positive step forward during each session. In this study, 20 to 30 minutes provided a realistic opportunity for progress to be made.

A one-to-one situation requires a high level of concentration, so the nurse should inform the patient that, although time has to be limited, it is also 'protected' and that problems can be discussed and goals set without interruption.

The assessment checklist

This will enable the nurse to assess whether stress management is appropriate for patients with specific problems (Table 3). The problems for which it has proved useful can be grouped as follows:
- Specific psychological disturbances eg, anxiety, tension, phobic symptoms, drug withdrawal, depression.
- Problems of daily living eg, family, work, unemployment, insomnia, smoking/alcohol.
- Problems related to ill health eg, hypertension, asthma, pain, heart disease.

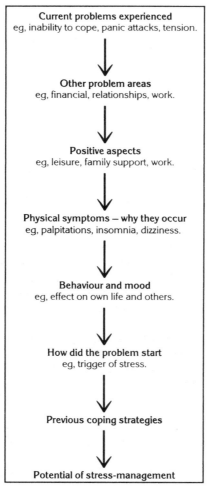

Table 3. The assessment checklist.

This list is based on the study, and is by no means complete but, in any case, if the nurse feels that stress management will help, it should be tried, providing it is monitored and evaluated with care. Signs of previously poor attempts at coping are also indicative that stress management retraining is necessary. The checklist also provides a useful guide for baseline measurements against which progress can be monitored and strategies evaluated. It is not intended to be used as a structured interview but as a guide for the nurse to lead the patient gently into a discussion which can reveal all aspects of the problem. It is essential that, after the initial discussion, both nurse and patient share a common concept of the cause of the stress.

Some people will deny that stress is influencing their health, convincing themselves that their symptoms are organic in origin. Rarely will they consider their thinking processes to be the source of the trouble. 'Acceptance' is therefore the first stage of recovery, and the nurse can facilitate this process by redefining the problem with the patient. The patient should then be able to make his or her own relationships based on personal values between symptoms and stressors. The patient can only work towards recovery if the problem is confronted, as avoidance can cause an escalation of pressure. Confrontation can bring long-term relief whereas over-reliance on limited coping mechanisms, which do not enable the patient to face up to the problem, may ultimately induce more stress.

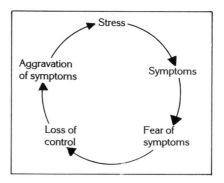

Stress frequently places people within a vicious circle from which it is difficult to escape (Figure 1). The sense of 'loss of control' is often central to the presenting problem, and by regaining control, relief from stress will occur (Table 4). Coping strategies should be planned to help restore the sense of control in the individual and provide a balance between counselling, education and exercises.

Counselling   Support interventions are those which accept the patient as he or she is without the pressure for greater awareness and change.

The nurse must know the patients and listen carefully to how they have assessed their own experience. Patients will then require time for emotional expression which may have been suppressed by others 'not understanding', and from this, greater self-awareness – necessary for exploring and sharing problems will evolve. Individuals can then be taught to recognise that they are active agents in their pattern of distress and that by talking through their difficulties they will regain a sense of cognitive control. Client-centred counselling should be used with all patients and, with stress-related problems, may be all that is required to bring relief.

Control	Nurse objectives	Examples of patient strategies	Effect
Cognitive control	Counsel. Show patient that he is an active agent in his own distress.	Focus on a positive thought. Plan attainable goals for the day.	Helps adjustment in any situation.
Special goals date			
Decision control	Redefine the problem. Identify stressors.	Decide to follow stress management programme. Plan a better diet. Choose to rest for a while.	Helps you make decisions in more demanding situations.
Special goals date			
Behaviour control	Teach exercises for symptom relief.	Practise techniques regularly.	Reduces discomfort and breaks the vicious circle of tension.
Special goals date			
Information control	Give information and facilitate learning.	Understand why symptoms occur and their triggers.	Helps you come to terms with stress in everyday life.
Special goals date			

The patient and therapist/nurse will discuss the special goals and the date by which they will be achieved.

Table 4. Regaining control.

Group 1
These exercises will enable your body to get the feel of tension and relaxation. To help cut down on distraction close your eyes.
1. Clench both fists and feel the tension in your hands and forearms, now relax.
2. Pull both hands upwards to touch your shoulders and tense your upper arm, now relax.
3. Straighten your arms tightly by your side and feel the sensation, almost of pain, now relax and leave your arms resting by your sides.

Group 2
Consider the sensation of touch where your head and shoulders are resting on the pillow.
1. Shrug your shoulders and feel the tension, now relax.
2. Gently press your head back into the pillow and notice how tension arises between the shoulder blades and upwards into your neck. This type of tension may happen frequently during your daily activity, leading to headaches or pain in your upper back. Now release the tension and feel that your head is once more resting back gently on the pillow.

Group 3
To push unwanted thoughts away that might be getting in the way of relaxation concentrate on seeing the word 'calm' written across your mind each time you now relax a muscle group.
1. Raise your eyebrows and feel the tension in your forehead, now relax and think 'calm'.
2. Frown and squeeze your eyes shut, now relax, think 'calm'.
3. Press the tip of your tongue upwards behind your upper teeth, feel the tension developing, now relax.
4. Press your lips together and feel the tension all over your face, now relax and let all of your facial muscles feel calm.

Group 4
The final sequence involves large muscle groups which, when relaxing, release lots of inner tension.
1. Breathe in deeply and hold your breath for a moment. Now breathe out slowly, in a controlled way, and release the tension in your chest. Now relax and continue comfortable breathing.
2. Pull in the abdominal muscles as tightly as possible, now release them and let go of the tension deep inside of you. Think of the word 'calm' as you let your muscles relax.
3. Straighten your legs and point your toes downwards, now relax and wriggle your toes slightly to help release the tension.

Table 5. The deep muscle relaxation groups.

Education   Opportunity should be taken to explore the patient's lifestyle, to identify factors which could help restore physical wellbeing. For example, health education relating to diet, the need for adequate rest and the pursuit of interests could be discussed. The patient may then be able to look at his or her day-to-day living more logically and plan goals which are easily attainable and help achieve enhanced physical health.

The Exercises
- Deep muscle relaxation;
- breathing techniques;
- quick relaxation;
- calming the mind.

Training in the art of relaxation will restore energy which has been used inappropriately to maintain levels of tension so often present in stress. All the techniques described are easy to learn but will require daily practice for at least three weeks for the patient to alleviate symptoms at will.

• Deep muscle relaxation
The technique described here is adapted from the Jacobson (1976) method and depends on the alternative tensing and relaxing of various muscle groups. The purpose of this exercise is to help the patient recognise when tension is developing and how to 'let go'.

Stand or sit to one side of the patient who should first learn the sequence when lying in a comfortable position. It takes about 10 minutes to work through the following groups of exercises, especially if enough time is allowed for pauses between each group. Quietly talk the patient through the groups as shown in Table 5.

Leave the patient for about one minute and then explain that the exercise is complete and that he or she can get up and yet still carry the feeling of relaxation. As well as the direct value of relaxation, taking 10 minutes out of the day to relax has great symbolic value to anyone who constantly feels under pressure from within or from others.

• Breathing techniques
The 'breathing square' (Figure 2) is an alternative exercise to the deep relaxation method. The patient should be told that this exercise takes the

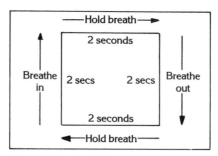

Figure 2. The breathing square.

'edge' off anxiety and can be performed in any situation unobtrusively.

Ask the patient to visualise a square or draw one as you describe the exercise. Allocate a time value, eg, two seconds for each side and ask the patient to breathe by working round the square as shown. Work round the square up to three times and then follow with calm and shallow breathing. The time value can be increased if necessary according to the patient's comfort. This exercise should be practised briefly before it is needed. Sitting in front of the television, working round the edge of the screen has proved useful.

- **Quick relaxation**

Introduce this method to patients who are familiar with the deep relaxation technique. Again, draw a diagram (Figure 3) to help explain.

The patient is told to count backwards from five to one allowing each

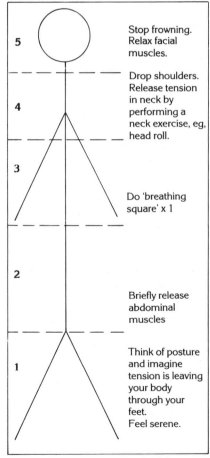

Figure 3. Quick relaxation checklist.

section of the body to release tension and relax before passing down to the next number. It is important to keep practising this techique throughout the day. Using a visual cue, such as several adhesive coloured spots placed in strategic positions, is one way to trigger the sequence. The patient is informed that the response to the cue will eventually fade but at this stage they should be able to relax at will when recognising tension developing.

- **Calming the mind**
The mind is the most difficult area in which to reduce tension, as it becomes filled with unwanted, restless thoughts which inhibit the relaxation process. This method for calming the mind has been adapted from Brande (1934) and has proved useful as a quickly learnt technique:

Simply close your eyes with the idea of holding your mind quite steady, but feeling no urgency or tension about it. At first the sensation may only last a few seconds, but it is essential that the procedure is repeated once a day over a few days.

If this exercise is at first difficult choose a simple object that you can 'cup' in your hands. Hold the object and confine your attention to it calling your mind back to it if unwanted thoughts start creeping back. When you are able to think of the object and nothing else for some moments, take the next step. Close your eyes and continue 'looking at' the object thinking of nothing else.

When you have succeeded, even just for a few seconds, allow the feeling of stillness and calm to refresh and surround you.

Evaluation of progress
Evaluation of progress will take place quite informally during each session. Patients are usually interested in the fact that the exercises are so simple and easy to practise and have obvious beneficial results. Some problems will remain resistant to this type of therapy alone, but patients will appreciate the additional care from the nurse who can use counselling skills to support those undergoing stress. To help patients help themselves is an effective solution to many problems, but an evaluation process must be included to measure the effect of such help so that the nurse will be able to plan which strategies are best for each individual.

An active part
The stress management regime works from different assumptions to the medical model, which provides a diagnosis and treatment – with patients often taking a passive role. Stress management works from the position that patients must develop their own resources and coping mechanisms and therefore take an active part in their treatment. Much of the success of this form of therapy relies on how well the GP or nurse 'sells' the idea to the patient. This depends on whether the doctor or nurse understands

and believes in stress reduction techniques as a means of overcoming stress and increasing the efficiency of the self-healing capacities of the body. Nurses must appreciate that in every disease there is scope for alleviation of physical distress by psychological means and real attempts to improve a patient's ability to cope may prevent a deterioration in health (Wilson-Barnett, 1982).

References
Bond, M. (1986) Methods of dealing with stress. In: Managing Care Pack 16. DLC, South Bank Polytechnic, London.
Brande, D. (1934) Becoming a Writer. Harcourt, Brace and Co, London.
France, R. and Robson, M. (1986) Behaviour Therapy in Primary Care. Croom Helm, Beckenham.
Jacobson, E. (1976) You Must Relax. Souvenir Press, London.
Kratz, C. (1979) The Nursing Process. Balliere Tindall, London.
McLeod, J. (1988) The work of counsellors in general practice. RCGP, London.
Wallace, A. and Michie, A. (1988) Stress management in general practice. Unpublished report for Northern RHA.
Wilson-Barnett, J. (1982) Neuropsychiatric aspects of stress. *The Practitioner,* **226,** 1580-82.

58

A terminal case? Burnout in palliative care

Ann Nash, SRN, DipN, RCNT

Nurse Consultant, the Macmillan Education Centre, Dorothy House Foundation, Bath

Working alongside patients and families coping with the problems of advanced disease is a stressful field for healthcare professionals, yet the specialty attracts large numbers of nurses and other professionals. This chapter reviews the significant literature, attempting to throw light on the incidence of burnout in palliative carers.

Stress

The concept of burnout is not new. Florence Nightingale was aware of the strain and pain of caring, and acknowledged carers' responses and reactions to that stress. The term 'stress' was first used in this context by Cannon in 1925. He coined the word 'homoeostasis', suggesting that the body would normally return to a steady state after such disturbance within the system.

Selye (1956) defined stress as a state of wear and tear, experienced as fatigue, uneasiness or illness, and described a basic biochemical model of adaptation to stress. There is no doubt that this biological reaction is significant, and can be observed. Mind, body and behaviour are closely intertwined, and this leads to a potentially healthy adjustment to the demands of daily living. Appropriate responses to stressful situations enable us to function usefully (Schafer, 1987).

Caring for dying people

Hingley (1985) observes that the public image of stress is generally negative, and explores what elements of nursing give rise to negative feelings of being under stress. In Hingley's work, nurses identified dealing with death and dying as a specific stressor, and this was linked to the expectations that patients will be cured and restored to health by the medical profession. Dying is a normal activity, yet these expectations of cure and health can lead to feelings of inadequacy and, where dying is accepted as inevitable, nurses may also feel unable to cope with the special demands of that specialist role.

The activity of dying, however, is not limited to patients. Nurses who work with the dying and bereaved are brought face to face with their own mortality. This self-awareness can lead to a higher level of stress than the nurse can cope with (Bond, 1986). On starting to work in terminal care, most nurses have high ideals. Idealistic nurses can be exciting, innovative and enthusiastic (Swaffield, 1988), but some of their ideals are unattainable and unrealistic. Standards are not always achievable due to financial, environmental or personal constraints and limitations, and the burnout response in idealistic nurses in such situations may be infectious, affecting a whole group of carers.

Significant stressors

Ward (1985) and Lunt and Yardley (1986) investigated the working patterns of specialist home care nurses in palliative care and observed that, while the stressors involved in caring for the dying and bereaved are undeniable, the major stressors identified as leading to burnout were to do with relationships with other professionals. Those professionals were identified as managers who did not understand or support the aims and objectives of the service and members of the primary health care teams, notably GPs and district nurses, who sometimes blocked the way to good care by their ignorance or in their response to a perceived professional threat. The inability to achieve good pain control and family support led to overwhelming stress in nurses, causing them to question whether the effort was worthwhile.

In her investigation of nurse training for terminal care, Simms (1984) identified the specific stressors for this group, which are lack of specific boundaries leading to overwork, and the inability to limit caseloads and workloads due to an ever increasing demand for specialist input. So these nurses appear to be subject to two major areas of over-stress – lack of useful management of time and objectives, and specific relationships with powerful colleagues who might influence outcomes negatively.

Need for support

Managers and educators involved in developing specialist roles have a specific responsibility to prevent burnout in these nurses, and having recognised the signals of distress, must develop useful interventions (Wilkinson, 1987). Supportive interventions may form a useful basis for the development of coping strategies (Heron, 1986), but the concept of nurses needing personal and professional support is still not widely accepted. Most nurses turn to colleagues informally for such support, but Adey (1987) suggested that it was lacking from teams and managers, and that most nurses felt inadequate in accessing appropriate support when needed. If it is to be effective, this support is needed before this stage, and to enable nurses to deal with the dilemma of reality vs. idealism, it must be available formally and regularly (Nash, 1985).

The implications for nurses of this development of self-awareness of death and dying, when caring for patients in a cancer ward was explored by Baider and Porath (1981). Using the group process, the nurses were able, in a formal setting, to reveal and share their feelings of frustration, anger and sadness. Such team support can be catalytic and cathartic, but can lead to a certain anxiety and wariness about the depth of shared feeling. This group was, in fact, abandoned as a consequence.

Personal involvement

The combination of high technology areas with extremely vulnerable patient groups, as in paediatric oncology units (Waters, 1985) and bone marrow transplant units (Pot-Mees, 1987), demands an acknowledgement of the need for prevention, awareness and early treatment of burnout. Nurses are, therefore, encouraged towards self-help, self-awareness and self-knowledge (Bleazard, 1984).

This development of knowledge of self, acknowledgement of personal reactions and awareness of own needs is essential to useful helping. Such personal work enables a level of involvement and helping which has more to offer the patient, but requires built-in supportive/supervisory intervention. Bailey, Burnard and Smith (1985) organised a workshop for managers involved in supporting staff, to examine methods of preventing and dealing with burnout. They used experiential exercises to raise awareness of the potential effects of burnout. Their concept of 'degrees' of burnout could enable managers to interrupt this process. The group was able to plan preventive measures.

Such workshops allow professionals to acknowledge that stress exists, that over-stress can be dangerous, and that we must learn to recognise the early stages of burnout in colleagues and, hopefully, in ourselves. Only when stress is accepted as an inevitable consequence of striving for high standards in a climate of severe constraints will we plan and be ready to tackle consequences effectively.

Growth

As we have seen, if such stressors did not exist, there would be little impetus towards improving standards of care. The starting point is the acknowledgement that nurses are people too (Holland, 1987), and that they are reacting to life and death both within and without the work environment; growing and learning about themselves among others. Caring for the dying and bereaved provides an opportunity for personal growth, working alongside professionals who also struggle with the problems of growth and change. While the stressors are huge, the rewards and satisfactions (both personal and professional) in palliative care are enormous.

References
Adey, C. (1987) Stress: who cares?. *Nursing Times,* **83,** 4, 52-53.
Baider, L. and Porath, S. (1981) Uncovering fear: group experience of nurse in a cancer ward. International *Journal of Nursing Studies,* **18,** 47-52.
Bailey, C., Burnard, P., Smith, R., (1985) Breaking the ice. *Nursing Mirror,* **160,** 1, 26-28.
Bleazard, R. (1984) Knowing oneself. *Nursing Times,* **80,** 10, 44-46.
Bond, M. (1986) Stress and Self-Awareness: A Guide for Nurses. Heinemann, London.

Cannon, W.B. (1935) Stresses and strains of homeostasis. *American Journal of Medical Science,* **189,** 1.

Heron, J. 1986 Six Category Intervention Analysis. Human Potential Research Project, University of Surrey.

Hingley, P. (1985) Stress in nurse managers. Royal College of Nursing Research Society, June.

Holland, S. (1987) Stress in Nursing. *Nursing Times,* **83,** 21, 59-61.

Lunt, B. and Yardley and Hospital Support Teams for the Terminally Ill. Cancer Care Research Unit, Southampton (unpublished).

Nash, A. (1985) Bereavement: staff support. *Nursing,* **2,** 43, 1288.

Pot-Mees, C. (1987) Beating the burn-out. *Nursing Times,* **83,** 30, 33-35.

Schafer, W. (1987) Stress Management for Wellness. Holt Reinhart and Winston, New York.

Selye, H. (1956) The Stress of Life. McGraw Hill, New York.

Simms, M. (1984) Nurse training for terminal care. *Senior Nurse,* **1,** 34, 21-22.

Swaffield, L. (1988) Burn-out. *Nursing Standard,* 14, 2, 24-25.

Ward, A.W.M. (1985) Home Care Services for the Terminally Ill: A Report for the Nuffield Foundation. University of Sheffield Medical School.

Waters, A.L. (1985) Support for staff in a Paediatric oncology unit. *Nursing,* **2,** 43, 1275-77.

Wilkinson, S. (1987) The reality of nursing cancer patients. *Lampada,* **12,** 12-19.

Managing Aggression

59

Handling aggression

Ruth E. Smith, BSs, RGN, RMN, DN Cert.
Support Worker in Rehabilitation, Lothian Regional Council, Department of Social Work

"Aggression is not necessarily destructive at all. It springs from an innate tendency to grow and master life which seems to be characteristic of all living matter. Only when this same life force is obstructed in its development do ingredients of anger, rage or hate become connected with it." (C. M. Thomson, 1964).

We all have an understanding of what we mean when we describe someone as "aggressive", "hostile", "frustrated", "angry" or "violent", but each of these terms can be used to describe a variety of states, and Table 1 gives reasonable working definitions.

Aggression: Activity by which a person intends to inflict physical damage or pain upon a person who seeks to avoid such attacks, or physical change to an inanimate object. We usually consider the negative and potentially harmful (dysfunctional) effects of aggression but it can also have positive or creative (functional) effects.

Hostility: Antagonistic speech or action which does not inflict physical harm but which is directed against a person who seeks to avoid such behaviour.

Frustration: Feelings resulting from being thwarted or prevented from pursuing a course of action or achieving a goal. Feelings of frustration may build up to form feelings of anger.

Anger: An active feeling of antagonism toward a person or object which, if expressed, will result in aggression or hostility.

Violence: Intense, powerful, and impetuous activity intended to result in damage to property or injury to a person or people. Violence may be used by someone exhibiting aggression.

Table 1. Working definition of terms.

The nature of aggressive behaviour

Aggression can be expressed in many different ways. The two most extreme forms are *passive* and *overt* aggression, which could be defined by using some of the criteria outlined in Table 2. Aggression is manifested in a variety of thoughts, feelings, bodily responses, and actions (Table 3).

It is important to distinguish between assertion and aggression. In assertive behaviour, the subject gives legitimate expression to his own interests; there is *no intention* to inflict pain or damage.

Included in the normal patterns of human socialisation (development of social skills) is the control of aggression, and in our society this can often result in inhibiting its direct expression and its indirect expression in "acceptable" behaviour. Individual differences in the exact nature of the expression seem to result from the individual learning and satisfaction gained from the process of socialisation. Feelings of aggression may be displaced into acceptable outlets — such as sport — and a single-minded determination to succeed in whatever field a person chooses. Equally, it can be displaced into unacceptable or harmful outlets.

Factors that may contribute to outbursts of aggressive or violent behaviour

Aggressive behaviour may be seen as the culmination of a number of contributing factors. Klein (1957) states that "the capacity for both love and for destructive impulses is to some extent constitutional though varying individually in strength and interacting from the beginning with external conditions."

The sources that may contribute to an individual's aggressive behaviour can broadly be divided into *intrinsic* (physiological, psychological, and psychopathological) and *extrinsic* (environmental and sociological) factors,

Table 2. Comparison of passive and overt aggression

Criteria	Passive/Latent	Active/Overt
Content of speech	Self-derogatory "I can't"	Other-derogatory "You never!"
Tone of voice	Quiet, cold	Loud, demanding
Interpersonal space	Distant	Invasive
Underlying message	"Hard done by"	"I'll get you!"
Measure of control	Moderate	Minimal
Feeling expressed	Resentment	Anger

and several from each group may be involved. The source of aggression may have some bearing on the way in which the aggression is expressed.

The physiology of aggression

The body has a biochemical system which results in the emotions and actions that we call aggressive. The arousal of emotion serves the purpose of preparing the body to take action. This is the "flight/fight" reaction which is mediated by the release of adrenalin and noradrenalin by the hypothalamus. The release of these is normally under inhibitory control by the cerebral cortex, but when a threat is perceived this control is released and the flight/fight response begins. Increased levels of adrenalin and noradrenalin in the blood cause increases in pulse rate, blood pressure, the rate of respiration, and other physiological changes (Table 3), which prepare the body for flight or fight, and if the opportunity for flight is denied (or inappropriate) the person will "fight" or become aggressive. These bodily responses are similar when an individual experiences *stress* which is perhaps usefully seen as an inwardly directed aggressive response.

Thoughts

Acknowledgement of want or need; Misperception; Distortion of reality; Impaired judgement; Diminished concentration

Feelings

Powerlessness; Annoyance; Anxiety; Frustration; Resentment; Anger; Hostility; Hurt; Humiliation; Vengeance; Defensiveness; Fury; Rage

Bodily responses

Increased blood pressure, pulse, and respirations; Muscle tension; Perspiration; Flushed skin; Nausea, vomiting; Dry mouth; Yawning; Flatulence; Itching; Blushing; Paling; Impotence; Frigidity

Actions

Direct: Argumentativeness; Verbal assaults; Blaming others; Domineering; Demanding; Belligerance; Manipulation; Physical control; Combativeness; Violence — fighting, rape, homicide, suicide. *Indirect;* Forgetting; Misunderstanding, Procrastinating; Being late; Failing to learn

Table 3. Manifestations of aggression (adapted from Trygstad and Jasmin, 1979).

Certain physiological conditions may increase the likelihood of an aggressive outburst, for example: hyperactivity of the thyroid gland (thyrotoxicosis) which causes an individual to become over-excited and irritable; epilepsy (particularly temporal lobe); and brain damage (either temporary or permanent) are examples of these. Agents, such as alcohol, other drugs, or anaesthesia can also precipitate aggressive behaviour; they appear to lower the individual's level of inhibition.

There has been considerable research into the observation that a high dietary sugar (sucrose) content increases the likelihood of aggressive or violent behaviour. Schauss (1975) discovered a strong correlation between the level of sugar intake and delinquent or violent behaviour among young offenders in the USA, and other studies have shown that a society's increase in sugar consumption is paralleled by the rise in violent crime.

The physiology and psychopathology of aggression

An individual's unique personality plays a large part in the exact manifestation of aggressive feelings and behaviour. Personality also affects the levels to which fear, anxiety, stress, pain, and insecurity are experienced, and therefore modify the effects that these factors have in contributing towards aggressive or other responses.

Psychological disturbances may play an important part in an individual's perception of reality and their responses to it — this is particularly true of any illness in which the patient suffers from delusions or hallucinations. A delusion may be defined as a false belief (out of keeping with the patient's background) which cannot be corrected by appeal to reason. Hallucinations are false perceptions without any sensory basis — the most common being auditory or visual hallucinations. The illnesses most commonly associated with these symptoms include schizophrenia, mania, depression, and toxic states induced by either drugs or alcohol. Illnesses that cause blunting of affect and loss of inhibition may cause the individual to exhibit behaviour he would normally control. Senile and pre-senile dementia, particularly Alzheimer's disease, are examples of this.

Environmental and sociological factors in aggression

It seems likely that many factors in a person's environment may contribute toward feelings of aggression, and these are the subject of considerable research. Inadequate housing, inappropriate education, and unemployment may all be factors in aggression for different individuals. A sudden or substantial change in a person's environment may also contribute, and this is a factor that nurses can significantly affect.

If a person becomes ill and therefore reliant on medical and nursing intervention, particularly if this involves a dramatic change in physical environment (such as admission to hospital), this may contribute toward feelings of aggression. A hospital may be seen as a "total institution" as defined by Goffman and exhibiting the problems he describes — frustration due to lack of privacy and enforced companionship, the restrictions imposed by all daily activities occurring in one building, and the helplessness experienced.

Balancing the needs of the individual and the restrictions of hospital policy may be one of the nurse's most difficult tasks. As Smeaton and Field (1985) suggest "Such (aggressive) behaviour may occur in situations which the individual perceives to be oppressive and which appear to enforce undesired behaviour or change.

Sociological factors that contribute toward aggressive behaviour are the subject of considerable research. Factors studied in this regard include: the effects of peer group pressures, life experiences, and expectations; aggression within the family; and limitations imposed upon the individual by society. The work of Milgram (1964) suggests that individuals within *groups* have a different sense of responsibility for their actions from that which the same individuals would exhibit if acting independently.

The socialisation process that occurs during childhood affects the way in which individuals develop their responses to factors that may contribute to aggression — and also their responses to aggression itself. As Smeaton and Field (1985) state ''There is some support for the suggestion that hostility in adults rises from elements of repressed hatred in childhood, perhaps as a result of having had repressive parents. The adult conscience should be able to reconcile itself with external authority but a conscience developed in childhood under the threat of extreme punishment is likely to carry a great deal of resentment and hostility.'' The effect of portrayals of violent or aggressive behaviour in the media on the development of aggressive responses is the subject of continuing debate.

The nurse's role
Various factors that may contribute toward someone becoming aggressive inherent when an individual becomes a patient include: the illness itself and the associated pain, anxiety, uncertainty, insecurity, and loss of independence and privacy. A major change of environment (such as the move into a hospital) also constitutes a predisposing factor. Certain nursing procedures, and the rigid routine of many hospital wards also contribute. A nurse's responses and attitude toward her patients could also predispose a patient toward aggression. Huffington and Brunning (1985) in their research show nurses as a group to be most insecure about their role — the majority of nurses feel that their opinions and training were not valued by other members of the ward team. This insecurity and feeling of lack of support may be reflected in nurses' responses to patients — feelings of frustration and resentment being displaced onto the patients.

Preventing aggression
Consider your own working environment carefully and try to identify any factors in it that may contribute towards feelings of aggression on the part of patients, their relatives, your colleagues, and yourself. Consider, too, the relevant factors related to the patients' illnesses.

If these factors can be identified, then steps can be taken to make changes in procedures and routines which make then less frustrating to patients and/or staff; and to improve the style and level of communication between staff, patients, and relatives, thus improving these relationships and establishing a valuable level of trust between individuals. If a patient is becoming frustrated or angry, assisting them to express their feelings and to develop better coping mechanisms (perhaps by directing their feelings *constructively*) may prevent an aggressive or violent outburst later. A supportive attitude towards the patient will help to increase their self-esteem, and enable them to take things less personally and to establish a sense of responsibility towards the control of their own feelings.

How to respond if aggression occurs

As Glynn Owens and Ashcroft (1985) state "Because of the rich variety of human behaviour and the number of ways in which people may respond to what goes on around them, it is not possible to give rigid guides on how to behave in an aggressive incident". The following guidelines may be of help, however.

1. Recognise that aggressive behaviour may occur in any situation not solely in psychiatric or casualty units.
2. Try to prevent violent behaviour occurring rather than planning how to manage it. This involves getting to know the patient's past strategies for dealing with anger, disappointments, and frustration. Is he more anxious at certain times of day, or when he is surrounded by people; could his anger/frustration be diverted into other channels?
3. Do not respond aggressively since this will increase the chance of further aggression. Face the patient, speak gently, slowly, and clearly, telling the patient who you are, using his name, and telling him what you want him to do. Nonverbal communication is equally important — an aggressive stance that challenges or confronts the patient, such as holding your arms crossed or your hands on your hips, increases the likelihood of further aggression. The aim is to calm the patient and decrease the chance of violent behaviour. This is not easy because anger tends to excite anger in others.
4. If the threat of violence is imminent, try to avoid potentially dangerous locations such as the top of the stairs, or restricted spaces, or where there is furniture or equipment that could be used as an offensive weapon. Ensure that you have a means of escaping from the situation and that at least one other person is aware of the situation and can get help if necessary.
5. Never be alone with an actively violent person; keep a comfortable distance from them and do not invade their personal space. Be prepared to move; violent patients may strike suddenly. Legally you may only use the minimum reasonable force to restrain a patient or you may find yourself charged with assault.
6. Effective communication must be established or re-established after the violent outburst. This involves the setting up of a trusting relationship which can only be based on mutual respect. The patient can be encouraged to identify their own feelings of anger and to explore alternative ways of coping with or directing these, and possibly establish techniques for cooling off, such as relaxation. The patient's responsibility for their own behaviour should also be explored, and the acceptable limits of behaviour established and defined with the rationale for them given. The consequences of going beyond them should also be explored and limits enforced if they are transgressed. Positive feedback should also be given when limits are adhered to.

Bibliography

Atkinson, R., Atkinson R., and Hilgrad, E., (1983) Introduction to Psychology, 8th edition. Harcourt, Brace, and Jovanovich, New York.

A good reference book covering all areas of psychology.

Glynn Owens, R., and Ashcroft J.B., (1985) Violence – A Guide for the Caring Professions, Croom Helm Ltd, Kent.

Views the problem of violence from three different perspectives (biological, social and psychological) and includes research findings. Detailed reading in the study of violence.

Morris, D. (1979) Manwatching. Jonathan Cape Ltd., London.

Enjoyable reading which will tell you a lot, not only about others' behaviour but also your own.

Royal College of Psychiatrists and Royal College of Nursing (1985) The Principles of Good Medical and Nursing Practice in the Management of Violence in Hospital. RCN London.

Practical suggestions for nursing/hospital policy and 'on the ward' situations. May be available in Nursing/Medical Libraries.

Storr, A., (1968) Human Aggession, Pelican Books, England.

Worth reading for an overall view of aggression.

References

Glynn Owens, R., and Ashcroft, J. B., (1985) Violence — a Guide for the Caring Professions. Croom Helm Ltd., London.

Goffman, E., (1968) Asylums. Pelican Books, London.

Huffington and Brunning, (1985) Altered Images. *Nursing Times,* 31 July, 24.

Klein, M., (1957) Envy and Gratitude. Tavistock Press, London.

Milgram, S., (1964) Group Pressure and Action against a Person, *Journal of Abnormal Social Psychology,* **69,** 137.

Schauss, A., (1975) Diet, Crime and Delinquency. Cancer Control Society, USA.

Smeaton, W., and Field, J., (1985) The Nature and Management of Hostility. *Nursing,* **2,** 1033.

Storr, A., (1968) Human Aggression. Pelican Books, London.

Thomson, C. M., (1964) Interpersonal Psycho-analysis. Basic Books, New York.

Trygstead, and Jasmin, (1979) Behavioural Concepts and the Nursing Process. C. V. Mosby,

60

Violence and the organisation

Andy Gibb, RMN
Nurse Teacher at Wycombe Health Authority

For many years violence in psychiatric hospitals has been a matter of concern. The focus is now widening to include other nursing specialties such as casualty departments and community nursing. Many reasons are offered for this increase in violence towards staff (Dewar, 1987). It has been said that society is becoming more violent in general and that this will be reflected in a nurse's sphere of work. Other excuses such as staff sickness and so on are also offered to explain away patient violence.

While working as a senior charge nurse on an acute psychiatric admission ward the author was alarmed at the frequency and severity of violent incidents and began to feel that these types of explanation were a barrier to acknowledging that violence can be controlled and reduced by altering methods of providing nursing care and by devising effective preventive strategies. It is important that staff and management do not come to expect and tolerate violence from patients as being 'part of the job' or that 'anything goes'. Such defeatist attitudes and acceptance of the unacceptable will only worsen the situation.

The perceived problem

A small multidisciplinary group was formed at the Maudsley Hospital to consider the issue of violence and how organisational factors may contribute to it. It was done to enable more control to be taken over the working environment when it was realised that staff remained at risk while waiting for management and government initiatives. Initial discussions revealed a wealth of knowledge and experience in dealing with violence. This had been gained through direct contact and by assimilating research findings. It seemed that staff were equipping themselves as individuals to cope with violence, and when they could no longer tolerate the environment, they left — taking with them their hard-earned coping techniques. The multidisciplinary group needed to know about these effective strategies and incorporate them into ward policy and practices. In this way, learning to cope with violence would be a shared activity benefiting the whole group.

Assessing level and severity

The emotive issue of violence creates responses that are not easily definable. It was important, therefore, to be certain that the frequency and severity of incidents were actually increasing and that it was not just the nurse's reactions to them that had increased. The hospital has maintained a 'Violent Incident Register' over the last 10 years to collate basic data, which is compiled from forms completed by staff after each incident of threatened or actual violence. A system devised by Fottrell (1980) enables the severity of the incidents to be rated (Table 1).

Contact incidents
1   No physical injury detected/suspected in victim.
2   Minor physical injury (bruises, abrasions, small lacerations).
3   Physical injury, large lacerations, fractures, loss of consciousness, special investigations needed.

Non-contact incidents
0   No physical contact, but threats and potential for violence apparent.

Table 1. Fottrell's rating system for violence.

A dangerous rating (D) was also added to this system for incidents that may only rate 0 but which are judged to be potentially dangerous. These tend to involve male patients whose threats are regarded as noninjurious, but where a weapon is involved. However, the D rating takes no account of the stress involved in such incidents for staff.

The system is computerised. In 1982 it was found that seven patients were responsible for 30 per cent of all violence, and 16 per cent of the most serious incidents (rated 2 or 3). Also, women were responsible for more incidents than men (64 as opposed to 54 per cent), although men caused more serious ones. Most of the attacks in 1982 were committed against nurses (53 per cent), while 36 per cent were against patients and 9 per cent against other staff.

In the past year it was found that not only had the number of violent incidents increased but they were also of greater severity than previously. Comparing this acute psychiatric admission ward with the rest of the hospital it could be seen that:
- It had more violence per inpatient day.
- There were more incidents of medium severity.
- More patients took no medication.
- Fewer patients were involved in only one incident.

The results also demonstrate a change in the pattern of severity of violent incidents. For example, for every incident rated 1 in 1982, there were three in 1983-84, although the level of incidents rated 3 remained much the same.

Compared to Fottrell's findings at Tooting Bec Hospital, London, the demographic data about patients in this hospital is parallel; the major difference is in the level of severity of violence. From the figures it was apparent that nurses on this acute psychiatric admission ward were exposed to a higher level of violence than other areas of the hospital, and indeed other hospitals, and that the levels were on the increase. This meant poor staff morale which was reflected in a high level of staff sickness and turnover, resulting in even greater difficulty in reducing violence.

The environment

This study led the investigating group to believe that factors in the ward environment were contributing to higher levels of violence. The possibility of manipulating the environment to control violence has been reflected in research findings. For example, Drinkwater and Feldman (1982) found that most violence occurred under the following conditions:

1. In the daytime.
2. When there are no planned ward activities.
3. During mealtimes in the canteen.
4. In the dormitory.
5. When most staff are occupied temporarily away from the ward.

   Drinkwater reviewed studies which demonstrated that administrative and structural changes affected levels of violence. She also looked at the organisational aspects of a ward and demonstrated that ward routine affected the behaviour of patients. McGuire (1977) looked at staff-patient interaction and its relationship to patients' behaviour patterns. He found that when interaction decreased, deviant behaviour, including violence, increased. These findings helped the group decide to take positive action regarding ward structure and organisation. One area considered was patient access to the nurses' office. Some nurses allowed this, others did not. Such inconsistency could have produced conflict resulting in violence.

Before, during and after an incident

Hospital guidelines about the management of violent incidents are available and are taught to all staff. There is also an emergency team which provides assistance when summoned by a bleep system. Dealing with incidents once they had occurred seemed to be effective.

However, these arrangements seemed to mean that staff could take effective control only after an incident had occurred. Aitken (1982) undertook a study on the ward which suggested that nursing staff were not accurate in their assessment of imminent violence, as they relied largely on verbal communication as a predictor. He devised a rating scale concentrating on nonverbal behaviour which provided greater predictive accuracy. His guidelines were not in use on the ward. If they were, intervention could possibly be made before violence actually occurred. In addition, Convey (1986) had noted that women were underestimated as aggressors. These provided useful suggestions about how to organise resources before any incident took place.

The multidisciplinary group felt it was important to meet as soon as possible after an incident to learn from the situation and provide support for the victim. It also considered it important to involve the patients in post-incident discussions. This would stress that violence affected everybody on the ward and it would also minimise the possibility of misunderstanding any nursing interventions. Uncertainty often produces fear and people occasionally react violently to a perceived threat.

Recommendations

The following recommendations were made:
1. Examine the primary nurse system. Produce role descriptions so that staff are aware of the extent and limitations of the role. As well as defining structure, it may enhance the quality of interaction between staff and patients.
2. Review the role of other disciplines with a view to establishing effective ward activity and routine.
3. Use the handover period to generate a plan of action for the shift. This may enable nursing staff to be proactive rather than reactive.
4. Prepare a ward profile defining ward policy and practices as a handout for all staff and patients new to the ward. Again, this would clarify

structure and expectations.

5. Hold meetings after a violent incident to discuss future strategy. Staff and patients involved in an incident should then meet to redefine therapeutic boundaries. In the event of serious incidents a group meeting should be held with all patients to discuss responses and consequences.
6. Work towards common practices regarding access to areas of the ward such as the nurses' office.
7. Use any information gathered to prepare a case for structural changes to the ward.

Evaluation

The main aim was to incorporate personal experience into ward practice. The author has contacted the current senior charge nurse who advised that 15 months after the recommendations were made, five had been fully implemented (1,2,4,6,7), and two were partially implemented (3 and 5). Certainly, he felt that nursing staff were more optimistic about their environment, and although there are no statistics yet available, he felt that concern among staff about violence had decreased.

Several broad conclusions relevant to all areas of nursing can be drawn from the exercise, and the following advice offered to nurses:

1. Become involved in examining violence in your area of work.
2. Don't accept violence as part of your work.
3. Don't accept bland explanations which offer solutions from society.
4. Keep a record of violent incidents in your area. Use it to:
   (i) form a basis of comparison with other areas;
   (ii) identify 'flashpoints';
   (iii) present your case to management;
   (iv) measure the effects of your interventions against violence.
5. Get to know local policy for the management of violent incidents. If none exist, prepare some for management agreement.
6. Share your experiences and encourage sharing between others.
7. Learn from experiences. Don't allow an unpleasant situation to arise more than once.
8. Seek out research findings and relate them to your area.
9. Bear in mind that you can positively influence your environment and organisation.
10. Don't wait until violence affects you. You can minimise the risk by taking action now.

The Department of Health is currently seeking details of local initiatives. You can write to them via Mr. J. Tait, DH, Alexander Fleming House, Elephant and Castle, London, SE1 6BY.

References
Aitken, G. (1982) Assaults on staff in a locked ward. Prediction and consequences. *Med. Sci. Law*, **24**, 3, 199-207.
Convey, J. (1986) A record of violence. *Nursing Times*, **82**, 47, 36-7.

Dewar, M. (1987) Violence. Who cares? *Nursing Times,* **83,** 23, 16-19.

Drinkwater, J.)1982) Violence in Psychiatric Hospitals. Reviewed in; Feldman, P. Developments in the Study of Criminal Behaviour, **2,** 111-27.

Fottrell, E. (1978) A study of violent and aggressive behaviour amongst a group of psychiatric in patients. *Med. Sci. Law,* **1,** 18, 66-9.

McGuire, M.T. (1977) An ethological study of four psychiatric wards. *Journal of Psychiatric Research,* **4,** 13, 211-14.

61

Violence: is enough being done to protect you?

ANN SHUTTLEWORTH, BA

Editor, The Professional Nurse

Anyone whose job brings them into contact with the public is at risk of violence. For many nurses the risk can turn into a frightening reality – especially in the community, in psychiatric facilities and in A&E departments, where it does not require much imagination to see how nurses can end up on the receiving end of verbal abuse, threats, and physical assault. Indeed, the problem is sufficiently serious for the National Association of Health Authorities to have produced The Directory of NHS Security (NAHA, 1988) giving advice on reducing theft and vandalism, and on dealing with violent. But what can be done – and who exactly is at risk?

A report by the Health Services Advisory Committee (1986) on violence towards health service staff found that nurses and ambulance staff are the target of most violent attacks. Four levels of incident were identified: those resulting in major injuries requiring medical assistance; those resulting in minor injuries requiring first aid; those resulting in no physical injury but involving a threat with a weapon and those involving verbal abuse. A random sample of 3,000 NHS staff in five health authorities and all occupational groups were asked whether they had suffered from violence at work in the past year: 0.5 per cent reported injury requiring medical assistance; 11 per cent had required first aid; 4.6 per cent had been threatened with a weapon and 17.5 per cent had been subjected to verbal abuse.

On the frontline

When these figures were broken down into occupational groups, 1.6 per cent of student and charge nurses had suffered major injuries – a rate second only to ambulance staff (1.7 per cent). No other profession reported more than 0.6 per cent receiving such injuries. The figures tell a similar story in the other three categories – nurses, especially at junior grades, and ambulance staff had consistently suffered more violent attacks than any other occupation – often up to six times more than others involving patient contact, such as hospital doctors.

Such violent attacks are costly, and not just in human terms. They cost the organisation dearly in disruption, days lost due to sickness and in lowered staff morale and efficiency, which may also lead to staff loss. Employers are required under the Health and Safety at Work Act to identify the nature and extent of the risk their employees run of being victims of violent incidents, and to devise meaures which would provide a safe workplace and system of work. Strange then, that only 12 per cent of·the respondents in the study reported having received any training in handling violence; most of these were referring to their basic training, and only 16 per cent of them had found it 'extremely useful'.

Reducing the risk

It is obviously impossible for the NHS to tackle the root of the problem – violence in our society – but steps can certainly be taken to reduce the risk of violence to staff. Poyner and Warne (1986) describe a practical step-by-step method of tackling the issue. The problem must first be identified – whether any staff are being subjected to violence; then information can be collected to ascertain who is at risk. Here, a purpose designed channel of reporting incidents needs to be set up and all staff should be made aware of it. Incidents should then be grouped into types where possible, after which a methodical search for preventive measures can begin and a strategy set up and implemented. Once this is underway it should be monitored carefully to ensure it is effective.

There is a wide range of preventive measures open to the NHS and its staff, tackling different components of the problem (Poyner and Warne, 1988). Often, simple measures such as providing more information can reduce frustration in people waiting to be attended to. Employees may benefit from training in assertiveness, interpersonal skills, the causes of violence and how to recognise and defuse tension. Junior staff are more often targets of violence because of their inexperience in dealing with potentially violent situations. Apart from training courses, they may benefit from deployment with a more experienced staff member, to learn from them how to avoid confrontations. Staff are also likely to feel more confident in handling aggression if they are aware of their authority's policies on the subject.

A better environment

Environmental factors can influence people's state of mind, and while little can be done about this in the community, some relatively simple steps may do much to make NHS environments appear less hostile, particularly A&E. An easily identifiable reception allows incoming patients to be properly received, and means they know where to address queries. Provision of sufficient information also lessens the risk of assault – even the most well-balanced individual can become agitated in unfamiliar surroundings when faced with unknown procedures.

Lighting should be glare-free, but bright enough to ensure there are no dimly lit corners, and people should be given enough personal space to ensure they do not feel crowded and threatened. Noise can be a potent stressor, and can be reduced by provision of sound absorbing surfaces and materials, while colour should be subdued, but brightened by plants and pictures. Boredom can increase anxiety, but may be relieved by reading materials or a wall mounted television, and access to a pay-phone means people need not get anxious because they cannot contact their families. Furniture needs to be robust and not capable of being used as a missile, but also needs to be comfortable enough for long waiting times.

In the community, nurses often have to rely on their own competence to recognise and prevent dangerous situations, but there are measures which can help them. A plan of staff whereabouts, with periodic reports to base allows management to identify when things go wrong more quickly, while assessing the potential or actual risk from either patients or the area in which they live alerts everyone to critical situations. Extra security may be necessary for visiting 'high risk' patients – visiting in pairs may help here and can also allow an inexperienced staff member to accompany one who is more used to handling potentially violent patients, while personal alarms may be useful for nurses to carry when visiting high risk areas. It may also be advisable not to wear a uniform if it is likely to identify the nurse as a potential source of drugs.

An issue to be tackled

Violence towards health service staff is an issue which, if the HSAC's study is an accurate reflection of the NHS as a whole, appears to be pushed under the carpet to a disturbing degree. Employers need to realise that, while steps to protect staff may involve some initial outlay, not only is it their legal and moral duty to provide them, but in the long-term they are likely to pay for themselves in fewer days lost due to sickness, improved staff morale and decreased staff wastage, and less disruption of the workings of the service. It is surely time they acknowledged this responsibility and set about protecting their staff to the best of their abilities – and ensuring that those who are subjected to violence are given proper support and compensation for any injuries they may sustain. Directories are not enough – health professionals need to know their working environment is as safe as possible.

References

Health Services Advisory Committee (1986) Violence to Staff in the Health Services. Health and Safety Commission, London.
NAHA (1988) Directory of NHS Security. NAHA, Birmingham.
Poyner, B. and Warne, C. (1986) Violence to Staff. A basis for assessment and prevention. Health and Safety Executive, London.
Poyner, B. and Warne, C. (1988) Preventing Violence to Staff. Health and Safety Executive, London.

62

A way forward: challenging behaviour in a day care setting

Patricia Brigdon, BSc, DipClinPsych
Principal Psychologist, Basingstoke and North Hampshire Health Authority

Margaret Todd, RNMH, RMN, RGN, FETC
Staff Development and Education Coordinator (Mental Handicap), Basingstoke and North Hampshire Health Authority

Hospitals for people with learning difficulties in our health district, in common with those in the rest of the Wessex Region, are being run down, and a community service is being developed for local clients. The parent hospital which had normally admitted from this catchment area stopped doing so five years ago, and since April 1988, the district has provided a self-sufficient service, including provision for those people who exhibit aggressive behaviour (now termed challenging behaviour).

Challenging behaviour is any behaviour which deviates from accepted norms. This can range from the relatively trivial, such as pouring bottles of milk down the sink to extremes such as physical assault, which are at worst life threatening. It is the latter category which we are considering. The district's 10 year strategy is to set up an 'ordinary life' (Kings Fund, 1985), service based on group homes, with day care provided in a range of settings under the auspices of health, education and/or social services. The shift to community care (House of Commons Social Services Select Committee, 1985), is posing some awkward questions about how challenging behaviour can be handled effectively and safely.

Traditionally, when adults with learning difficulties behaved aggressively in the social services community placement, they were excluded from such services and responsibility for care would be taken over by the health service. If the problem behaviour could not be dealt with adequately in the community – and it should be remembered that the health service is having the same problems as other agencies in the community – they would be admitted to hospital. In cases of exceptionally aggressive behaviour, the person would be moved from ward to ward as each situation broke down. This would contain the situation rather than alleviate it.

Since community care is based on the philosophy of an 'ordinary life', this strategy is no longer feasible or desirable. The implications of this are twofold: aggressive clients cannot be excluded from a service because of their behaviour, and the problems cannot be passed from one environment to another. The strain on staff and families is considerable, and it is increasingly important that psychological interventions are not only effective but can be rapidly applied. This paper explores some of the issues raised when working with a client who attends a day placement for people with special needs and who was referred to the community mental handicap team (Sines and Bicknall, 1985) after seriously injuring a member of staff.

Aggressive behaviour

Mark has a lifelong history of aggressive behaviour which has led to his exclusion from several schools. Prior to starting at the day centre there had been a history of episodic aggression at the health service day care service, and the psychologist had been heavily involved with the client. Mark started attending the centre on a part time basis when the special needs base opened. This attendance had been successful for 16 months – there had been occasional incidents of aggression, such as kicking, but the staff felt confident to deal with these episodes. It was decided to offer him a full time place at the centre, but this led to a rise in the level of challenging behaviour. Incidents of physical aggression became almost daily occurrences, and although most were managed effectively on some occasions he had to be physically restrained by four members of staff. During one of these incidents a staff member received a severe bite. Staff injuries escalated in the three months after Mark started full time attendance. The incidents were usually kicking, so staff started to remove Mark's shoes when he entered the unit, but he then started to punch staff, which he had not done previously.

The incident which resulted in the community mental handicap team becoming involved occurred when a member of staff intervened in a dispute between Mark and another trainee. The staff member received a blow to the head, and suffered a fractured skull.

The policy of the day centre is to try to ensure that clients are not excluded because of aggressive behaviour. However, due to the severity of the incident, Mark was excluded for a week. During this time an emergency case conference was called and arrangements were made to draw up and implement a programme which would enable Mark to be gradually reintroduced to the centre.

Mark is known to have brain damage and complex partial epilepsy. Many of the drugs used to control this are contraindicated because of exceptionally severe side effects experienced by Mark – his aggression. His abilities are patchy; he is able to read and write and do simple arithmetic at a six-year-old ability level, and his expressive language and overt behaviour are obsessive-compulsive in nature. Interrupting an obsessive-compulsive sequence results in violent behaviour such as kicking, biting and hitting, but much of the violence can be avoided, especially in recurrent behaviours. For example, he has repeatedly refused to come out of a cupboard where he repeatedly throws quoits at the electric meters, threatening his own safety and the likelihood that the electricity supply will be fused, but can be tempted out by the invitation to lock the door and replace the key in the office.

Mark's behaviour varies according to whether epileptic seizures are imminent and is presumably due to temporal lobe auras. Staff must therefore be able to perceive these warnings and adapt their behaviour accordingly. When Mark is in a cooperative mood he will join in activities willingly, provided they are ones in which he is interested and enjoys. However, if his behaviour is of an obsessive-compulsive nature he should be allowed to set the pace for the day's activities: a flexible routine and constant empathic handling are crucial.

Conflicting accounts

The psychologist and community nurse were faced with a bewildering array of conflicting accounts about the build up to the serious injury which had resulted in Mark's exclusion. Antecedent, behaviour and consequences recording charts designed by a psychologist were used as specific incident forms in the centre. The antecedent column describes the events before the behaviour, including a description of the background in which the behaviour occurred, such as time of day, what activity was in progress. The behaviour column states in clear unambiguous terms what behaviour was actually observed, while the consequences column describes the events immediately after the behaviour (Barker, 1985). This information is collected to ascertain the reasons for the behaviour, and to gain some ideas on how to prevent it in the future or to develop effective handling techniques. If this information is collected systematically over a period of time, a pattern can emerge, such as an incident occurs five minutes prior to a meal, or every time a certain activity occurs (Yule and Carr, 1980). In our experience, this approach did not yield sufficient information regarding the antecedents, but this may be due to the policy of integrating special needs clients with the main centre clients, which effectively reduces staffing ratios from 1:3 to 1:11. Due to these staffing levels and the large number of clients, staff often observe the incident and its consequences, but the factor which sets off the incident may not be known, as it is not possible to observe one person at all times.

The approach decided upon involved either the community nurse or psychologist accompanying Mark to the centre every afternoon. This enabled them to observe him and determine the antecedents. They were also able to act as role models and implement a plan for Mark's reintroduction to the centre.

The reintroduction plan

Phase 1 Mark attends for two hours per day, accompanied by either the community nurse or psychologist. Initially the activity occurs in a quiet room with individual attention.

Phase 2   Two hours per day based in a quiet room, but joining in some group activities. Community nurse/psychologist gradually moving into the background but remaining on hand to intervene if Mark displays signs of agitation.

Phase 3   Lengthen the time from two hours to a complete half day in gradual steps, otherwise as for phase 2.

Phase 4   Staff start to take over the role pioneered by the community nurse/psychologist, who gradually withdraw from the programme.

This approach ensured Mark's gradual reintroduction into the normal activities and the phasing out of the community nurse and psychologist. It was felt that it would be effective because it enabled staff to become desensitised to specific anxieties that had built up about Mark's behaviour. Desensitisation is used to enable people to cope with irrational fears (Sainsbury, 1980). Although it is acknowledged that the staff had some justification for being afraid, the level of that fear was thought to be excessive, as the majority of injuries and incidents had not been serious. The importance of exposure to real life phobic situations is an important part of treatment and staff need to be able to relax during the exposure. Initially, the exposure was minimal and gradually increased as staff's fears lessened and became manageable. As the desensitisation programme worked and staff became more relaxed and confident, Mark's behaviour improved, as he could tune into the staff's feelings. This approach has been used effectively three times in similar situations with Mark when the placement appeared to have broken down, and further interventions were not necessary for one to two years after each occasion. Though this treatment can be criticised as too time consuming in its early stages for the community nurse and psychologist (Ehart, 1987), it does have advantages:

- The desensitisation programme alleviates staff's anxieties.
- The community nurse and psychologist can identify antecedents for themselves, enabling practical advice on behavioural management to be offered which will be of value to that setting.
- Organisational problems can be identified and listed.
- Mark can be occupied during the day outside his home setting.

Organisational issues

Several organisational issues were identified as potential precipitating factors in Mark's aggressive incidents.

1. There appeared to be little structure to the afternoon timetable. This leads to clients being left unoccupied for long periods, resulting in boredom. It is well documented that boredom precipitates aggressive incidents (Burrows, 1984).
2. The range of activities offered were limited. On three consecutive days a music session occurred, the content of which involved a member of staff playing a guitar, leaving the clients only passively involved.

Alternatives were not available, and the activities that were arranged appeared to be done at the whim of the staff and did not relate to identified needs of clients. There was no forward planning.
3. Staff's attitudes to clients who exhibit challenging behaviour were negative – they did not appreciate the need to use avoidance strategies. It was felt that all clients should be treated the same regardless of the possible outcomes (Altschul, 1977).
4. When dealing with clients of differing abilities, materials and equipment should be available to suit everyone, but the attitude of the staff was such that equipment was not purchased according to individual needs.
5. There appeared to be no quiet area for individuals to be alone when they wished to work quietly or in small groups.
6. There was no continuity of staffing in the establishment, which makes it difficult to ensure continuity in the client's care (Jay, 1979).

Many of these organisational issues have not yet been resolved, although discussions are on going.

After the programme had been operating for a few months, the staff felt confident enough to cope with Mark on their own, and the community nurse and psychologist withdrew. One year after the incident occurred, the staff are now thinking about increasing Mark's time at the centre to full time. This will be phased and monitored over two months with gradual weekly increases, an approach which has been used successfully with other clients exhibiting similar problems. We believe this approach could be adopted and used effectively in other community care settings where similar problems exist.

New approaches to coping with challenging behaviour in the community need to be developed urgently, as the alternative is admission of the client to private hospitals or secure units, an excessive and expensive response from which rehabilitation can be difficult. Mark's progress shows that given time and effort, people with challenging behaviour *can* be kept in community services and out of hospital.

References
Altschul, A. (1977) Psychiatric Nursing. Ballière Tindall, London.
Barker, P. (1985) Behaviour Therapy Nursing. Croom Helm, London.
Burrows, M. (1984) Nurses and violence. *Nursing Times,* **80,** 4, 56-58.
Ehart, K. (1987) The cost-quality balance: an analysis of quality effectiveness, efficiency and cost. *Journal of Nursing Administration,* **17,** 5, 6-13˘
House of Common Social Services Committee (1985) Community Care with Special References to Adult Mentally Ill and Mentally Handicapped People. HMSO, London.
Jay, P. (1979) Report of the Committee of Enquiry into Mental Handicap Nursing and Care. HMSO, London.
King's Fund (1985) An Ordinary Life. King's Fund Centre, London.
Sainsbury, M. (1980) Key to Psychiatry. HM. and M. Publishers Ltd, Aylesbury.
Sines, D. and Bicknell, J. (1985) Caring for Mentally Handicapped People in the Community. Harper Row Publishers, London.
Yule, W. and Carr, J.)1980) Behaviour Modification for the Mentally Handicapped. Croom Helm, London.

Product Appraisal

63

Product appraisal

Brenda Pottle, SRN, SCM, DN (Lond)
Senior Nurse, Research and Quality Assurance, East Surrey Health Authority

The nurses' involvement with purchasing decisions

In many purchasing decisions, the nurse on the ward or in the community has an important role. She uses many items of equipment and supplies every day, and also has the most detailed knowledge of the needs of the individual patient.

There has been, and often still is, a very large gap between the contracting supplies officer and the nurse on the ward, in the department, or in the community. This can widen if, for example, a company representative shows nurses products that are not available to them because there is a regional contracting system for purchase which excludes these products on grounds of cost or unsuitability. To be involved with decision-making at ward and regional levels nurses must be aware of the cost and be systematic in their appraisal of products. This information must then be circulated to the appropriate people, and used effectively in reaching purchase decisions.

A system for product appraisal

A product appraisal system was devised by Doreen Norton by which to obtain basic facts about products in use (Norton, 1982). In such a survey, the nurses using the item are asked to complete a product appraisal form (Figure 1), having had experience of using a product for three months. The opinion of nurses in different specialties can be included in the survey. The forms are then collated onto the product appraisal result form (Figure 2) for analysis and for use in decision making by the appropriate person or department.

This information gathered from the completed forms does not in itself constitute a rigorously researched evaluation of the product, but it does give a practical survey of the opinions of nurses and should reveal which products are suitable for purchase. The survey may indicate that further evaluation should be carried out.

This simple system can be used successfully in conjunction with a monitoring and costing exercise, for example examining three different types of wipe or cleaning tissue for incontinent patients.

Different manufacturers' products 1, 2, and 3 were each used for one week on one ward, over a period of three consecutive weeks. The product appraisal forms were completed by all nurses working on the ward during the trial and the results were collated onto the product appraisal result form. The results were as follows:

Product 1: A + B = 75% Y + Z = 25%
Product 2: A + B = 25% Y + Z = 75%
Product 3: A + B = 100%

This information was then forwarded to the contracting officer with the recommendation that **Product 3** should be selected for the regional contract (Smith; Unpublished Report).

A system for evaluation

More detailed evaluation of products may be required, and this will take more planning and research than the simple example just given.

To evaluate means ''To determine significance or worth of usage by careful appraisal and study'' (Webster, 1977). This means that there must be a commitment by staff, and in many circumstances patients, if the evaluation is to take place and be of value. A protocol must be written first to establish the criteria and the plan for the research.

Conclusion

Nurses have a vital role to play in appraising and evaluating resources, but the necessary research must be done in a systematic way and be carefully planned and properly documented. If the need for this discipline

Figure 1. Product appraisal form

```
┌─────────────────────────────────────────────────────────────────────┐
│  PRODUCT APPRAISAL RESULTS          Ref. No. . . . . . . . . . . . .   │
│                                                                       │
│  ITEM . . . . . . . . . . . . . . . . . . . . . . . . . . . .   Date . . . . . . . . . . . . .   │
│                                                                       │
│  MANUFACTURER/BRAND . . . . . . . . . . . . . . . . . . . . . . .      │
├───────────────────────────────────────────────────────────────────────┤
```

Number P.A. Forms completed . . . .

Question 1-4:   4 × . . . . = ... (100%)

ANALYSIS OF RESULTS	A	B	Y	Z
	Strongly Agree	Agree	Disagree	Strongly Disagree
1. Product easy to use				
2. Quality about right				
3. No major disadvantages				
4. Suitable for the job				
TOTALS				

Total of **A** + **B** (favourable) . . . . (. . . . . . %)
Total of **Y** + **Z** (unfavourable) . . . . (. . . . . . %)

COMMON COMPLAINTS: in order of frequency of mention, with approximate number making comment.

	Number
. . . .	
. . . .	
. . . .	
. . . .	
. . . .	
. . . .	
. . . .	
. . . .	
. . . .	
. . . .	

5. Would like product available for ordering
     number . . . . percentage . . . .

ACTION TAKEN

Figure 2. Product appraisal result form

is recognised prior to an evaluation, this will surely stop the use of so-called "trials", in which one or two products are used with only one patient and then one product either praised or rejected. Incorrect decisions are often made as a result of inadequate or insufficiently documented factual information.

Nurses are increasingly involved with the decisions made on purchase. Ward budgeting is used in some hospitals and is a system that is likely to become more widely adopted in the future. One of the results of this system is that the ward sister or charge nurse may now be accountable for sizeable budgets for ward-based purchases. We owe it to our patients, our employers, our colleagues, and ourselves to make the best decisions.

References
Norton, D (1982) What's in Store? *Nursing Times,* 1221.
Websters Dictionary (1977) Cassells, London.

64

Product evaluation

Brenda Pottle, SRN, SCM, DN (Lond)
Senior Nurse, Research and Quality Assurance, East Surrey Health Authority

Ward budgeting is a system that is used now in some hospitals and it is likely to be more widely adopted in the future. As a result, ward sisters may be accountable for sizeable budgets and they need to know how to make the best decisions on ward-based purchases of equipment and supplies.

A system for evaluation

In the last chapter the nurse's involvement with purchasing decisions was discussed and it was stressed that to be involved with decision making at ward and regional levels nurses must be aware of the cost and be systematic in their appraisal of products.

A simple system for product appraisal was illustrated which can provide a practical survey of nurses' opinions and reveal which products are suitable for purchase, but sometimes a more rigorous and detailed evaluation of products may be required, and this will take more planning and research.

To evaluate means "To determine significance or worth of usage by careful appraisal and study" (Webster, 1977). This means that there must be a commitment by staff, and in many circumstances patients, if the evaluation is to take place and be of value. A protocol must be written first to establish the criteria and the plan for the research.

Protocol for product evaluation

Purpose   There may be a number of reasons for undertaking product evaluation. A new product may have become available and an existing product in use over a number of years may not now be the best choice. Suitability of a product for a particular group of patients may be questioned. A comparison of products may be required and the cost-effectiveness of each may need to be evaluated.

Products to be used   All products to be included in the evaluation must be listed; details are taken from the manufacturer's specifications and literature.

Costs   These should be carefully defined and VAT included where applicable. The unit cost if a bulk purchase on a regional contract is made should also be known. If the product is not available on prescription, evaluation of it with patients in the community should be questioned, and the value of assessing these products considered carefully.

Literature search   Has anyone been down this path before? If so, what did their research cover and what were the results? Should those findings be tested again, or new methods employed?

Criteria to be tested   The manufacturer's literature can be used to draw up some of the questions that may be asked in finding out if it is suitable for the patient and the nurse to use. For example, a bandage to be evaluated has in its manufacturer's literature (Johnson and Johnson, 1984):
''Easy to apply and remove
Stick only to themselves
Easy for home and ward use
Aid compliance
Do not stick to hair or skin
Less discomfort and skin trauma
Tears easily to length without scissors
Conforms even on awkward sites
Extremely comfortable
Highly absorbent and permeable
Kind to skin
Fewer complications and fewer changes
Can be worn in water
Radiolucent''
   These statements can be used to draw up a questionnaire to assess the practical use of this product. Other criteria may include suitability for different groups of patients (such as children or the elderly) or the effectiveness of use by untrained personnel, who could include relatives.

Method of evaluation   The method used in the research must be planned out in detail. This should include the following:
Length of time in days, weeks, or months
Staff to be consulted
Numbers of patients and locations in hospital and/or community
Ethical issues
Instructions for using the products (company representatives could be
   involved here)
Design of the forms and questionnaires: Should these be piloted?
Monitoring the use of detailed forms. Is someone able to give the time
   personally to monitor the evaluation? Time and staff must be available
   to collate the results.

The research   With this planned out in detail, the forms and questionnaires devised (and if necessary piloted), and all the staff fully briefed, the information gathering can begin.

Results Once the forms and questionnaires are collected, it takes time to collate the results. If a computer is available time can be saved, but monitoring forms and questionnaires must be designed before the research with full knowledge of the computer's potential in order to make best use of this resource. The limitations of the research must also be clearly identified (for example it may only be appropriate for one group of patients, or one setting for care). The problems encountered while undertaking the research should also be reported.

Report This needs to have all the details of the evaluation, limitations, problems encountered, costs, results, conclusions, and recommendations in a clear, typed format. Before writing the report, consideration must be given to its future use. It may be circulated to other nurses, administrators, or supplies officers only, or it may be made more widely available to the manufacturers or even for publication.

Reports are best written as soon as possible after the research is completed so that the most up-to-date information is made available to colleagues. Imposing a deadline for the completion of the report may help with this. The report must be circulated to appropriate colleagues, including the nurses involved with the evaluation and the budget holder.

Conclusion

Incorrect decisions on purchasing are often made as a result of inadequate or insufficiently documented factual information. Nurses have a vital role to play in appraising and evaluating resources, and the necessary research must be done in a systematic way, with careful planning and proper documentation. Recognition of the need for such discipline prior to an evaluation should avoid the use of so-called "trials", when one or two products are used with only one patient and then one product is praised or rejected on this basis.

References
Johnson and Johnson Ltd (1984) New Secure and Secure Forte Literature.
Norton, D. (1982) What's in Store? *Nursing Times*, 1221.
Websters Dictionary (1977) Cassells, London.

65

Measuring product performance

Doreen Norton, OBE, MSc, SRN, FRCN

Retired; formerly Nursing Research Liaison Officer, South West Thames RHA and Professor of Gerontological Nursing, Case Western Reserve University, Cleveland, Ohio

Evaluation means measuring performance against prescribed criteria. The first step to conducting a reliable trial of a product is writing the prescription for the performance, as these criteria are the basis for planning the data-collecting form or questionnaire to be used in the trial. 'Measuring' means the information sought and obtained must be capable of interpretation in numerical form.

This chapter offers guidance on these aspects of product performance trials. It is written in terms of a single product but the same principles apply when two or more of the same kind are subjected to comparative

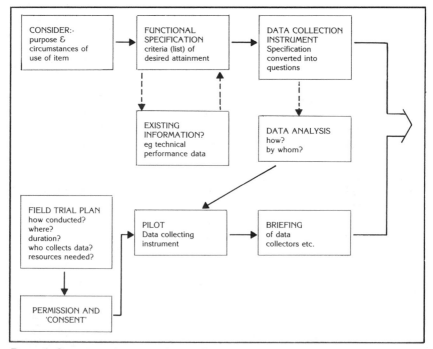

Figure 1. Steps in equipment evaluation field trial.

evaluation of performance. Any field trial must be systematically planned (Figure 1) and based on scientific principles.

Criteria prescription

What is the purpose of the product and the general circumstances of its use? Write a concise statement answering these two questions (Figure 2). This is not always easy, but worthwhile because it focuses the mind and throws up issues which can easily be missed through familiarity with the nursing tasks involved in using such an item.

a) Roughly list all the functions and properties which, ideally, are desired of the product in fulfilment of its purpose and in the circumstances of its use. Note any information supplied by the manufacturer, particularly technical specifications, and adjust the list accordingly.

b) Now examine each entry critically, with a view to revising the list by deletions and modifications. Extract and record separately, for example, any factor which would require to be tested other than in the field trial, such as a bacterial test in a laboratory. Bear in mind throughout that demands made of the product must be realistic and that each stated requirement will later involve framing questions to ascertain if, and to what extent it is met in performance of the product.

c) Assemble the remaining entries into some form of order, eg grouping of related factors or an appropriate logical sequence.

d) Against each entry, record into which of three categories it falls — essential (it shall), desirable (should), permissible (may). The terms in brackets will apply when finalising the wording of the criteria.

e) Prepare for the revised list by dividing a large sheet of paper into two sections, one headed **Requirements** and the other **Explanation and Constraints.** Now comes the brain-teasing part — not to be rushed! It is advisable to study the example (Figure 2) at this stage.

f) Make each entry under 'Requirements' a precise statement in terms of functional performance. (Do not specify design or materials — express only the properties required of them.) Try to make the statements in the positive, ie what the product must, should or may do, rather than what it must not do. (The 'must nots' should become apparent under the other section heading). Under 'Explanation and constraints' record information which clarifies the entry opposite. Indeed, it is advisable to work through such information and assemble any extrinsic facts necessary before attempting to finalise the wording of the statement of Requirements.

Data collecting instrument

Whatever the plan decided for conduct of the trial, the criteria have to be converted into some form of questioning of observers about the product's performance under working conditions.

The kind of questioning varies with the nature of the requirement; it can be a direct question or a statement for agreement/disagreement. In either, a 'yes/no' type of answering may be appropriate for some factors

REQUIREMENTS	EXPLANATION AND CONSTRAINTS
MATERIAL 1. Shall be reasonably non-generating of static electricity.	(i) Cap worn in the presence of anaesthetic gases.
2. Shall allow ventilation.	(ii) Operating theatres have a temperature of 18-24°C and humidity of 40-50%; therefore the head covering must not impede heat evaporation from the scalp nor generate its own heat.
3. Shall remain intact when handled (donning of cap) and throughout use.	(iii) Must not disintegrate, stretch or contract under conditions of heat and humidity (ii).
4. Shall be non-irritating to skin.	(iv) Length of time in contact with skin (v) and environmental conditions (ii) increase risk of skin irritation.
THE CAP 5. Should be reasonably light in weight and softly flexible.	(v) Cap may be worn up to eight hours and therefore should not give awareness of weight or rigidity in the interests of comfort.
6. Shall be easy to put on.	(vi) —
. . .etc. . .	. . .etc. . .

Figure 2. Criteria specifications.
ITEM: Disposable theatre cap.
PURPOSE: To keep hair enclosed for (a) hygenic reasons and (b) uninhibited vision and movement.
MAIN SITUATIONS OF USE: Operating theatres and intensive care units.
This example of prescribed criteria was developed as an exercise with a group of nurses from East Surrey Health Authority in 1982.

but for others allowance usually has to be made in the data collecting instrument for recording degrees of the product's compliance with the requirement. An even number of degrees (say, four or six) is preferable to an uneven number (say, three or five) as this allows for a balance of degrees towards satisfactory and unsatisfactory and avoids the less helpful 'middle of the road' reply. The more degrees there are the more refined the information obtained but it is often necessary to strike a compromise between the amount and sophistication of information sought and the resources available for collecting and analysing the data.

Scoring of points
To achieve measurement of a product's performance, a weighted value of points is allocated to the optional replies to a question. Maximum points are given for total compliance with the requirement (completely satisfactory) to nil for no compliance (completely unsatisfactory). The number of intervals between depends on the number of degrees of compliance allowed for, eg four degrees will be in the order of 3,2,1,0

in value, but in any event the points' 'weighting' must be proportionately equal in their graduation steps.

Measurable analysis

The sum of the maximum points obtainable to all questions gives the 'ideal' performance score. The points scored by the product are then totalled and this figure calculated as a percentage of the 'ideal' score.

Example: Ideal score 58; obtained score 38.

$$\frac{3800}{58} = 65.5 \text{ per cent compliance with the criteria.}$$

If the product is a disposable or requires treatment before being used again (such as laundering) it may be decided to record observations at each incident of use rather than to collect data at the end of the trial period. In this case, the formula for analysis is to multiply the 'ideal' score by the number of times the item was used and the total of the obtained scores calculated as a percentage.

Example: Ideal score 58 x 110 incidents of use = 6380 max.

Obtained score total = 4125.

$$\frac{412500}{6380} = 64.6 \text{ per cent compliance with the criteria.}$$

Refinement of results Irrespective of when data are collected, a refinement of results can be obtained if desirable. Namely, by isolating those requirements earlier identified as essential (shall) and applying the same procedure to their respective total of maximum points possible and the obtained score. It may be decided that the product is unacceptable if it fails to satisfy any one of these requirements or achieves less than, say, 90 per cent, in respect of these, however well it rated overall.

Comparative evaluations When two or more products of the same kind (and used in the same way) are to receive a field trial to determine the most suitable, the principle is the same as for a single product. That is, the performance of each is measured against the prescribed criteria (and not simply compared with each other) and rated accordingly. All, however, must be subjected to the same trial conditions and, preferably, using the same observers.

It was mentioned at the outset that reliable information is the key to products being designed suitable for purpose and acceptable in the work situation. Manufacturers are starved of such information, and weaknesses in the design of products can be generally attributed to the failure of health care professionals to produce user-specifications. A performance criteria drawn-up for trial purposes and a user-specification are one and the same, so performance criteria made known to manufacturers can influence future design for the better. In any event, a full report of a product trial (including details of the methods) should always be sent to the manufacturer concerned.

Bibliography

Buckles, A.M. (1980) How should we dispose of our used needles and syringes? *Nursing Times*, **76**, 34, Journal of Infection Control Nursing, ICNA, 5-11.

An evaluation of four different types of containers for the disposal of sharps which serves as a good example of a comparative type of field trial using product performance measurement.

Norton, D. (1978) Equipment fit for purpose. *Nursing Times*, **74**, 19, Occasional Papers, 73-76.

Describes in detail the principles of specifying and evaluating equipment and for conducting field trials.

Index